GARDENING IN THE LOWER MIDWEST

Gardening
IN THE LOWER
MIDWEST

A Practical Guide for the
New Zones 5 and 6

Diane Heilenman

Indiana University Press

BLOOMINGTON AND INDIANAPOLIS

Photograph of Diane Heilenman and Buttons
by Pam Spaulding

The paper used in this publication meets the
minimum requirements of American National
Standard for Information Sciences—
Permanence of Paper for Printed Library
Materials, ANSI Z39.48-1984.

™

Manufactured in the United States of America

Library of Congress
Cataloging-in-Publication Data

Heilenman, Diane, date
    Gardening in the lower Midwest : a
practical guide for the new zones 5 and 6 /
Diane Heilenman.
        p.   cm.
    Includes bibliographical references
(p.   ) and index.
    ISBN 0-253-32811-X (cloth). — ISBN
0-253-32813-6 (paper)
    1. Gardening—Middle West.   2.
Gardening—Kentucky.   I. Title.
SB453.2.M53H45   1994
635'.0977—dc20   93-33827

1 2 3 4 5 00 99 98 97 96 95 94

CONTENTS

Introduction: Garden Smarts

Many Missouri orchardists have heard cautionary tales about the "Armistice Day Freeze." That's the memorable day in November 1940 when the temperature dropped sixty degrees in three hours. Not surprisingly, many fruit trees—among other plants—were killed to the ground. There is no record of the response among orchardists and gardeners, but we can pretty well guess.

More recently, there was the devastating single-digit and below-zero killer cold in December 1989, which hit us before plants were fully dormant, decimating gardens. It took out so much nursery stock that professionals and amateurs alike considered quitting. In fact, every year has its moments. Some years we'll have a drought; other times we get too much rain, say, three inches in half an hour. We have windstorms, ice storms, tornadoes. Early one morning in October 1988, before the leaves had fallen, Bloomington, Indiana, received two inches of wet, heavy snow. All day long, tree limbs and entire trees were crashing down all over town.

And, as I write, 1993 has brought the "storm of the century." For us, it was a typical spring—balmy one day and bitter the next. The line of deep snow and bitter cold began about eighty miles east of my garden, at Lexington, Kentucky. It essentially missed us, but gave gardeners in Tennessee and Georgia a once-in-a-hundred-years taste of what midwesterners suffer yearly.

If you are reading this book, presumably you garden or contemplate gardening in hardiness zones 5 or 6 of the Lower Midwest. If you have gardened here even one season, you know these are the Zombie Zones. Everybody likes to think his or her weather is the worst, but we live where wild temperature swings are normal.

It's close to a certainty in the quixotic zones 5 and 6 that one year—or even two or three in a row—you may have winter lows so high that the plants think they've died and gone to Tidewater Virginia, and the next year you may have temperatures so low the plants just die.

However, the problem may be the opposite. Our summers can get too hot too soon, which has greatly influenced my decision not to grow delphiniums in the Ohio River Valley. Our springs can swing like a pendulum. Winter warm-ups may be accented by dots of yellow blossoms on forsythia bushes, which everyone knows don't have the sense to stay dormant more than a week, followed by spring frosts ill-timed for your horticultural ambitions in the realm of peach, almond, pecan, and magnolia flowers—among others.

This book is about how to get along with such difficult and trying weather in the Zombie Zones. It also is a distinctly personal account of how I think you might go about the business of being a modern gardener, a role that has broadened in the late twentieth century from cutting the grass and growing a few tomatoes and dahlias to an entire lifestyle sometimes fraught with moral responsibility, social mobility, and political correctness.

My viewpoint is from northern Kentucky, which may seem an odd perch for writing about the Midwest. Indeed, as a native Kentuckian, I was brought up to believe in the southern nature of this state. It was a small family joke that my mother, who was accidentally born on the other side of the Ohio River in nearby Cincinnati during a visit, was a northerner. There are some social and political reasons for this icono-clastic notion. Kentucky was once part of Virginia, definitely a southern sort of place, and the artificial boundary of the Mason-Dixon line separating North from South in the Civil War corresponds to the Ohio River.

But when it comes to gardening, Kentucky is a close cousin of the Midwest and a mere distant relative to the South. It takes only a little travel to perceive geographic similarities among Ohio, Indiana, Illinois, Missouri, the lower reaches of Iowa and Michigan, and the upper reaches of Kentucky. Our soils may be different; our levels of humidity vary; but we all stand in the vast drainage basin of the Mississippi River, which was created to God's own scale and extends from the Appalachian Mountains to the Great Lakes and the Rocky Mountains.

It takes only a little experience with the endless round of putting on and taking off of coats in this region to perceive that we are at the center of some of the continent's great weather battles. We live and garden in a big transition area between cold, dry polar air and moist, mild tropical air.

Meteorologists tend to symbolize these forces as vast sailing ships. They even call a cold swing across the country an "Alberta Clipper." To my mind, it is more like two flocks of birds. One travels unimpeded and quickly, moving across the Great Plains to sweep in along

Only local gardeners really know what grows well in their region. That's why the United States Department of Agriculture sensibly looked for volunteers to tell them which among a list of 2,000 plants grew well where. This hands-on observation is the basis for the plant recommendations in the *National Arboretum Book of Outstanding Garden Plants,* keyed to the new zones in the USDA Plant Hardiness Map, redrawn in 1990. The book is a strong addition to any serious gardener's library. Its plant lists are based on satisfactory growth rather than mere survival. The map—a Herculean effort, worthy of applause—pretty effectively regains any ground the superseded USDA map had lost in popularity. It is now, generally, the map published in most plant catalogs and garden books.

A fast visual tour of the new USDA map reveals, logically enough, that the warmest areas (a new Zone 11) comprise the tip of Florida, its southern islands, and pockets of superwarmth in the depths of southern California. Here it is frost-free all year. Logic triumphs again as the coldest Zone 1 is in the frozen north, where temperatures *average* under –50 degrees. After that the zones from 2 to 9 snake about, wrapping the U.S. in sinuous bands that form a multicolored profile of that crafty, shifting entity called climate.

Hardiness maps based on winter temperatures suggest that folks in Illinois can grow anything folks in Seattle or Philadelphia can. The working gardener knows this is not true. For instance, there may be no more widely badly grown plant than rhododendrons. They adore the moist, cool climate of Oregon's Zone 6, but struggle in the steambath heat of Indiana's Zone 6.

Discrepancies exist even within our region. English hollies can be grown along the shores of the Great Lakes, a pocket of mild-mannered climate tempered by the water, but seldom survive harsher conditions a few hundred miles to the south and inland. Apple tree varieties that thrive in Michigan give up in Illinois. All this means is that Mother Nature doesn't read. She sees no problem with saying "No!" even when the map says "Yes!" One of a gardener's first lessons is to keep one ear tuned to Mother Nature and thus avoid that dread horticultural disease, zone map blindness, which can lead to a debilitatingly high buy-and-bury ratio.

There's more to hardiness than temperature, of course. There's humidity, wind velocity, summer heat highs, rainfall, soil composition, not to mention the human hustle factor, which can keep things alive by sheer willpower sometimes.

By the Lower Midwest, we mean upper Kentucky, all of Ohio,

Iowa, turn right at the Mississippi, and drop like a rock through Illinois and Indiana, thence to hover over Kentucky and Ohio, where it is stymied by the southern "flock" of warm air beating its way slowly up from the Gulf of Mexico, winging through Louisiana and the South, bringing moisture along like a trace scent of algae in the air. Some members of each flock may drop out, hovering in one area for a time and causing pockets of rain or cold or wind that have one gardener ecstatic and another a mile away cursing. Such effects are basically transitory. Droughts occur over large areas, and a wet winter tends not to be spotty.

Knowing *your* weather's patterns year after year is what allows you to say a winter is mild or brutal. It gives you as a gardener knowledge of the climate, or larger changes that occur on a bigger scale in a region. If you know your climate and your plants, you can come up with a personal and fairly accurate definition of hardiness.

Interestingly, plants rather than weather were the basis for classification of climates—"tropical wet," "tundra," "highlands," "warm summer continental" (that's us), or "cool summer continental." It may startle you to realize that our region's climatic counterparts are in Japan, China, and a block of Eastern Europe including parts of Ukraine, Bulgaria, and Rumania—not in England and Europe, whence some gardeners think we should buy all our plants. Those are part of "cool summer continental" regions and are only marginally like us in gardening terms. They do not have the wide swings of our Zombie Zones. (Incidentally, the person who worked out all these geologic regions around 1900 was a Russian-born meteorologist and climatologist, Wladimir Köppen.)

You may be able to cook authentic Japanese cuisine in Kansas City and swim indoors year round in Indianapolis, but palm trees still falter in St. Louis and the radiant blooming dogwoods of temperate forests wilt under the chill, dry winds of the Upper Midwest.

It can irritate, challenge, thrill, or amuse you, but the truth is that climate rules, no matter what the hardiness zone maps say. These maps have all the benefit and risk of generalities based on averages. Hardiness zones are a handy device for the newly hatched gardener looking for rules, but it takes very little seasoning to realize that hardiness is a relative term. This is because, thank goodness, gardening is an outpost of regionalism in a world otherwise largely rendered homogeneous through television coverage, interior climate controls, outdoor irrigation, "overnight" distribution systems, and deforestation of our world for suburban shopping mall parking lots.

Indiana, Illinois, lower Iowa, all of Missouri, and the lower parts of Wisconsin and Michigan. These are part of zones 5 and 6 but by no means all of those zones. The USDA map also pegs the water-soaked Pacific Northwest and the arid elevations of New Mexico, Arizona, and Nevada as parts of zones 5 and 6.

This book is about garden smarts—the kind of common-sense gardening done with a sense of geological destiny. It is the only kind of how-to gardening book I can write because I am a self-taught gardener with most of my experience in the Lower Midwest. By education I am an art historian who makes about half of a living writing about art and architecture and the other half by writing about gardening. I do both for the *Louisville Courier Journal*.

One of the most enjoyable things I do as a garden columnist is meet other gardeners, from whom I get to borrow ideas and expertise. Moreover, it makes me part of a large and generous, casual but important association of people who acknowledge the earth. I have met many gardeners who have forgotten more than I'll ever know. I am not always able to sort out what I've learned on my own from what I've picked up from others along the way, but I think it is important for garden writing to get away from what I call the seamless expert stance and acknowledge debts whenever possible. I will try to name names.

I also want *Gardening in the Lower Midwest* to reflect American gardens as more regional than national in nature despite recent books that attempt to shoehorn the whole country—and its dozen hardiness zones—into a single frame. The healthiest trend I've noticed is the movement slowly gathering force in the landscape-design community toward making gardens that reflect their surroundings. It is a legacy begun by Brazilian artist, musician, environmentalist, and landscape designer Roberto Burle-Marx, whose gardens reflect his consuming love of native flora and grand, tropical-sized design gestures. It is continued with great common sense by California designers such as Ron Lutsko, one of the first to concentrate on drought-tolerant native plants for a water-hungry region.

Gardening is regional, but there are immense, overarching issues that we must all know about and decide about. Overpopulation, deforestation, pesticides and the disappearance of toads, synthetic fertilizers and the contamination of groundwater, mega-agriculture vs. intensive, sustainable at-home agriculture, recycling, animal rights—if you can articulate your stance on issues like these, you are well on the way to forming a gardening philosophy that will inform your plant and design and tool choices.

All of this is true no matter where you garden—in the fertile floodplain of the Wabash, in the gritty city dirt of Chicago, among the rolling hills of Illinois, on the flatlands of Iowa, in the knobby hills of southern Indiana, or atop Kentucky limestone. I have lived in Arizona, Indiana, New York City, and northern California, and gardened most places. I have family in Iowa and on North Carolina's Outer Banks, and I have watched and helped them garden there as well as in their other lives in places like Virginia, Chicago, and Louisiana.

Like many midwesterners, I came home, and now live near where I grew up. My five and a half acres is large enough to be a bother but is mostly a blessing. It's a wonderful bit of property, with a creek and a little bog, patches of old and new woods, arid and scrabbly hillside, and a nice, sunny, deep-soiled plateau at hilltop. It has taught me a lot about yielding my gardening notions to the land and the climate.

GARDENING
IN THE LOWER
MIDWEST

First Lessons

MANY GARDENING BOOKS begin with sections on soil and how to improve it—and presumably oneself—by engaging in a little garden task called double-digging. Mine begins with gardeners, improved or not.

You can be a card-carrying gardener without once double-digging a border. Indeed, a fair portion of a gardener's education is derived from trying to avoid such wrenching work, on the premise that minds may last longer than bodies. Which is not to say that you blithely ignore a time-honored and, I concede, occasionally useful skill. It's just that not all known skills—or plants—have to find a use in your garden.

Some of the skills you need to navigate the modern and determinedly sophisticated world of gardening revolve around making informed decisions, and I don't merely mean which European market lettuce to sow or which roomy pair of mail-order trousers to order.

You learn these gardening lessons as you progress in the classic evolution from an interest in growing a few vegetables and annual flowers to a gradual appreciation and greed for every perennial known to horticulture. This enthusiasm, in many instances kept from excess only by the fortunate circumstance of shallow pockets, is succeeded by arrival at a higher plateau of awareness of the role of the more subtle foliage plants, including trees and shrubs, until, finally, there you are, right back at a new appreciation for the vigor and honesty of annuals, with the cycle beginning again and each time deepening the gardener's aesthetic and horticultural skills.

Along the way you have struggled to understand the difference between annuals and perennials, broadleaf and needled evergreens, determinate and indeterminate tomatoes, grafts versus plants grown on their own roots. You have picked up on the grand peculiarities of biennial flowers, suffered your share of mail-order mistakes, and learned that there is more to houseplants than dracaena and African violets.

But there are harder lessons than these—bigger lessons, smaller lessons; lessons seldom mentioned, much less taught.

Lesson 1: Nothing Is Simple

Consider hardiness zones. Nothing could sound simpler. Here they are, neatly colored guidelines, rules—almost laws—about what you can grow where you live.

That's why the redrawn plant hardiness zone map published in 1990 by the U.S. Department of Agriculture may have shaken up a few gardeners. Even if your yard landed in the same number zone as before, the basis for the zones shifted a bit.

The USDA map replaces one drawn twenty-five years earlier and confirms what common sense has told us. Cities tend to be hot spots in their zones, mountains tend to be cold. However, the new map does not support the greenhouse effect or global warming theory and instead tells us that overall, notably in the Southeast, winters are a bit cooler than they were in the 1960s. The cold zones are advancing slightly in Kentucky, Illinois, Missouri, Ohio, and Michigan. States with weather or winter temperatures similar to those on the 1965 map include Iowa, Kansas, Nebraska, and Wisconsin.

There now are three hardiness zone maps to consult. That is because there are three versions of hardiness reality. (I know, you hoped there was only One Big Truth in gardening—the last bastion of honor and optimism that crosses all cultural, social, financial, and racial lines.) Although the USDA map is the most widely published, frequently reproduced in mail-order catalogs and gardening books, you should at least be aware of two others. The AA map, produced by the

Arnold Arboretum in Massachusetts years ago, is used in the indispensable *Wyman's Gardening Encyclopedia,* reprinted by Macmillan in 1986. The Rutgers University map, developed by the school's Cook College in 1990, is seldom seen. (The U.S. Forest Service produces its own specialized zone maps, but we can ignore these.)

The USDA map has eleven zones. It marks Zone 6 as having annual lows of −10 to 0 degrees and Zone 5 as having annual lows of −20 to −10. The AA map with nine zones marks a slightly different Zone 6 with a −5 to 5 range and the area just north of that a Zone 5 with −10 to −5. This puts northern Indiana in its Zone 4 with −20 to −10 range, or the Zone 5 range of the USDA map. The Rutgers map has twenty-three zones, and its makers compiled their zones based on a lot more than minimum air temperatures. They also factored in maximum air temperatures, precipitation, wind, sunshine, humidity, elevation, and length of growing season. Gardeners know these things make a big difference. It's often not the winter cold that kills, it's the rain that rots. It's not the heat, it's the desiccating winds. The Rutgers map, therefore, is perhaps the most accurate of the three. But accuracy is not the issue. The one to favor is the USDA map, simply because it is the one used by a majority of the folks who sell us plants.

This will horrify those who dole out microscopic carrot and beet seeds one by one in a furrow or who insist on engineered edges to the lawn and shrubbery, but the truth is that you should consult any zone map as a generalization only. In fact, you can garden without ever consulting a hardiness zone map of any description. Rely instead on local knowledge. That means buying from regional nurseries, which normally won't carry plants that are not 100 percent survivors in their area and yet may indulge in variety past forsythia, maple trees, Day-Glow orange roses, and Stella de Oro daylilies. It also means close observation of good gardens in your neighborhood. To be very clear about this, it means avoiding national discount stores that mount instant garden centers from March through June, staffed generally by workers chosen for the ability to lose plant labels and swear that everything they sell will thrive in your region.

Or you can play the game more dangerously, using hardiness zones as challenges rather than rules. *Washington Post* garden writer Henry Mitchell once commented on a widespread trait among gardeners—the desire to garden one or preferably two hardiness zones south of where they reside. The Upper Midwest gardener, for instance, longs to grow too-tender American pillar rambling roses, he said, while the Bostonian covets magnolias and evergreen hollies and the Tidewater Virginia matron looks at her boxwoods and yearns for oleander.

Which brings us to microclimates, one of the proofs that Mother Nature doesn't read hardiness zone maps.

A microclimate is a nook where conditions are different from those in the rest of the garden. There can be microclimates on both sides of what passes for normal in the Zombie Zones. Of course, we seldom hunt for the chill, exposed spot, searching instead for an area beside a wall or hedge or in the ell of a house addition that protects from wind and cold and tends to augment warmth, allowing us to grow spring-blooming jasmine where we should not be able to.

Practically speaking, a useful microclimate is a space where you can grow tender plants, like that jasmine, but it also can be any spot with a peculiar set of circumstances. Wind baffles occur beside walls, hedges, solid fences, earth berms, slopes, hills, retaining walls, houses, or woodpiles. Boggy spots can be found near gutter down-spouts or around an outdoor water faucet. I have a rather nice one that is boggy only in the growing season and not in winter, when many plants can't handle wet feet. It's where I toss out dog water and refill dog water dishes in the summer. Desert conditions can be found under a deep roof overhang on the south or west side, in planters, next to foundations, on the tops of hills. Extra warmth often occurs near heated buildings where radiant heat loss can add up to as much as one hardiness zone or ten degrees' difference. Even insulated houses tend to heat the outdoors a bit. You might as well take advantage of it.

To find your microclimates, stroll about and note where you are warmest in a winter wind, coolest in a summer heat wave. You can follow the cats around in early spring, too. They invariably locate a late-winter sunning spot in the heart of a microclimate. If you insist on being technical, buy two high-low thermometers and set one at plant height for a week in the suspect microclimate, the other in a less pro-tected area, and compare notes each day.

Lesson 2:
Sooner or Later You Will Speak Latin

You shouldn't call a pelargonium a geranium, but of course we all do. This is one of the more famous instances of the verbal confusion that reigns as gardeners mix common names with proper Latin names. The boldly colored, large-flowering annual plant we call geranium is really a pelargonium, "geranium" being the proper Latin name for a low-growing, pastel-flowered perennial ground cover also known as cranesbill.

A small understanding of Latin names will wow your relatives, cow inexperienced gardeners, and put garden center clerks on notice that you are not to be trifled with. Hook up with the Latin system and you open the door to a vast and orderly world of plant nuts past and present. It is especially helpful in catalog reading; once a workable familiarity is acquired, you can be free of the bondage of color-photo catalogs with their invariably higher prices and/or lower range of offerings. There really are gardeners who thrive on single-spaced plant lists with the only English appearing as the price in dollars and cents.

You can acquire this knowledge painlessly, if slowly, by simply keeping an open mind and being willing to write the proper Latin name on your orders, your labels, and your planning sheets.

When you come across *Acer palmatum* 'Dissectum', make yourself read rather than pass over the Latin for a maple (*Acer*) with finely cut ('Dissectum') leaves shaped like a hand (*palmatum*). It's not as bad as being raised on U.S. measures and learning to cook in metric, but self-taught Latin nomenclature can be sticky going at first.

Blame Swedish naturalist Carl Linnaeus. He made it his life's work about three hundred years ago to give systematic Latin names to all the plants he knew—some 7,700 species—and to classify them according to their sexual features. He was the first to classify in this manner. Eventually scientists all over the world adopted his standard of a two-name naming system, and it is continued today. This two-name system is similar to the way we file human names last name first—Heilenman, Diane—in order to show the relationship of the individual to a larger family.

Clearly, *Itea virginica* and *Itea ilicifolia* are related. The first, as you probably figured out, is a native of the southeastern U.S. Its common names are sweetspire, Virginia willow, and tassel-white. The second itea is from western China and is more mysteriously identified as having glossy leaves (*folia*) like ilex (*ilici-*), which is holly. This itea does not have a common name that I know of. One itea is not like another. *Itea virginica* is hardy in Zone 6 and is valuable because it grows in sun or shade and in almost any kind of soil. Its Chinese cousin is of no account to us midwesterners; it's hardy only in warmer Zone 7.

Let's take ilex for our next example. We know this wonderful family of mostly evergreen trees and shrubs as holly. Again, not all ilex are equal, as those of us who have lived through winter dieback and kill-off know all too well. There's a big difference between *Ilex aquifolium,* known as English or European or, sometimes, Oregon holly, which can grow along the shores of Lake Michigan and in the moist air of the West Coast but is not happy elsewhere in Zone 6 and certainly not in Zone 5, and *Ilex opaca,* known as American holly, a hardy fellow that will thrive in Zone 6 and often in Zone 5. *Ilex crenata,* the Japanese or box-leaved holly, is a zones 5-9 plant that can suffer winter browning if subjected to harsh winds. Some ilex jewels for midwesterners are our underused deciduous and evergreen native holly shrubs, including *I. decidua, I. glabra,* and *I. verticillata.*

The alert reader may have noticed that my first example—*Acer palmatum* 'Dissectum'—in fact had three, not two, Latin names. The first is the genus name. The second, never capitalized, is the specific or species name. If there is a third name—which, by the way, can be either Latin, Latinized, or English, and which is not italicized but instead set off by single quotation marks—it indicates the variety or form. This last is a descriptive word, almost an adjective, that refers to a distinguishing trait or an important person connected with the discovery or dissemination of that plant. The variety name can be crucial in determining if a plant is hardy in a particular zone, or has some special characteristic that is desirable to a particular gardener. For instance, one form of the tender *Ilex cornuta* (Chinese holly) is 'Burfordii', which some folks in Zone 6 may get away with growing. But if they simply order *Ilex cornuta* without specifying 'Burfordii', they don't have a prayer.

Juniperus chinensis 'Sargentii' is a juniper from China named after the man, Sargent, who discovered it. *Juniperus horizontalis* 'Douglasii', sometimes called the Waukegan juniper, is a low-growing juniper named after the nursery in Waukegan, Illinois, that discovered it. However, it is not the only juniper with a prostrate or horizontal growth habit. There is, for instance, *J. h.* 'Blue Rug'. All of these plants are the same species, but the varieties differ sufficiently to warrant having names of their own.

And then—if you're still not sold on the idea of using Latin rather than common names—there's the matter of laurels. Oregon's Forestfarm Nursery, which produces one of my favorite no-pictures mail-order catalogs, alerts us to nineteen plants called laurel that actually range through genera including kalmia, magnolia, rhododendron, and arbutus as well as laurus. To say it doesn't matter is like thinking all women named Diane are related. Obviously, knowing a little Latin is helpful if you want to get what you ask for.

At the beginning, the game plan is to try to absorb rather than study this minefield of Latin terms. Don't be afraid to be ignorant. When you run across a plant you love, get the proper full Latin name and write it down. I keep these scraps in my schedule book, in my wallet, on the car dashboard, and in my pockets. I also lose them with great regularity, but it's amazing how much you retain by the act of writing.

Eventually you get to the point where you know a lot of names without looking and will think of firs as abies and willows as salix, or even geraniums as pelargoniums.

But remember, Nothing is simple.

Sometimes they change the Latin names on you. The genus Funkia became Hosta in my grandmother's era, and in mine the species datura became brugmansia; many of the plants we grew up knowing as chrysanthemum have been sent to live with other existing genera such as ajania, dendranthema, and nipponanthemum. The botanists do this for important reasons that really have nothing to do with keeping us gardeners in our place—because of revelations along genetic lines or because a conflict of names has appeared.

That is why we have reference books.

The bible is *Hortus Third,* a dictionary and description of plants cultivated in the United States and Canada, compiled by Liberty Hyde Bailey and Ethel Zoe Bailey and revised and expanded by the staff of the Liberty Hyde Bailey Hortorium of Cornell University. It is big and heavy and expensive, over $100, but it is sometimes offered as a loss leader item by garden book clubs. Look for this and buy it then. The other, much smaller book is *Dictionary of Plant Names* by Allen J. Coombes, from Timber Press. It cross-references plants by common name and Latin name. It includes pronunciation guides and limited explanations of the names, and it's small enough to carry to the nursery in order to double-check names prior to purchase.

When it comes to pronunciation of Latin names, here is a secret known to art historians, teachers, and newscasters. Say it fluidly and with confidence. Don't falter, stumble, change your mind, or apologize. Fully two-thirds of the audience won't know or care if you are correct, and of the other one-third, I'd bet that a good majority will think they've been mispronouncing it all this time.

Still, it never hurts to look up the proper pronunciation; but if you are caught in field circumstances, here are a few tips to help keep your tongue straight:

C and g are hard, as in "cat" and "gate," except when followed by e, i, y, ae, or oe. Examples: catalpa, gladiolus; but acer, A-sir; gynandra, ji-NAN-dra.

A double vowel, such as ii, is generally pronounced with two syllables. Wiltonii is Wil-TON-ee-aye.

The diphthongs ae and oe have a long-e sound. Example: arborvitae, ar-bor-VYE-tee; rhoeas, REE-as.

Final vowels are always long (ah-STILL-bee) except for final a, which is an unstressed "ah."

Final -es has a long e sound: ribes, RYE-bees.

When a word begins with one of these pairs of consonants, the first letter is silent: cn, ct, gn, mn, pn, ps, pt, tm. Example: psyllium, SIL-i-um.

Y is pronounced as short i. Example: diphyllus, di-FIL-lus.

It also helps to learn a few of the most often misspoken names. Clematis is CLEM-a-tis. Cotoneaster is co-TONE-e-aster. Liriope is la-RYE-o-pee.

Lesson 3: Plant Origins Are Important

The deliberately anonymous proprietor of J. L. Hudson, Seedsman, of Redwood City, California, once suggested that the purpose of human occupation of the earth is to distribute plant and seed varieties. There is some basis for this philosophical observation, which the proprietor did not mean as a joke, even given the nature of his occupation.

Knowing where plants came from—even long ago—is a basis for understanding where they will be happy to live, and gives you another clue besides the zone map.

Admittedly, many once-exotic plants are such agreeable world travelers that we forget where they came from. Tomatoes and peppers are from Central and South America and advertise this in the fact that, to us, they are warm-weather crops not to be set outdoors until the soil has warmed past 50 degrees.

Tulips are from Persia, not Holland, although it was Holland that set the civilized world on its ear with tulip bulb speculations in the early seventeenth century and laid the basis for the modern Dutch bulb industry, which also grows Near Eastern natives like daffodils and crocus. The first tulips came to Europe from a trip made in 1554 to Constantinople by botanist and diplomat Ogier Ghiselin de Busbecq. They still advertise their origins by requiring, as do most spring-blooming bulbs from the Near East, a hot, dry period of dormancy in the summer. Hot, dry periods are not typical of Holland, as only slight reflection will attest.

The list goes on. The Siberian iris is from Russia. Sunflowers hail from North and South America. The great rose family was immensely vitalized when European roses met American roses and Chinese roses. It's hard to imagine American cities without Chinese ginkgo trees. It's hard to imagine suburban housing developments without Japanese hollies.

But sometimes a plant is miserable when uprooted and asked to live in an alien environment. We discover plants on the mountains and grow them on the plains. We press woodland shrubs into suburban service on front lawns constructed over former pasture. We extract trees from swamps and try growing them on city lots. Location in the landscape of origin can be important. Pines that grow on the lean and mean scrabbly hillsides of the Rockies may get too rich a diet in the river valleys of the Midwest.

The names will often give you clues. Many plants from China are too tender for us. China roses thrive in Washington, D.C., but not in Indianapolis or Iowa City. As mentioned, Chinese hollies are not reliable for Zone 6, much less Zone 5. The word "chinensis" is a scare word for me, whereas "canadensis" tells me a plant might do well in the cool, dry air of Zone 5 but be somewhat unhappy in the moist heat of a typical Zone 6 summer.

The National Arboretum wants plant sellers to adopt a universal letter code developed by the American Association of Nurserymen in order to avoid the Latin name/common name dilemma. I don't have any problem with spelling out the full name, *Acer rubrum,* instead of ACRRB, or *Hosta* 'Honeybells' instead of HSTHBHN. Moreover, I resent this code idea as one more attempt to force me into computer mode.

What I do wish that plant growers and label makers would consider is a code to identify plant origin, such as SENAm for southeastern North America or NEur for northern Europe or Aust for Australia. The system would break down with cultivars of Chinese origin developed in America or tulip hybrids created in Holland, but it would give a grower some real growing information.

And don't give me labels with little circles variously filled in with black to indicate light requirements. I'd like to know if a plant wants moist sun or dry shade, is alpine, ericaceous, boggy, or an actual water-dweller. Too often we go for the broadest range when it makes sense to grow plants in narrower ranges of adaptability. That's what regionality is about. Who wants lackluster foxglove if you can have outstanding bee balm? Who needs a disease-ridden pin oak or English oak if you can readily grow a magnificent red oak? Why bother with pest-prone Australian pine when our native white pine works fine?

Lesson 4: Gardeners Must Be Trilingual

Latin is not the only tongue you need to converse sanely in this horticultural adventure. In addition to that and Standard English, a certain familiarity with the colorful, colloquial dialect of Gardenspeak is handy. It is a language of the soil that does not always find its way into standard dictionaries. And, because Gardenspeak sometimes conveys images at variance with actual meaning, you can't always rely on common sense. But once you get used to Gardenspeak, it seems as inevitable as spring after winter. Here's an introduction.

Acid-lovers: Plants that prefer to grow or will grow only when soil is rated acid on the pH scale. This is a simple determination with various meters and materials, but generally areas of normal to lush rainfall tend to be slightly acid to neutral. The desert and Far West, where rains are scarce, have alkaline soils because the salts are not leached out by the rain but stay up near the top. The major acid-lovers are azaleas, rhododendron, mountain laurel, and blueberries, but plants like enkianthus, clethra, and leucothoe also are acid-lovers, just not so picky about it.

B & B: Shrubs and trees and sometimes even large perennials are balled and burlapped so they can be transported without losing so much dirt and breaking off the critical feeder roots. Many ornamentals are sold pre-dug and with the root ball wrapped in a fabric that used to be burlap but is sometimes a plastic, open-weave fiber. They can survive, if not thrive, in this state for some time.

Cut back hard: Cutting back plants is universally understood, but many gardeners are too tentative and cut back too high. "Hard" means to above the lowest pair of viable buds. It is often done to rejuvenate a senile or too-woody shrub through fresh young growth but also is done to get a leggy, lank, and top-heavy hedge to start over and bush out properly. Compare to "pinch back," which suggests nipping out only the top growth of each growing stem using finger and thumb, as is done to encourage profuse blooming in chrysanthemums.

Dig and divide: A command that implies activities undertaken on perennial plant clumps every two to three years, which range from gently tearing apart overcrowded plants with the wrist action of a four-year-old to chopping resolutely into the mass of stony roots with a spade or axe.

Double-dig: An English system of outdoor torture wherein the gardener and a single spade improve soil by systematically removing topsoil, mixing compost with subsoil, and replacing topsoil. Intelligent gardeners try to delegate this chore to others, as in "Honey, could you please double-dig the twenty-foot-long rose bed marked with stakes?"

Drip line: This is the roughly circular area where rain tends to drip off foliage. It used to be (and often still is) thought to correspond to the outer circumference of the root mass and so was used as a guide for where to dig for B & B or the critical area for fertilizer.

Eyes: It sounds crazy to mammals, but many plants reproduce via their eyes. An eye is a bud on a tuber or rhizome, such as a potato, iris, dahlia, or peony. Eye can also refer to a cutting with a single bud on it and to the dramatically marked center or "eye" of a flower, such as a black-eyed Susan.

Foliar feed: Plants are flexible creatures and will transport nutrients whence they find them, at the roots or on the leaves. At one time foliar feeding seemed a revolutionary panacea, but sober studies suggest it is a supplemental method to soil feeding. Because plants literally shut down at night, closing the tiny stomata on their leaves, foliar feeding is best done during the day. Some houseplant foods are made just for this.

Force: This is an indoor sport for gardeners who like to plan ahead. You can make bulbs and shrubs flower out of season by manipulation of their normal dormant and growing seasons, forcing mums for Mother's Day and tulips for Christmas.

Green manure: Not to be confused with fresh or unrotted manure, which can indeed be green, this term refers to a soil-building temporary crop grown to be plowed under, such as rye, clover, alfalfa.

Grow on: The horticultural equivalent of "etc.," this deceptively brief term instructs the gardener to inform herself of all pertinent cultural facts on a specific plant and apply them, as in "plant out and grow on."

Harden off: Home-raised or greenhouse-grown plants cannot be suddenly stuck outdoors and expected to thrive. They require a period of acclimatization of as much as two weeks. During this time, the leaves and stems become tougher, literally "harder," and better able to take what nature dishes out.

Hardy: One of the gardener's most slippery terms, it is subdivided into many maybes—half-hardy, marginally hardy, not reliably hardy, hardy with winter protection—all supposed to help you gauge a plant's tolerance to cold and heat and other elements of climate and weather in various geographic areas.

Heel in: A phrase with different interpretations. In some versions, the gardener's heel is used to score a trench for temporary planting of bare-root transplants. In other versions, the heel comes into play as the handy tamper of the planted trench.

Hill up: A number of vegetable plants including potatoes and corn are commonly grown along by periodic heaping up of soil around the stem to encourage more roots. Other plants are grown in hills, a practice that makes a small community of plants, such as pumpkins, watermelons, squash, and gourds. Strawberries are grown on hills to increase air flow and reduce mold. Roses are sometimes hilled up after the ground freezes in order to protect the lower stem and graft, if present, from winter damage.

Limb up: In this major pruning activity where lower branches of deciduous trees are removed, it's actually the limbs that come down and the light level under the tree that goes up.

On its own roots: One might well ask, Where else would a plant be? The truth is that many plants, especially apple trees and roses, are cuttings from one highly desirable but perhaps tender or touchy type grafted to the sturdy and undemanding roots of another type.

Plunge: Not so precipitous as it sounds, this is the act of digging a hole and burying a potted plant in it up to the pot rim. It is done to reduce stress on both plant and gardener and allow less water and worry in the summer. Amaryllis bulbs and agapanthus, or lily-of-the-Nile, are often handled this way.

Stick: Non-woody activity of gardener making cuttings and "sticking" them in rooting medium.

Strike: Non-violent activity associated with propagation that means a cutting has rooted; e.g., it has "struck" when it resists a gentle tug.

Well-behaved: A relative term, it mostly tells you what a plant is not. A well-behaved plant is neither "slow to start," which means it takes forever to grow and may die before it does, nor "aggressive," which means the blamed thing will take over the garden.

Lesson 5: Compromise Is a Way of Life

You will never be right. You will never be finished. Such are the challenges of parenthood, writing, and gardening.

But you can count on having to make compromises.

The basic one, which underlies all other garden compromises, is the conflict between desire and budget. Budget, of course, can be a euphemism for time, as we all know that those who have money to throw at the garden can buy a big tree rather than wait for a little one to grow; they can buy perennials by the dozen rather than in singles to be propagated into dozens over a period of years. But all of us have to find a balance on a number of other issues.

COMPROMISE ONE: ACCEPTABLE DAMAGE VS. THE IMMACULATE GARDEN

I am getting fairly fixed in my opinion that we must compromise unreasonable notions of neatness and order in the garden if we are to have any planet left on which to garden. This is not just an untidy gardener's wishful thinking.

No garden is unblemished. That is an unattainable goal, a fiction we've been sold through advertising and garden writing done without the reality of hands-on experience, I suppose. But we are to blame, too. Gardeners and produce consumers must not ask growers to render impossibly perfect plants and fruits.

A garden is not a living room. If you can't handle a few bugs and fungi, get out of the garden. If you opt to stay and play the game nature's way, you have to figure out an acceptable compromise position.

A few holes in your hosta leaves from slugs seems a small price to pay to avoid killing birds and household pets with slug bait. A lot of holes and a dead hosta are another matter. (Wood ashes will stop the slugs, but you must be more persistent than they.) The annual rain of sticky honeydew from aphids swarming on your big tulip poplar will not bother you if you refrain from parking your car near the tree during that season. Indeed, aphids in spring are often cleaned out by ladybugs, which also do a great job on overwintering scale on indoor plants brought outdoors for the summer. Powdery mildew on bee balm, zinnias, and lilacs is unsightly, but not life-threatening. You need not kill every moth that flutters above the cabbage; you can cover it with water-permeable horticultural cloth instead. Those black and yellow caterpillars on the parsley will turn into swallowtails if they live. Plant more parsley if you don't have enough to share.

A rough border of wild shrubs, blackberries, and such encourages birds, which eat bad bugs. It also hosts wonderful garden companions like toads and snakes and the shiny brown ground beetles which University of Kentucky entomologist Daniel Potter calls "the cheetahs and leopards of the insect world."

Compromise does not mean giving up, keeping hands off. Every weed you remove in May and June is worth three in August. Every adult Japanese beetle dispatched means fewer white grubs in the lawn.

The moral of compromise is that you can avoid much labor simply by timing what you do to its most efficient moment. Buried inside this lesson is yet another: You have to do some chores even when you don't feel like it.

COMPROMISE TWO: THE QUICK FIX VS. THE PATIENT GARDENER

An immaculate garden, a flawless lawn, and picture-perfect shrubbery are a snare and a delusion. Instead, the goal should be a garden that is "clean" in the sense of being balanced. There are checks and counterchecks to the buildup of disease and pests, of both the insect and the vegetative sort.

The monoculture of one-grass lawns, the use of the same shrubs and trees as everyone else for miles around, and the continued planting of the same vegetables in the same spots year after year all encourage pest and disease buildup. This in turn encourages the fast chemical fix, which we also now know destroys self-balancing environments.

In a balanced *attitude* toward gardening there is a place for fast workers like synthetic fertilizers and knock-out herbicides and pesticides, but most of us are wary of the environmental price paid by thoughtless handling of these things or by thoughtless land-clearing and timber harvest.

But gardener, heal thyself! When you hear a plant described as vigorous, invasive, or rampant, do you immediately want it?

Although some plants, such as water hyacinths in Florida, purple loosestrife in Minnesota, kudzu in Tennessee, and Japanese honeysuckle and multiflora rose seemingly everywhere, can have invasive growth patterns that rival those of the human species, there is nothing wrong with many other exuberant but controllable growers. These include Lombardy poplars, silver maples, forsythia, lamb's ears, ajuga, ivy, German iris, scouring rush, rose of Sharon bushes, white pines, soapwort, the grass called gardener's garters, gooseberries, sorrel, privet, barberry, common "ditch" daylily, and on and on—dwarf bamboo, Shasta daisies, dame's rocket, violas, campion, columbine, some roses, garlic chives.

As your gardener's education continues, you sometimes wonder why people pay money to have these things. They are so easy to propagate at home that many gardeners secretly use the extras to fill the interior of the compost heap. I swear there are some springs when I can hear the chuckles of greenhouse and nursery owners, humming like a cricket chorus as they fill orders for soapwort, ajuga, or lamb's ears.

But there is nothing wrong with these all-too-willing plants as long as you understand the compromise they require.

A fair amount of gardening is getting rid of stuff that is getting in the way of choicer plants. This is called plant management, and it requires stern discipline. Do not permit the common, sprawling soapwort into your tiny or formal garden no matter how many times someone calls it a pretty wildflower. It is, and it serves me well now that I have it struggling for survival on a dry bank, but it got there only after I spent an entire spring and part of the summer pulling it off the rock garden sedums, which it threatened to swamp and kill.

I have grown or still grow all the above monster plants—and more, I am sure, that I simply don't yet know are monsters. However, I no longer fret at snatching a few ajuga with the violets while weeding. I am reconciled to a polite lack of interest when I take a few paper grocery bags full of German iris rhizomes to work. I feel like a wise and silent earth mother when I hand out generous starts of buttercup and hear the recipients respond to my warning that it will spread rapidly with, "Oh, that's great. That's just what I want."

You know you have had a garden growing-up lesson when you can deadhead larkspur before it seeds, root out holly seedlings without sobbing, and keep any new, potential garden monsters safely contained in a pot or behind a ground barrier for a few years until you see their true intentions.

COMPROMISE THREE: MISTAKES AND THE INSISTENT GARDENER

Doctors bury their mistakes. Architects plant ivy. Carpenters nail on trim. Gardeners go out early with pruners and saw and then head for the compost pile.

Sometimes you must compromise your vision. It sounds simpleminded, but don't struggle on and on, trying to grow what doesn't grow for you.

This advice has to do with not pining for plants you simply can't grow—like avocados or artichokes or palm trees—because they won't survive winters near Lake Michigan, but it also applies to plants everyone but you can grow.

Just as there are people whose personal magnetic fields preclude their wearing watches, I believe there are gardeners with selective black thumbs. I can't seem to grow mignonette or bachelor's buttons. Sometimes I think I am jinxed with roses. All the ones I really, really want either die, fail to thrive, or get cut down accidentally over and over again by myopic mower-wielding relatives. Bee balm, which prospered for me at two other gardens, has twice died at this house. I have killed lady's mantle, bear's breeches, and thyme more often than I can recall. I can't seem to keep heliotrope going from pot to garden and back to pot.

By all means try twice, maybe three times. Change the location each time. There is a notion among well-seasoned gardeners that often it's the spot and not the plant (heaven forbid it might ever be the gardener) that is wrong. Then, if it still doesn't work, find a substitute plant or—the hard-core compromise—find a non-living plug, like rocks or bricks or mulch, or a garden gnome.

If you can't bear to toss or pave, you are left with that greatest of garden compromises, the holding bed. As long as there is hope—and I know a lot of us will stare daily at a dead plant from March to June in hopes it will change its mind—move it to your private horticultural nursing home. This is a secluded, bring 'em back to life planting bed or area in semi-shade with well-drained, sandy soil. All canny gardeners have nursery beds with or without cold frames where they bring on tiny plants and experimental plants. These are sometimes called reserve borders, because they are the place where you hold shrubs and flowers and trees in reserve for future permanent siting.

If in doubt about the viability of a plant that you do want to grow on and on, put it in a pot and plant the pot in the holding bed. Many plants like being snug around the roots, yet it is a frequent beginner's error to plant out material that is too small to survive.

Lesson 6: The Genius Loci Will Rise Up and Smite You

Sometimes we simply make wrong-looking gardens or parts of gardens. A little voice nags at us every time we stroll past that place. "Try again," it whispers. "You can do it better."

It is your genius loci, no doubt.

The notion of a spirit (*genius*) at your place (*loci*) just waiting to guide your gardening hand seems like either a beguiling thing or a fruitcake idea. This is one of those believe-it-or-not concepts that never quite go away. Even if you use the phrase only at an occasional cocktail party, it behooves the modern gardener to know about the genius loci—a pseudonym, I think, for a complex of cultural ideas.

The genius loci can be traced to classical gardens, which originated as courtyards centered around a statue of the local god in that patch of Roman countryside. Alexander Pope, an eighteenth-century man of letters and a gardener, commands us still:

> Consult the Genius of the Place in all;
> That tells the Waters or to rise, or fall;
> Or helps th'ambitious Hill the heavens to scale,
> Or scoops in circling theatres the Vale;
> In the Country, catches op'ning glades,
> Willing woods, and varies shades from shades;
> Breaks, or now directs, th'intending Lines;
> As you plant, and, as you work, designs.

Pope was one of the first to elevate a minor Latin deity of place to a new role as the spirit of inspiration and the embodiment of a site. It was a reflection of a highly conscious attitude toward gardening as art, a recognition that gardening is not mere survival but a flow of give and take between gardener and genius.

Through the centuries, the concept of a garden muse has become a nest of ideas. Buried inside Pope's understanding is the idea that there is a perfect solution to each site, a notion currently extended to suggest that the perfect garden should look as if it "belongs" where it is. It is harmony of place or, in contemporary talk, a sense of the "life rhythm" that makes a southern or West Coast garden different from a Midwest one.

This may be just a fancy way of describing cohesive and thoughtful landscape design that begins with really "seeing" the site and its surroundings rather than starting with preconceived notions about proper and improper plants, colors, paths, etc.

In the event it is not, the logical question arises: How do you meet your local genius?

Go outside.

The genius loci is the reason why it is often so much easier to figure out where to plant things while standing in the yard than it is while sitting at the kitchen table with graph paper, pencil, and erasers.

It is why the plethora of big, beautiful picture books of landscape ideas are not very useful to anyone but publishers and photographers, and why, no matter how much you like the unkempt cottage look, it seldom translates well to a small city plot. No matter how much you covet a rock garden, it can look like riprap accidentally dumped in a backyard.

It is not always easy to contact the genius loci. This is because we are so far back in the reception line. We have allowed politicians, developers, and—now that 41 percent of American farmland is in the hands of people who don't actually, physically farm it—accountants and corporations to stand in front of us.

When we fill in wetlands, superimpose grid subdivisions on rolling farmland, and get rid of all those pesky woods in order to provide parking lots, we not only displace and kill our fellow creatures and jimmy up ecological balances, we also create a lot of Anywhere, U.S.A. places.

It is a fact of modern life that development, like the magnificent gardens of Versailles, is all about isolation and manipulation of the genius loci rather than harmony with it. Wouldn't it be nice if we could convince politicians, who could convince developers, who could convince contractors, who could convince bulldozer operators, about the reality of this genius? There are a few landscape architects and building architects who might brush up on the notion, too.

However, it is a cop-out to lay all the blame on other, more abstract shoulders. What with the modern gardener's insistence on aesthetics and frills (viz. the popularity of the edible landscape idea pioneered by Rosalind Creasy of California and others), we ourselves are frequently guilty of superficiality, collecting styles and trying to apply them like a veneer.

Consider what has happened with the lawn.

The genius loci was a guiding principle for A. J. Downing and other American designers of the naturalistic school in the first part of the nineteenth century. But we have largely been happy to accept mistranslations of Downing, without worrying that his principles were already a translation. And so we have turned the great meadow of the English landscape school of design well away from its original notion of serpentine lines and softly rolling grasslands punctuated by copses or little groves of trees. That is a silly sort of thing to try to visit upon small plots, although it still is a good design strategy for those blessed with a few acres.

Yet, the weight of unexamined tradition makes us feel good when sowing grass on any and all bare spots regardless of slope, degree of shade, unsuitability of soil content, or ridiculously small size. Thus we find the gas station owner growing grass on a mattress-sized raised bed between highway and gas pumps, and the urban dweller sowing grass on an unmowable eighty-degree slope of front yard separating house from sidewalk. Had we listened to the genius loci, we might be spared a lot of grass cutting, not to mention lawn mower accidents.

Lawns are a pretty easy target these days, what with all the noise over groundwater contamination by fertilizers, the environmental and personal hazards of misapplied pesticides and herbicides, and the need to compost lawn and leaf litter rather than send it to beleaguered landfills. There are other garden design notions that your genius loci might not necessarily recommend and that need to be examined for suitability before automatic use.

My quarrel with the increasing interest in planting landscapes to encourage birds and wildlife is that they are often a halfway commitment. I call it the Bluebirds Only approach. Please, no hosta-nibbling deer, delphinium-gulping bunnies, clever and ravenous raccoons, or—those wonderful garden companions for whom we must still discover a purpose compatible with gardening—groundhogs. A wildlife border is feasible but hard to maintain side by side with a basic American mindset for neat and prissy yards.

Another item on my list is simple-minded veneration for native plants, which becomes an astounding and reactionary isolationist movement against non-native species in one bit of legislation introduced in 1991 in Minnesota and tabled in 1992. It calls for labeling as suspect all plants not found growing in the state (a political boundary not recognized by flora and fauna) prior to 1800, and getting rid of any deemed invasive. (To be fair, Minnesota has had more than its share of woe from purple loosestrife and zebra mussels.)

Contemporary gardening is much more than a stress-relieving activity for baby-boomers, although it is that, too. It is a symptom of a radically changing view of the human position in the world. The danger of the current gardening boom is that it will reinforce the simplistic view of gardening as a hobby, or at best a means of improving the value of real estate through landscaping. (I recall one "fact" I have trouble believing, that $500 worth of landscaping can translate into $5,000 more in resale value!)

The nature of gardening is immensely complex. Perhaps the final lesson is mystical. We are part of circles inside circles. Gardening is a compromise between one's ego and the genius loci. I have a theory that gardeners are imprinted with extra optimism as well as a special gene for seeing things as they are *supposed* to look instead of as they actually *are*. This affliction (I call it the Scarlett O'Hara syndrome) is why we are able to so long ignore the large and serious issues floating about the garden in the late twentieth century: chemical vs. organic, small vs. big, sustainable vs. spendthrift, bioengineering vs. conventional propagation, agribusiness and us.

All the way back to the original, mystical Garden that appears in so many cultures, we have been trying to recreate or reorder the natural landscape. In the process we sometimes destroy the beauty, the balance—the genius—of what we are trying so hard to possess. Perhaps it is this notion of possession that trips us up so badly. The basic propulsion behind a garden is ego, a bit of stubbornness in the face of futility. We all know that gardens die when the gardener does. (Sometimes earlier. All you have to do is go on vacation for a month in June.)

It might seem that the final gardener's lesson is that a garden is temporal; the genius loci is not.

The eco-gardener in me worries that we find it good to chop up farmland into suburban ghettos of overlarge homes on undersized lots aggressively landscaped with plants pretty much the same as those next door. The frustrated city planner in me frets that all the while suburban developers are putting money in the bank, similarly scaled dwellings in the city go to waste.

In my thinking, the have-nots are not just poor city folks. They include all of us, and the bluebirds, hawks, foxes, toads, and butterflies which are being squeezed off the land to make way for our so-called gardens—and the genius loci, too.

2 *Gardens*

THE GOAL OF all gardeners is a garden. Therein lies the glory and the problem. What is a garden? Definitions are as individual as gardeners. For some, the garden may be a rectangular plot for growing vegetables and a few flowers. For others, it may be the hardscape—the framework of walks, walls, patios, pools, stairs, terracing, and other design features which one "infills" with plants. For still others, it may be a metaphor for an ideal world.

The garden has long been understood as a key to a culture's relationship with nature. And that, it now seems, is a metaphor for us.

A Brief History of Garden Design

Our earliest gardens were havens, sanctuaries where we, our animals, and perhaps some crops were kept safe—especially at night—from a harsh and rapacious nature. This notion of the garden as an enclosed world away from the "other" world was refined under the influence of different regions, climates, and cultural and religious thought.

In the Middle East, gardens were quadrants formed by a cross of irrigation canals that permitted the growing of scented flowers and edible plants. The quadrant was a sacred form, the symbol of heavenly paradise promised to Muslims by Mohammed. In the Middle Ages in Europe, the mingled herbs and other useful plants in enclosed monastic gardens served as practical medicine chests, while the enclosed garden and covered arbor of the medieval castle were a welcome escape from dark, dank, chill, and largely unprivate life indoors. By the sixteenth century the Italian mode of compartmentalizing garden space into formal outdoor rooms reflected an increasing exclusion of nature, made very evident by the prescribed symmetrical control over the garden.

By the seventeenth and eighteenth centuries such control became self-indulgent. The concept of nature comfortably tamed appeared in such conceits as the shrubbery maze and the popular and often elaborate "water joke," an automatic jet triggered by an unsuspecting stroller. (An intriguing contemporary parallel appears in theme parks with water features where visitors pay to ride rides that will "surprise" them in a similar, highly controlled manner.)

Geometric, formal gardens continued to be fashionable in the Western world until landscapers in eighteenth-century England developed the romantic notion of gentlemen's parks in the picturesque country style. Broad lawns and pastures bounded by swooping curves, dells and bosks, swales and lakes were testimony to the almost insolent human control over once-feared nature, a control so confident it could feel safe imitating the disorganized look of real, raw nature. Organic curves and asymmetrical, naturalistic plantings affected the later development of many of America's public parks under the influence of Boston designer Frederick Law Olmsted.

In the Orient, the story is one of organized naturalism. The tension of such an apparent contradiction of terms typifies Chinese and Japanese garden traditions, where the garden is an homage to nature, a symbol of the world often imbued with profound religious and philosophical overtones.

Japanese garden traditions are highly refined experiences. For instance, a "stroll" garden of whatever size is created to cause the stroller to deliberate on vistas, labor up hills, pause at certain points and choose a new direction or path. It is a garden that is a clear metaphor for life. The tea garden form is a symbolic journey from garden gate to house. A dry garden captures an entire environment in miniature, using a flow of gravel to symbolize water or rivers, rocks to mimic the mountains, and moss to suggest hillsides of flora.

American gardeners, largely unschooled in any gardening aesthetic or tradition and more accustomed to anything-goes design, can find this Japanese attitude rigid and non-experimental. Even some contemporary Japanese designers complain that the weight of these principles is too inflexible, perpetuating static garden design. Such complaints can be leveled at many design traditions in both West and East, but one element of Japanese and Chinese design I find valuable is that the design is based on shaping the viewer's perceptions. As gardens, they remind me most clearly of some contemporary participatory or environmental art, often called "site-specific art." Both art and garden are made to be activated by the observer rather than to be a simple, pretty picture like the all-American front-yard decor.

As even this brisk summary shows, to make a garden is no simple thing. One of the fascinations of gardening for me is the realization that my actions—many of them almost automatic rather than closely examined—add me to the long list of people who have sought to clarify their relationship to nature by modifying their surroundings.

It is equally fascinating to watch the many small and large shifts in desire and philosophy that mark the end of the twentieth century.

American Gardens Today

Although there seems to be no end to suburbia's sprawl and the proliferation of houses ringed with a necklace of evergreens studded each summer with pink begonias, there are clear indications of a more "insider" attitude—a desire for plants and gardens that attract birds, butterflies, bats, bees, and other easy-to-live-with wildlife. As nature is increasingly locked out of our lives, we see a meadow makeover, a paraphrase of a prairie, or a bit of marshy bog as the modern paradise.

They are, of course, laborious and rather mannered illusions to create in places where generations before us have labored to obliterate nature, clearing woods and making pastures which they little knew would become subdivisions.

Roger Swain writes of a philosophy he calls editing: gardening along the lines of least resistance, culling the woods or weeding the wild meadow rather than planting either. It is a cooperative notion that resembles the preferential-treatment gardening our ancestors must have done to slowly domesticate and improve crops and livestock. By not cutting a wooded patch, or cutting very selectively, you can in a year or three have a respectable-looking copse or small forest. If the neighbors and town ordinances do not get in the way, you can simply let a lawn "deteriorate." By neglecting it except for a once-over cut in the fall, you can have a labor-free meadow. It may not resemble the meadow of advertising agency dreams, but it will be real.

This intellectual shift—reflected in various statistics that close to 80 percent of Americans call themselves environmentally aware and 73 percent do enough yard work to consider themselves gardeners—seems a clear product of several realities of late-twentieth-century existence. One is a realization and fear that the weight of our impact on the world may be so heavy that we as well as nature are subdued. Another is the increasing urbanization—or more properly suburbanization—of our country, the abandonment of family farms and self-sufficiency in favor of a specialized society that allows many people a visual rather than personal relationship to land. Notwithstanding the accompanying mania for gardening appurtenances such as $2,000 teak benches, colorful clogs, and fancy tools, gardens are more than appearances. They are a means of escape from the now-uncontrollable "artificial" world of work and industry to a personal paradise, where physical labor is suddenly satisfying. The battle is no longer with nature; it is a person-to-person and nation-to-nation fight over the proper use of our little world.

Anthropologist Margaret Mead wrote an article for the journal *Daedalus* in 1960 on "Work, Leisure, and Creativity." She closed with a thought we gardeners might remember as we toil:

> We have so sedulously sought each his own view, swept clear of the hand of man, that we have failed to recognize to what extent our house or garden has become the "view" of others in this crowded world. We none of us take joint responsibility for the city streets, the combination of water tanks and occasional pleasant pinnacles which we call a skyline, on which our children's eyes must be fed, and so we learn to turn a blind eye to ugliness. Our unplanned towns and sprawling developments, our unwillingness to adapt a new building to the line of the buildings already there, have bred a people who expect beauty to be a piece of private property for which they take no responsibility.

Where all this will lead is unclear, but it is certain that to make a garden is to engage in a journey that only seems private, but actually is part of a gardening continuum. Perhaps what kind of garden you make is not so important as the fact of trying. If you want to try, here are a few garden types to consider.

The Night Garden

I once thought I had an original idea here. It came to me one evening upon my return from a summer's day downtown, indoors, slaving over a word processor, then home just in time to miss the garden: *I need a garden that peaks at dusk—a night garden.* Since then I have learned that I stand in a long line of gardeners enamored of scented, night-opening flowers and the soft mysteries of nighttime shadow and illumination.

Part of the magic is that in a night garden the senses are shifted and displaced. It no longer matters so much if you can see with your eyes. It is like a walk on the beach at night, when the ground under- foot is taken on faith and you can suddenly hear and smell and intuit what was masked during the day by sunlight.

The night garden is lit from within, a world of black voids and glowing paleness where the sense of smell becomes suddenly keener. Like a moth you are drawn to the sources—the sharp sweetness of night-opening brugmansia and its dramatic "angel's trumpet" flowers or the fugitive floral scent of four-o'clocks and *Nicotiana alata,* or flowering tobacco, whose flowers unfold only in the afternoon after a day of slumber.

There is magic in realizing that the night-blooming jasmine is on, full force, one sudden August night. The flowers are so ho-hum and small and appear so long before they mature enough to be fragrant that you forget about the plant. But when jasmine flowers release their destiny, it is a strong and tender, heady and beguiling fragrance that occurs only at a remove from the flowers. The unseen waves of aroma roiling in the dark that stop you in your tracks are silently calling to the moths. If, in the dark, you approach the jasmine, you will feel rather than see moths at the flowers, their wings moving as rapidly as a hum- mingbird's as they hover and sup.

The night garden is normally a world of gentle movement. Cater- pillars crop silently on leaves. Slugs glide about, absorbed in their task of forage. Butterflies hang frozen under leaves or twigs, asleep for the night. The fireflies, each somehow stirred to flight by another, begin rising like a shaken-out blanket of light points that move skyward to- gether. It can be quite a sight if you are lucky enough to stand watch over a meadow or large lawn. If you are very, very lucky indeed, you may feel and then see bats flicker overhead, intent on the capture of mosquitoes and other flying insects.

In my garden, it is usually 9 P.M. before the evening primrose buds declare themselves awake for the night. With a mild quiver, an edge of yellow unfurls from the green sepals, then pauses as if exhausted. After about ten minutes, some inner tension we cannot perceive has built, and the pale yellow flower opens in a slow whirl, released for one night to live its life as a chalice for moths.

A night garden provides quiet, intense entertainment. Built into it is a sense of privacy, of night worn like a cloak. Those who keep night gardens learn to stroll with the moon, to see without flashlights or streetlights, to slip through the night and the garden with a light presence.

The Japanese make moon gardens as variations on their stroll garden designs, where they meander about on carefully plotted walkways that control pace and open and close views before and behind them. Herbalists and symbolists construct their brand of moon gardens, which may be a circular space filled with crescent beds and planted with silvery plants or plants associated with the moon.

I know at least one such, conceived by feminists as a garden of metaphors related both to the Greek moon goddess Diana and to the monthly reproductive or lunar cycle of women. It is a wide-open theme, limited only by the maker's ability to make associations. The use of silvery-leaved plants, such as lamb's ears, mulleins, and artemisias, is an obvious design strategy that is visually effective at night. This is the simplest level, enlivened perhaps by equally obvious plant choices like the pulmonaria or spotted lungwort named 'Mrs. Moon'. But there could be a subtext, as well. You might grow plants long associated with women, such as pennyroyal, used to relieve menstrual cramps, or shepherd's purse, used to dispel afterbirth.

The presence of brugmansia or angel's trumpet is more complex in a feminist garden. The plant is a stunning tropical night-bloomer with long, trumpet-shaped flowers that emit an incomparable, sharp scent. It is a cousin of the ordinary jimsonweed or thornapple, and belongs in any night garden, I think, despite the toxic quality of the plant, especially the seeds. All of the tropical brugmansia clan are highly decorative semi-shrubs and small trees, which grow fairly fast. They are tender in the Midwest and must be hauled into the house each fall, when they often are so bushy you must cut them back hard. Until recently known as datura, they contain tropane alkaloids, which

produce atropine poisoning, symptoms of which include dilated pu-
pils, flushed skin, elevated temperature, and anger that can border on
the manic. Horticultural scholars now say that rubbing leaves of any
species of the genus datura or brugmansia on the body, especially in
the vascularly rich genital area, could indeed create the sensation of
flying.

The association of dark and private actions with gardens may surprise some readers. But, of course, flowers and plants have mutiple
levels of use and meaning. That is part of their fascination. Think of
Nathaniel Hawthorne's strange and compelling story "Rappaccini's
Daughter," wherein the brilliant Rappaccini, an "emaciated, sallow,
and sick-looking man, dressed in a scholar's garb of black," cultivates
an enclosed courtyard of strange and deadly flowers he distills into
medicines "as potent as a charm." The flowers themselves are so potent that only his beautiful and doomed daughter can touch them as,
indeed, in this garden the scent of these deadly flowers is what keeps
her alive and beautiful. She can never leave, and no one can touch her
or the flowers without becoming a similar captive. A night-blooming
garden is not usually that potent, perhaps, but all gardens are sensual,
and a night garden is overtly so.

My night garden is a very loose and personal ramble. I have
tucked night-blooming or night-lovely plants here and there as it
makes sense to me for a moonlit stroll. Some plants also are placed to
be seen and/or smelled when we are simply sitting out on the porch in
the dark, or, in the case of the night-blooming jasmine, positioned so
their perfume will waft through the screens of bedroom windows.

A day-and-night garden benefits from plants with pale flowers or
foliage, including airy gypsophila or baby's breath; gray-foliaged
plants including pussytoes, lamb's ears, and the artemisias; and—
some of my favorites because they add the element of sound—rustling, silvery ornamental grasses such as the head-high miscanthus
group or the dramatic ten-to-fifteen-footers like giant reed grass
(*Arundo donax*). Evening stocks (*Mathiola bicornis*) did not like me,
or perhaps they were sown too late in the heat of the summer.

I enjoy having evening primroses outside my bedroom window,
where I can see them first thing in the morning. The primroses are
biennials, but some annual plants that are suitable include the white
flowering tobacco (the colored nicotianas are not night-openers), best
grown to cascade from a tub or to sprawl over shorter neighbors;
moonflower vine (*Calonyction aculeatum*), which grows best with
cool feet and a hot head, like clematis; and four-o'clocks (*Mirabilis*

jalapa), which reseed prolifically or can be held over winter by digging the tubers and storing them in a dark, frost-free place.

Another must-have potted plant for your night garden is the night-blooming cereus, a tropical vine that combines what may be the world's most dramatic and pungent flowers with the least attractive foliage. The flowers are for night owls, opening from 11 P.M. to just past midnight for me in late summer. They are so photosensitive that they will close up if you hold a flashlight beam on them too long. It takes the plant several years to produce flowers—seven precisely, says my mother-in-law, who gave me a start from her grandmother's plant.

Many daylilies are night-bloomers, opening in the afternoon and staying fresh until the next day. Specific nocturnal varieties include 'Happy Returns' and 'Evening Belle'. Some white and pale roses, too, are basically at their best at night, including 'New Dawn', a superlative shrub and climbing rose for the Midwest, and the tall shrub 'Nevada'. Strongly scented roses are especially delightful.

One night-blooming perennial I am hoping to find is called abronia or sand verbena. It is a perennial of light sandy soils in the Lower Midwest with white flowers clustered in an open clump.

The Container Garden

What I like best about planting in pots is how it turns gardening into an upright pursuit. That's quite a consideration for those of us with iffy knees and backs. Such an upright, self-contained, and mobile garden also is perfect for landless apartment and condo dwellers as well as folks who plan to move and want to take the garden with them. It is easy to monitor watering and feeding and, perhaps best of all, you can shift things about to get just the right amount of sun and shade and wind protection.

The pleasure of a container garden is just this mobility. If you think of the regular planted garden as a sort of collage, where you can tug up and reposition an element (a plant or shrub or tree) that's been pasted (planted) in the wrong spot, then a container garden is an unpasted collage, a fluid design to play with.

It is amazing how handsome some plants look potted when in the ground all they look is puny and undergrown. Bulbs do especially well. In the ground they can look skimpy if not planted full enough, but it is a simple matter of crowding them into a pot to get a lush, expansive look. Many tender spring- and summer-flowering bulbs, such as agapanthus and clivia, are happiest crowded anyway. Mannered gestures like roses grown as standards or little lollipop trees always look best to me in pots rather than in the ground.

Herbs lend themselves to pot culture. Favorites include a more or less matched pair of bay laurels, indispensable kitchen herbs that also are good-looking small trees; marjoram and thyme to curl and cascade over the pot lip like an unruly haircut; and stiff, upright rosemary, always in need of a quick pinch to make it bushy and strong.

And there is something appealing if contrived about containers full of well-grown, healthy lawn grass.

CONTAINERS

Just as a collage can fall apart and be no more than too many colored pieces of paper, so your container garden can become a messy forest of pots unless you spend some time arranging and rearranging pot positions, and unless you take care to suit pots to plants and to avoid too much variety. It's hard to beat simple clay pots, although they can be pricey in the big sizes and rather fragile, too, and tend to break and chip if left out all year with soil in them. The wooden half-barrel obtained from distilleries and sold in the spring through garden centers and groceries is getting to be a cliché that avant gardeners sneer at. I don't, primarily because I can't think of anything more economical and useful. If fitted with a plastic liner, available at pond and garden shops, they can be pretty little water gardens.

Tires are the latest trendy container, and the more paint and the more outrageous the folk-artsy treatment the better. This does not appeal to me; I probably grew up too close to driveways lined with old tires planted with petunias.

Window boxes made of metal are so often flimsy and too small that it makes sense to buy or build your own using cypress or redwood. They should be at least eight inches wide and deep and as long as you need them but not unwieldy.

Pots come in a variety of sizes, textures, shapes, and even colors if you get into the plastic line. I prefer clay, and find that twelve- to nineteen-inch pots have the most pleasing proportions. Much bigger is too heavy. Much smaller and you need groups of three to make a visual point.

Don't forget odd pots, such as chimney pots, strawberry pots, or flat-backed wall pots. I am always on the lookout for stands, and have been pleased to locate an old wire trash-burning basket, the bottom of a fifties magazine rack, old metal stools, and a wonderful pair of funeral home plant stands.

Hanging baskets are a matter of taste. I think they are greatly overdone, although fuchsias, ivy-leaved geraniums, chenille plants, and—an admitted favorite—black-eyed Susan vine do seem to sell well. But hanging pots, however lush their growth, are usually too small to have sufficient presence hanging from porch rafters, tree branches, garage eaves, or street signposts.

If I make up any hanging baskets, I prefer the wire kind with sphagnum moss as a liner to the ugly, round-bellied plastic pots, even if the latter do require marginally less watering. The flat-backed hay basket is also a nice option.

Sinks and troughs—the real thing, old, weathered, and moss-covered stone—are pricey, rare, and very heavy. You can make your own substitutes by stirring up a batch of hypertufa, a mix of peat with cement and sand developed by rock-gardening fans (for recipes, see chapter 5). The traditional plants for troughs are alpines, sedums, and dwarf conifers. Troughs normally are displayed set up on two square stones or atop a retaining wall.

SOIL

Do not use garden soil in containers. It is probably weed-seed-infested and may be heavy, non-draining clay to boot. Container gardening allows you to fine-tune each pot to its population, so you can grow a lime-hating heath next to an acid-loving azalea. Another nice thing about container gardening is that you can fill your pots and "till" your soil without worrying that the ground is too muddy in spring.

PLANTS

There are very few plants that can't be grown in a container. Bonsai, miniaturized trees and shrubs, is the ultimate in container gardening. Most of us start with easier projects, like herbs and annuals, but many vegetables can be potted, too. A kitchen garden in containers is a good first project. Use bush or dwarf varieties of squash, okra, broccoli, and tomatoes—'Sweet Million' tomato is my top choice for pots. Full-size beans, peas, cucumbers, and other vines can be grown with a sturdy trellis inserted in the barrel. Carrots, beets, eggplant, lettuce, spinach, and peppers both hot and sweet are all about the right size in normal-size plants. You can even expect a few potatoes and onions. A number of vegetables and herbs are very decorative as well as useful: rhubarb, strawberries, globe or round-headed basil, hot peppers, and a variety of colored lettuces.

Perennial plants, shrubs, and small trees require very large containers to winter over without root damage; even then, many must be trundled off with a hand truck to a sheltered, unheated porch or garage to avoid root freeze. Or else you have to engage in fairly elaborate mulching practices.

The Water Garden

Water is magical in a garden.

Given the world's history of great gardens with great water features, from elaborate Italian water theaters to the carefully casual path and pond aspect of the traditional Japanese stroll garden, it is no wonder that we sometimes think you can't have enough of a good thing.

Consider Monet's brilliantly planted tangle of flowers at his water lily haven and gardens at Giverny; the fifteen hundred water jets at Longwood Gardens in Kennett Square, Pennsylvania; the serene, butterfly-shaped ponds at historic Middleton Place in South Carolina; the eerie beauty of mossy cold springs at Hanging Bog Nature Conservancy near Cedar Rapids; the exuberance of the Fort Worth Water Garden, so unexpected in the hot Texas climate; or the unassuming shallow fish pond—a holding tank for dinner—that is part decoration and part practicality at Thomas Jefferson's masterwork, Monticello.

Gardeners who are blessed with a one-acre pond or a ten-acre lake may find that planting it and keeping things tidy is daunting maintenance for one person. Gardeners on more limited land may discover that the idea of making a naturalized artificial pool is easy. Getting it to look right, to look professional, is another story.

Yes, it is true that you and a friend with good shoulders can dig and line a pool with plastic in a weekend. This does not guarantee that it will look like anything much more than a depression filled with plastic, water, and a few expensive water plants. The plastic liner has put water features in range of gardeners without a construction background or big bucks, but like many good ideas it has become its own cliché.

Louisville pond designer and maintenance expert Tiffany Scofield levels a little scorn at the notion of the liner as foolproof. She prefers whenever possible to go for concrete, which on a limited level is not beyond the scope of do-it-yourselfers capable of digging a two-foot-deep pond and wrestling with fifty to one hundred pounds of liner. The crucial points, she says, are adequate pump and filter systems and a willingness to get in there once a year with muck up to your knees and clean it out.

The initial problem for most of us is making it look right. After touring a lot of homemade and professionally designed water features, the best tip I have for creating a pleasing and perhaps extraordinary water feature in an ordinary yard is to opt for a small, geometrically shaped pool and to keep it simple. It's hard to improve on a circle set in a ring of flat flagstones. Rectangles are also nice. Flagstones can be set in mortar to overhang the edge slightly, creating a deep, well-like look. Rectangles need not be swimming-pool size to be effective. They can be compressed into long, slim channels or expanded to canal status, even raised above grade with masonry to form a lip just the right height for perching and meditation upon aqueous themes.

About the easiest way to get your feet wet, so to speak, is to buy a wooden tub, line it with plastic, and use it to hold a water lily and one or two other small plants. A large ceramic jar can be fitted up as a summer abode for a goldfish if you are willing to monitor the water and keep it clean just as you would a fish tank indoors.

There are so many options to the now overdone kidney-shaped hole in the ground ringed with rocks and set about with iris, hosta, and ferns that the first step in planning a water garden should be field research and not a trip to the garden center.

Here is an inventory of some historical water garden ideas that I like. Water is used in two basic ways: moving and still. Moving water can be a fountain, a rill, a cascade, a drip, or a torrent. Still water in moats, canals, and pools is often useful as a mirror or reflecting device.

Catch-basin and pipe is a derivation from Japanese design; you begin by disguising a hose or pipe by inserting it in lengths of bamboo. The hardest part here may be finding the bamboo. When you do, position the bamboo to allow the water to trickle, splash, or rush into a catch-basin. The catch-basin can be a homemade concrete platter, wooden tub, ceramic jar, metal pot, mound of stones, whatever.

Canals can be created by digging a ditch. The scale is up to you, from a narrow, long line traversing the lawn to a more pool-like six-foot-wide canal with a step-down on both sides.

Fountains of the stand-alone type with spouting winged cupids or fish often turn out hokey-looking. They are the garden equivalent of "plop-art," the urban habit of buying a large-scale sculpture and setting it on the first handy city plaza. Neither fountain nor sculpture tends to look very much at home in such circumstances. Think of the fountain and the setting together.

Water ramps or stairs, also known as cascades, are an old Italian device whereby one pool runs into another, lower one, which runs into another, lower one, etc. The scale is up to your yard and your budget. It can be a series of steep steps or a gentle descent from one pool to another. Cascades usually are done on a large scale.

Water curtains are a fall of water in a solid sheet along a wall face. They have many important precedents in twentieth-century landscape design, notably in the South American gardens of Brazilian-born designer Roberto Burle-Marx, with quiet, brim-full raised pools that empty into each other, and in Manhattan's well-known Paley Park with its more active, cooling, and noise-dampening water curtain.

And, of course, a natural pond or stream can be tidied up and planted on the verge with marsh marigolds, Japanese iris, hosta, astilbe, primroses, ligularias, ferns, and some of the moisture-loving sedges. You can use your natural water flow as a hydraulic source, to create cascades over a downhill slope or a series of created steps, or if the force of the fall is enough you can run fountains off the flow. For centuries natural hydraulics were the only means of pumping water in great water gardens, including Chatsworth in England and Versailles in France. Today's technology includes a handy little submersible electric pump and filter system that gives you many aqueous alternatives, even on flat ground. It is possible to connect it to an outdoor faucet and let it drip all summer, but it's more economical to rig a recirculating device. Exactly how to do this and how best to conceal the hardware in your design are questions that can be answered only on site.

Other water features require a bridge, ranging from a plank laid bank to bank to stepping-stones set irregularly in water, rustic sod bridges, and the somewhat overused arched Oriental-style foot bridge.

Here are some other challenges to consider in your planning.

Almost full sunshine is necessary for success with many water plants, especially water lilies. Avoid too many trees nearby. A scattering of golden leaves on the pool may look exquisite for a week in autumn, but eventually decaying leaves cause oxygenation problems.

Plants and fish do not always live together harmoniously, and both tend to expand their populations beyond the capacity of your pool if they are happy. Go easy on initial purchases and be especially wary of hardy water plants. The famous modern "water joke" is about the woman who spent the outrageous sum of $50 on water lilies and then five years later had to pay $5,000 to have them removed from her pond.

Water plants will require up to a two-foot depth if they are to be successfully submerged and wintered over outdoors. Ditto for hardy goldfish. However, bog plants that grow near the pool edges are normally lifted up on concealed rocks so that they sit in only a few inches of water. Almost all submerged plants are kept in pots, and the planting medium is held in place with wire.

Do not be talked into invasive, undesirable plants let loose from pots. Cattails can be thugs, so are some of the loosestrifes; the scouring rushes—named after the scouring action of tiny silica particles in the leafless stems—and hardy bamboos that "run" underground rather than clump can take over in short order. All require more elbow room than most gardeners have to spare.

Hardy water lilies, some of which were developed at the Missouri Botanical Garden in St. Louis, generally open during the day and have fairly small flowers. Recommended varieties include 'Pink Sensation', red 'Attraction', yellow 'Sunrise', and the fragrant white *Nymphaea odorata*. Tropical water lilies, which must be taken indoors to live in warm water over the winter, include nocturnal bloomers and amazingly large-leaved water-platters in the Victoria species that can have leaves up to six feet across. Look for tropicals bred to smaller sizes, such as 'St. Louis Gold', 'Shell Pink', the white 'Mrs. George Pring' (named after the St. Louis hybridizer's wife), and night-flowering 'Missouri'.

Pretty aquatic flowering plants hardy in the Lower Midwest include sweet flag (*Acorus calamus*) and yellow water iris (*Iris pseudacorus*). The arrowheads (*Sagittaria species*) and pickerel rush (*Pontederia cordata*) can tend to get pushy if planted in earth but are good for large water effects. One way to get around thugs is to buy new but rapid-growing tender aquatics each year once the water has warmed up. These include water cannas, umbrella palm (*Cyperus alternifolius*), and the Egyptian paper reed (*Cyperus papyrus*). You discard them at the end of the summer.

Now that you are dreaming of lush and lavish water effects, it may be the moment to mention that a pool kit from liner to plants, pumps to chemicals, and fish to fish medicine can run from around $350 for a small pond suitable for a single lily to close to $2,000 for a pond barely big enough (a 120-square-foot surface) for six water lilies and a few bog plants.

Hardy but unhyped water lilies can be bought for $25 or less each. You can lust after the water lilies with three-figure price tags, but wait to grow them until you are a pond master. Baby goldfish run a few bucks at the local pet store versus imported exhibition koi worth $150 each.

The Flower Arranger's Garden

Gardeners who entertain are often faced with an agonizing last-minute decision. Which is the greatest good—to leave the hostas (or peonies or roses or iris) in bloom at the front walk where guests will see them, or cut the blooms for an indoor arrangement?

The answer is neither.

There is no good way to have your flowers and cut them, too. No way, that is, unless you have a garden of flowers and foliage created just for cutting. Commonly called a cutting garden, I prefer the kinder, gentler term "flower arranger's garden."

You may start with a strip of zinnias in a spare row past the okra and arrive, eventually, at a large plot complete with paths and cold frames and raised beds, a place of propagation and experimentation that's often more appealing than the stiff and proper, no-slip-showing garden out front. A flower arranger's garden is a can't-go-wrong place in which it matters not if heights are not properly arranged back to front or if colors clash.

Many a flower arranger has been called forth from the bosom of a tender-hearted or parsimonious gardener wondering what to do with all those extra iris, daylilies, hosta, geraniums, rose of Sharon bushes, and so forth. Eventually, you get to the point of selecting plants you like for cutting flowers and foliage that suit your house or, as was and perhaps still is often the case, to use for the church altar.

Annual flowers are traditional subjects. It is fun to experiment with different ones each year. Some good ones are cosmos, zinnias, snapdragons, celosia, and many of the everlastings such as statice, sweet Annie, and gomphrena, which will just about dry themselves if stood in a vase. I also enjoy cutting various perennials and shrubs, including the dramatic foliage of the plume poppy, which is a small effort as the stems must be seared with a lighted candle as they are cut to keep them from drooping. Mine the vegetable and herb garden, too. I love the unexpected gaiety of tiny radish flowers borne aloft on high-branching spikes. If you don't know the spires of hedge hyssop (blue) and anise hyssop (pink), you are in for a treat.

Other good perennials and shrubs for cutting include old-fashioned tall, tender red cannas, which are hardy on the south side of my house but iffy elsewhere in the yard; Asiatic lilies, peonies, roses, buddleia, lacecap hydrangea, hosta, artemisia, euphorbias (which drip a white sap when cut), yarrow, clematis (float the blooms), peonies (cut in bud stage), grasses, forsythia, witch hazel, mock orange, baby's breath, asters, chrysanthemums, globe thistles, perennial phlox, Shasta daisy, and coreopsis.

The time and method of cutting count. Go to the garden before 10 A.M. If your feet stay dry it means the dew is gone, the sun is out, and the plants are drained of moisture. Go back inside and wait until the evening or next morning. If your feet get damp, fetch a bucket of tepid water and a sharp knife or shears. As you cut, immediately put each stem in the water and, if possible, keep the bucket in shade. Some flowers have toxins in their sap that make other flowers unhappy. These include daffodils, heliotrope, and the campanulas. Either make single bouquets or stand the offensive ones by themselves in a jar of water overnight.

Because you want your flowers to be clean, you may have to provide cages or stakes for those that can be beaten down in storms, such as lilies, peonies, and roses. Amazingly, the eight-foot-tall plume poppies hold their own most of the season and are felled by only the most severe storms. A handy plant cage can be had by simply using the knee-high round wire tomato cages sold everywhere that are too small for tomatoes. Bamboo stakes (tie with twine) or even branches stuck in the ground will work, too. Save your fancy plant labels and supports for the decorative border.

The Cook's Garden

Good cooks are often good gardeners. A lot of understandable pride is passed along with the dishes when the cook can boast that such-and-such is made entirely with home-grown ingredients. When I was a kid, my mother often laid on the pre-dinner praise, pointing not to heaven but to her garden as the source for the potatoes, the beans, the onions, tomatoes, corn, even the pickles. It got to be an overlong litany after she started raising chickens, too, and that's probably why we always discouraged her ambition to have a milk cow.

The vegetable plot has changed since my mother's day. In this new age of cooking, eating, and gardening, we make kitchen gardens, cook's gardens, *garni* gardens. It's fun, if you don't have to bear the weight of planting and digging enough potatoes to serve your family of four for a year, or canning enough green beans and tomatoes to last until next July.

The cook's garden is no mere patch of much-tilled dirt into which herbicides, fertilizers, plants, and pesticides—in that order—are injected. It has permanent paths, raised beds, a cold frame or two, a tidy compost heap, and a thick mulch of straw or newspaper to suppress weeds. It is festooned with trellises and tepees worthy of a first-year architecture student. It is planted with an eye equal to that of a freshman art major. Corn is interplanted with bush beans in a decorative diamond pattern. The pole beans bloom red and the bush beans grow purple. Lettuce is a year-round crop. Entire gardens are put together to serve a favorite cuisine, from Tex-Mex to Chinese. It is a little more trouble than that old rectangular plot, but a whole lot more fun.

A cook's garden requires some experience with how plants grow, so you don't get messed up with corn on the south side, shading the tomatoes, or sowing lettuce seed in July, when it is unlikely to germinate because of the heat. It requires diligent attention to providing fertility through strategies like green manure cover crops (e.g., winter rye, crimson clover, or buckwheat) and the use of genuine manure, preferably horse and preferably well rotted. It also requires vigilance so that unwanted cross-pollination among plants in the cucurbit family of squash and pumpkins or among corn varieties does not occur.

The cook's garden often is intensive, which means plants are closely spaced and attention is paid to succession, bringing one crop on in the same space as another which matures at a different time. Companion planting of plants thought to deter pests looks pretty and doesn't hurt. Absolutely critical, however, is the time-honored daily inspection tour to catch disease and pests before things get out of hand. The gardener-cook wants to avoid using pesticides and other compounds that have possible long-term negative effects in the garden and on the people and animals who use it. This means becoming familiar with organic and IPM (Integrated Pest Management—see chapter 7) techniques.

When you make your cook's garden, put it close to the back door. You will want to stroll in it and look out on it. A picket fence is a nice touch, if you can afford it, but I also like the simplicity of a frame and wire homemade fence with swinging gate.

Half the fun of planning a cook's garden is being creative about the style. This is a garden that delights in ingenious space and support solutions. The other half is in plotting how you will make patterns and combinations.

Lay it out with some formality. A four-square design is helpful, as you will have to rotate crops, or move the plants around each year, to avoid a buildup of pests and disease. Be sure to set aside a border or central island for perennial crops like asparagus, rhubarb, horseradish, and fruit. These also can be corner markers in your quadrants.

As you plant annual crops, borrow design elements from the flower garden. Use herbs and lettuces to form borders. Grow beans on arbors. Arrange broccoli like a hedge. Consider colors, too. Chives blooming pink next to feathery bronze fennel make a good combination. Bright green broccoli is stunning facing off the leggy okra with its hibiscus-like flowers.

Rustic supports are *de rigueur* if country is your theme. Consider making a framework for raspberries of straight branches lashed with baling twine to forked branches buried in the ground like fence posts. Construct a giant wire gateway trellis by bending large-gauge wire fencing in an arc and holding it in at the ground with stakes. Use neatly trimmed tree branches for garden peas to climb.

Fancy techniques to acquire include making standards, small tree-shaped plants, from bushes of currants and gooseberries; learning to grow the new dwarf fruit trees on wires, or espaliered into closely trimmed, decorative, and productive shapes; and growing woody herbs such as rosemary and bay leaf in topiary shapes in pots that are set out in the garden each season.

One of the greatest gardening pleasures is trying out unfamiliar plants. Some that you may want to include in your cook's garden are forcing endive, cardoon, salsify, crambe or sea kale, alpine strawberries, Egyptian or walking onions, elephant garlic, currant tomatoes, and climbing or Madagascar spinach. I do not recommend Jerusalem artichokes unless you just adore these crisp tubers. If you are not rigorous about digging them all up each fall, you will end up with a Jerusalem artichoke forest.

Other avenues to pursue are the many wonderful-tasting and wonderfully decorative peppers and heirloom or open-pollinated vegetables such as moon-and-stars watermelon, winter radishes, and fancy potato varieties. Choice fruits include kiwi, grapes—as long as your area is not plagued with Japanese beetles—and the prolific, delicious, and decorative midwestern sand plum or sand cherry (*Prunus besseyi*), which makes a fine informal hedge of stout proportions and a dandy jelly. Unlike its relative the beach plum, the midwestern sand cherry can handle dampish soil, but be sure it is light and not clay.

Be generous with flowering herbs to attract bees for cross-pollination. The ultimate touch for the dedicated cook might be a bee-hive.

The Cottage Garden

The cottage garden is really nothing more than a cook's garden done up with roses in swags, phlox in droves, and teak benches in four figures. Or, at least, so it seems to me. It has all gotten to be rather a bit too much of an American dream of a British fantasy, a romance of rural living that has less to do with earthy country plots complete with privy, well, and pigsty than with the current decorative fashion for the soft, blowsy, and unkempt garden—a sort of living chintz.

You can have a wonderful, casual garden that merges culinary and pleasure garden elements without devolving into a cluttered dependency on iris and black-eyed Susans, but it takes a great deal of plant knowledge, vigilant maintenance, and diligent deadheading to make a casual sprawl look good. If you want to try, think of making a working yet pastoral garden inside your larger garden framework. A cottage garden is a part of the whole, not the whole shebang. Therein lies its charm.

Just as a tidy fence is nice for the cook's garden, a sturdy wall around your cottage garden is required. It need be brick and higher than your head only if your pockets are deep and if the style suits your house.

British designer John Brooks writes in *Gardens of the World* that the cottage garden of today is a misinterpretation of the philosophy of British garden doyenne Gertrude Jekyll. We have, he suggests, picked up only on rustic mannerisms, such as roses tied to brick walls and clematis sprawling through trees, missing the point that a cottage garden is not decoration but a symptom of a holistic lifestyle in which gardening is necessary to living.

Think practical and spare, rather than romantic, lush, and soft. Over time, nature and human sloth will tend to soften the edges anyway. With that in mind, a cottage garden becomes a very achievable midwestern notion. We are, after all, the region of backyard vegetable plots, side-yard orchards with chairs set about, and front porches vined with morning glories and moon vines on which we sit to snap

the beans or shell the peas. We don't need to imitate the English countryside; we *are* the American countryside.

Here, at least in areas that have not become homogenized subdivisions modeled on Williamsburg, all we need do is indulge in a little
editing. Turn that side-yard orchard into a small meadow. Let it bump
up against a closely cut lawn for croquet and horseshoes. Tidy up the
vegetable plot and put in walkways. Plant a circle of herbs. Keep a
small collection of daffodil varieties in three neat rows along the drainage ditch out front. Let sumac grow up on the fencerow. Pull out the
barberry and put in clove-scented currant bushes. Forget 'Blue Boy'
holly and 'PJM' rhododendron. Admire that old snowball hydrangea or
bridalwreath spirea.

It may be that all you need to do to achieve an American cottage
garden is unthink convention. Mow the edges of your yard in curves,
not angles. Plant a deep border of fruiting and flowering shrubs and
trees. Have a picket fence out front, or an old-time (and admittedly
laborious) clipped privet hedge. Keep a gravel drive. Plant the public
sidewalk with flowers and herbs. Shade your front door with a trellis
and roses.

In short, pay homage to the old-fashioned American yard. Its
plants are proven stayers and its design is a true, unstudied, unsophis-
ticated cottage garden of its own type, well worth preserving.

The Garden of Grasses

Speaking of American classics, it had been suggested that the new
American garden is one composed of tall, bold ornamental grasses
such as those popularized in the past ten years through designers and
plantsmen including German transplants Wolfgang Oehme and Kurt
Bluemel.

There's no doubt that the ornamental grasses, which range from
mophead sedges to bamboo-like *Arundo donax,* are striking on their
own or as part of mixed borders. And they have a prairie look to them
that is very appealing in the Midwest. But the mere notion of an American garden style, much less a new one, is hard to believe in. This
country is too large to have just one gardening style.

Still, the grasses are a strong addition to a gardener's arsenal.
They are plants that are simultaneously the inspiration for and symptom of rethinking our garden emphasis. When you line up this rethinking in a sequence, it becomes a fascinating comment on what
might be called the nature nostalgia of this century.

GRASSES AS CENTERPIECES

Plain old front-yard grass planted in chocolate pots and wooden flats and used as dinnertable and fireplace mantle decoration may strike some midwestern minds as an excessively city-folks mannerism. However, as a former New Yorker I can testify that you do get real homesick for real land. Another thing I like the look of indoors is a tiny piece of sod at the feet of narcissus forced to bloom in a pot over winter or even at the base of a tall and woody houseplant.

GRASS AS FLORAL CARPET

This essentially rustic English notion is a very simple way to garden in small spaces such as courtyards, the strip between sidewalk and street, city lawns, and traffic islands. The turf is planted with a seasonal series of small bulbs, whose ripening foliage will not interfere with timely grass mowing. The sequence might run from white crocus in early spring to short-statured species tulips in later spring to tiny alliums in early summer with, in autumn, the unexpected punch of fall crocus.

The carpet effect can be much looser with a larger space. Here, your garden might be a lawn of different heights with an edge allowed to ramble into a near meadow until it is cut in summer.

GRASS AS SPECIMEN PLANTING

It can be no coincidence that the last great age of enthusiastic gardening was roughly a hundred years ago with the Victorians, and that they too valued the drama of a great clump of tall, feathery-flowering grass growing in the lawn. The grass most people think of is pampas grass, which is not hardy in the Midwest. We need to use either Ravenna grass (*Erianthus ravennae*) or *Miscanthus sinensis* for those arching clumps or, if we want a more bambooish effect, the tall and stemmy *Miscanthus floridulus* or the truly giant *Arundo donax*.

Do not grow bamboo unless you have space for it. The types that are hardy in the Midwest are generally the running types, which are best controlled by mowing around them in a twenty- to thirty-foot swath.

GRASS IN THE MIXED BORDER

The smaller the grass, the more important it is to use it in groups of three or more or in swoops or borders. Be sure to plant back from the edge to allow for a graceful overhang.

Grasses have a softening effect. They also can have very specific and special effects in a border. The larger grasses act like shrubs and small trees. They provide a sort of sliding-scale, up-and-down movement in the border as they grow fully up from the ground each year, changing from cut stubble to magnificent inflorescences of seed, which may be airy and beautifully insubstantial like calimagrostis or feather reed grass, or solid and substantial like the miscanthus group. The smaller grasses and sedges are terrific edgers and fill-in plants. Many make good ground covers. The festucas and pennisetums are sun-lovers. The sedges are woodland plants and like shade and moisture.

Pamela J. Harper, in her wonderfully useful book *Designing with Perennials,* calls grasses "see-through" plants that can go at the front of the border even when they are relatively tall. The plants growing behind are not totally concealed by the fountain of grass leaves and flower spikes.

GRASS ALONE

Wonderful effects can be created by grouping grasses. They are easy to handle, are virtually pest-free, and produce stunning effects from the early fresh green to the rustling browns and golds of late fall and early winter. Select with an eye for different heights, colors, textures, and bloom periods.

There are only two major maintenance times. The first is late winter or early spring, when you cut back the old dry growth to a few inches from the ground. This helps the plant renew itself each spring and avoids the awkward look of new green coming through tattered old stems. (In my yard, the grasses look great until around February, when winter rains and snows have taken their toll.) I also cut back low-growing grasses that tend to peak early and then go dormant, such as ribbon grass, once in midsummer to kick-start them again. Around the Fourth of July is a good time for the haircut.

The major grasses for midwestern gardens are the stately miscanthus clan, sometimes called Chinese silver grass, which comes in several variations; the pennisetum family of fountain grasses, which have spiky bottlebrush flowers and attain a medium height, blooming in early summer; phalaris, the ubiquitous ribbon grass or gardener's garters, knee-high with ivory stripes; panicum or switch grass, with a loose shape and a bright red color, effective in large colonies; calamagrostis, tall, upright, and very appealing; and the festuca clan of short, stiff, bluish mounds—common but still effective as a low border.

Gone Wild Gardens

This category is perhaps the main garden thrust of the future. There is an upsurge of interest in gardening for birds, butterflies, and other wildlife, using all-native species, making meadows, bog gardens, and woodland walks, reconstructing prairie, and generally letting go of the older, neater ideas of nature rigidly contained and disciplined.

But, as I have said elsewhere, wild gardening is more labor-intensive than is often realized. A casual-looking garden that is neglected will go to pot quicker than a neglected formal garden. It takes years to get a perennial meadow or prairie sturdily on its way so that you can back off a bit, and even then the patch requires regular mowing and some weeding.

Here are a few variations.

BUTTERFLY GARDEN

The quintessential butterfly haven will lie in full sun—the winged beauties don't fly unless the temperature is above 60 degrees—and will have stone paths, walls, wooden fences, or just open flat dirt areas for the insects to bask in the sun and get up to flying temperature. It will incorporate a wild and grassy meadow area with dandelion, nettles, and alfalfa. Borders will be planted in masses of flowers all the same color rather than a plant here and there in a variety of colors.

While the flora you need to plant to entice butterflies to linger in your garden will vary with what butterflies are around, there are a few almost universally appreciated plants for nectar sources and, equally important, as host plants for the caterpillars. These include butterfly bush and milkweed. Both will attract butterflies from afar.

A list of "universals"—which I have arranged in a rough sequence of bloom because you want to provide a full season of nectar, not just a spring tonic—might include the following: lilac, dandelion, dame's rocket, sweet William, daisies, larkspur, lavender, pink stonecrop, thistles (with awareness of pestiferous self-sowing and the fact that they may be outlawed in rural areas), mock orange, honeysuckle, zinnias, hyssop, coneflowers, black-eyed Susan, milkweeds, morning glory, passion flower, hops, butterfly bush or buddleia, phlox, and asters.

You should also have foliage plants, including carrot and parsley for the swallowtails (they are almost a sure repeat and breeding visitor to my vegetable border), cabbage family plants, mints, oak, clover, and a variety of grasses.

Refinements for butterfly pleasure include installation of a mud puddle or barrel of damp sand that you periodically salt. Mud puddling is a favorite behavior. The insects obtain critical moisture and salts as they congregate in seemingly convivial crowds.

Some butterflies, such as viceroys and red admirals, hang out near woods and eat sap, dung, and rotting fruit. If you live near a wooded area, you might indulge them with a feeding platform, which is no more than a table set up about four to five feet high and stocked with rotting fruit and bowls of sugar water (a 4-to-1 water-to-sugar ratio). Clean up the platform once or twice a week to avoid fatal molds.

A simple hibernation box can be made from a stack of long logs, covered with a tarp to keep the 'flies dry. Or use up those old coffee cans: fill them with dry leaves and bark and set them on their sides in the shade. You can, of course, also buy specially made butterfly boxes that are long, tall wooden affairs with slits for entry.

The only other rule of butterfly gardening is so obvious, it seems almost silly to mention it. No pesticides!

PRAIRIES AND MEADOWS

There are no hard and fast rules on creating made-at-home meadows and prairies. The simplest way I know is to just stop cutting the grass and see what happens. Usually you have to cut over the area—burning also works—once a year to keep the woody seedlings from taking over. As many farmers will tell you, a lawn may be merely a decade away from a cedar grove.

A more organized approach, which might suit suburban neighbors better, is to let your grass grow in four formal quadrants, separated and surrounded by neatly mown lawn. The quadrants will harbor an amazing amount of wildlife, particularly insects that attract birds. You maintain the quadrants at the degree of wildness you like by cutting over. It's best to do this in a regular sequence, so that only one quadrant is cut per year.

If you want to make a meadow or prairie from scratch, here are some specific tips.

First, pick your spot with care. Meadow plants like rich, moist soil. Prairie plants grow on dry, poor land.

I've tried plowing and seeding and all I can say is, begin with plants. Either buy them all or buy a few and propagate your own from cuttings, division, or seed. You can spend a year or two doing this because the construction of a meadow or prairie garden requires a lot of advance planning. Ground preparation, for instance, takes at least one year.

Do not plow. It will simply bring weed seeds up and allow them to germinate. Instead, let the area grow for a full year. Tell your neighbors what you are up to if there are local ordinances that can force you to mow the plot. Put up a sign: "Meadow in the Making. Thanks for Your Patience."

Or, mow as high as possible until around June, at which point let 'er rip and let annual grasses flower, set, and scatter seed.

Start small. You can always go bigger if you are successful. A ten-by-thirty-foot wild border may sound small compared to nature's scale, but for most human gardeners, it can loom large at digging, weeding, and raking time.

After the first growing-on year, mow the nascent meadow/prairie and let the cuttings lie. Then, plant your plants in early spring, perhaps March and certainly by April. Water every few days as necessary to get them established. This is critical. Go buy the amount of hose you need, hook it up, and keep it in place all summer so you will water.

If your ambitions run to a plot larger than a border, do islands and long patches with paths in between done in something low-growing like buffalo grass. The flower patches should expand annually, sometimes dramatically, because you are keeping down competition and, of course, watering that first year. Watch for visiting plants. Goldenrod and asters are very mobile in my yard. Of course, if those are plants you want, great; but if not, root them out or cut them back to avoid self-sowing. Aim for a good proportion of grasses to flowering plants. I think a ratio of 60:40 or even 80:20 is nice. Most people err with too many flowers.

Once it is established, leave your meadow or prairie in place until spring. This gives insects a place to overwinter and allows seeds to self-sow. Burn each spring, or cut and rake. If you do not rake, you will be smothering certain seedlings. A hand scythe works well. Avoid tractors and riding mowers, as they compact the ground.

Add new species as your plants grow. Be ruthless about removing woody seedlings. Once the meadow or prairie is established, you should not have to water it except in extended drought, if then.

Meadows might include ox-eye daisies, blue-eyed grass, wild yarrow, dame's rocket, fescues, foxtail, broom sedge, switch grass, redtop, timothy, wild strawberries, fleabane, clover, plantain, chicory, Queen Anne's lace, boneset and snakeroot, larkspur, Joe-Pye weed, ironweed, the yellow goatsbeard that produces distinctive round balls of airy seed, sunflowers, mullein, sorrel, dock, butterfly weed, bee balm, hawkweed, and liatris. I grub out thistles, white morning glory weed, and any plants that set burr-like seeds that cling to my dogs.

Prairies might be heavier on the grasses and could include buttercups, phlox, rattlesnake-master, coneflowers, dock, shooting star, and

Culver's root. Tall grasses will tend to take over, while the smaller grasses are most suitable for small areas with a few of the tall species as accents.

If all this is beginning to sound like work, remember that a homemade meadow or prairie is a garden, not a gift from nature. It will take about four years to have something approaching your vision that will even begin to take care of itself.

The Herb Garden

Sweet and simple and yet so complex, the herb garden is in many ways the basis of gardening and botany. If I could have only one garden, it would be of herbs.

The use of herbs forms the underpinning of many disciplines. The flower garden derives from the herb garden, although by the Renaissance they began to have separate lives as the aesthetic garden versus the practical one, forming the basis for modern notions of horticulture versus botany. In literature, the fast-forward history is that herbals evolved into either flower books (which led to the genre of flower painting or bouquet portraits) or herbal recipes, which branched in various ways to form the basis of the pharmaceutical and cosmetics industries.

Early garden layout is a fruitful subject for modern gardeners to pursue, providing lots of ideas for transforming the typical city or suburban plot. Herb garden design encompasses many classic elements of design in the need to have handy access to many different types of plants. The early garden, known as the *hortus,* was a rectangular enclosed place with a central path leading to the historical equivalent of the toolshed. The central path might be elaborated a bit to form four rectangular beds with a border of plants around the wall. Patterns of bedding might run to a grid of small squares divided by paths, diamond shapes, or elaborate "knots" and parterres formed by plants clipped into intricate patterns. Or you may try hub-and-spoke designs, island beds, mazes, and simple rows. One of the most memorable herb gardens I have seen is at Inniswood in Westerville, Ohio, just north of Columbus. It involves a meandering plan of paved walks and raised beds filled with herbs and shrubs and even small trees.

However you shape your herb garden, it will require almost full sun and well-drained soil. Many herbs grow well in gravel, a fact to remember if you ever want to turn a driveway into a courtyard.

Herb gardens are masterpieces of textures, foliage colors, and scents. The blue-green of rue contrasts with the silvery green of artemisias, the mahogany of bronze fennel, and the dark purple of some basils. The tropical look of soaring angelica merges with stately foxglove spires, and the felted leaves of mulleins make a foil for the dark, airy leaves of chervil.

It is not all subtle. There is ample justification for including showy flowers such as the old shrub roses, lilies, violets, and poppies, which had medicinal or culinary uses. And there is a good argument for having some shrubs and small trees, because most herbs die back over winter, leaving your garden bereft of structure. That is why it is so nice to have a strong pattern of paths and structural plants. If you want to keep it pure and low, go for short hedges formed from mostly evergreen woody herbs such as hyssop, germander, and even boxwoods.

Scissors will be your most important tool. Be reconciled to clipping, pinching, and shaping. Most herbs from floppy marjoram to bushy santolina need it and welcome it. One exception is the tiny, naturally globe-shaped spice basil, which makes a charming and primarily decorative border plant.

Make room for potted herbs, too. A large potted bay tree is a traditional central feature in an herb garden. They are easy to grow but hard to find. They are tender in these parts, and must be taken indoors over winter. Most rosemary varieties need protection, too, although I am growing a variety called 'Arp' that is said to be and seems to be more tolerant of hard freezes.

Planting low-growers like thyme and chamomile between paving stones seems a charming idea but has not always worked for me. I think it is much easier to plan for them to sprawl over the border edge onto the walk than to grow them successfully where gardeners tread.

Budget for a few bought plants, notably bay, rosemary, tarragon, and lavender (get *L*. 'Grosso' for hardiness in cold climates), which are all propagated by cuttings rather than seed. Most other herbs come readily from seed, except thyme, which is one plant I have great trouble growing well. I fuss with it either too much or too little, I guess.

Beware of sorrel and garlic chives. Both are pretty and useful enough—sorrel for soup, and chives for late summer flowers and leaves chopped for *garni*—but both will run you out of garden space in two years if you don't keep seed heads cut off.

The Collector's Garden

When in doubt about what kind of gardening you do, you can always fall back on the collector's garden. The tag can be a euphemism for an unordered tangle of plants in pots and in the ground, or it can describe the logically ordered garden of a botanical connoisseur.

Collecting goes in predictable stages, from early mild interest to final consuming passion that can turn a Sunday gardener into a home hybridizer.

Whatever, a family of plants is a lot of fun to play with. Doing so will speak to the botanist who lives within each gardener, and it will considerably boost your Latin plant name vocabulary. Some plant families that have long inspired rabid collectors include primroses, dwarf conifers, alpines, daylilies, roses, daffodils, hollies, hostas, and ferns. A fernery is one of my ambitions. If I ever get there, it shall be a sunken space, with grotto and pool. Another ambition is a bank of sedums, all dry, dusty, and splendidly subtle as to textures and colors. I have played around a bit with roses, but that is such a vast category that it is easy to be discouraged by the cost and depth of field. I am now interested mostly in climbers, but have been beguiled by the new English roses developed by David Austin. I continue to be fascinated with the *Umbelliferae* family, which includes celery, Queen Anne's lace, dill, chervil, parsley, parsnip, hemlock, and many other medicinal, culinary, and poisonous plants.

It goes without saying that the collector's first task is to duplicate the suitable environment and to do it with enough clarity of design that the collection is displayed rather than merely planted.

One caution: a collection of all one thing such as iris or peonies can be splendid once a season, but then that's that. This is why fanciers of old roses often end up clematis fans, too; the vines can clamber over the shrub and bloom after the roses are long gone. It's why iris lovers tend to become daylily lovers also. It's why it's hard to grow daffodils without some hostas or ferns to come along and cover the brown leaves.

A Word on Design

Rules are made to be broken, and it is often only in the breaking that you begin to understand why the rule works. It gets to be fun to try to understand the thought processes behind garden design elements rather than simply copying the effect. Still, there are some elements of design that can't be beat.

• A path or system of walkways is vital. Gardens are places to experience, in the American vernacular, although the Japanese style encompasses the notion of both a tea or stroll garden to use and a contemplative or Zen garden made to be viewed from without.

Many gardens are strolling gardens, deliberate if not always conscious metaphors for humans wandering through nature, sometimes cutting straight swaths of rigid control and other times designing gentle meanders that lie on the land like rabbit paths. A hill creates a journey that may have one path up and several choices when it comes time to descend the other side. The way may not always be clear or easy. Stepping-stones converse with the feet, eccentrically but cleverly placed to demand slow pace and a downward glance, which might be rewarded by a choice plant. When paving makes the way forward easy, perhaps a vista is opened.

• Buy one late-blooming plant, shrub, or tree for every spring-bloomer you acquire.

• Calculate space for behind-the-scenes and ancillary garden activities from compost heaps to toolsheds, from sandboxes to garbage cans.

• Be prepared for a long run. You can't make a garden in one year, or even two or three. You've got to stay put if you want a garden and not a yard.

• A sense of enclosure is critical, as it provides clarity and order even in the most spontaneous-looking garden.

A small city lot provides its own containment, usually, and the issue becomes how to avoid the claustrophobic. A suburban lot has set borders as well, and here the issue is often how to avoid the boring and expected three-sided border with a patch of central lawn. Larger spaces are equally problematic, and I have found that my five-acre plot would seem chaotic and unsatisfying without walls and halls formed by shrubs, paths, fences, buildings, and sightlines.

• Another and almost infinite point that can be made about making gardens is that they tend to—perhaps must—have a theme, a purpose, a point, a clarity, or some way to limit what you will do. Often the site suggests the context, such as a steep grade that becomes a natural rock garden. More often we are living on land sectioned off from former pasture, and the suburban plot has no more depth of context than a boxy city lot full of broken glass, cinders, and cat smell.

Take your inspiration from looking around you, not from standing at the nursery staring at pot after pot of euonymus and juniper. At those times when the floral muse does not visit, I do a quick run-through of tried-and-true design features, trying to figure out if any will suit a rethinking at my house.

Here are some of my favorite inspiration-provoking design elements.

Borrowed scene: What you can see from where you stand that is not part of your garden per se. It may be a glimpse of ocean or river or a hole punched in trees to reveal a far-off horizon. It may be the alley, which can be all right, too. The point is that even enclosed gardens need an occasional window. The light at the end of the path is often what draws you forward.

Canal: Straight and narrow waterways may be tiny bars in tiny gardens or broad water courses suitable for boats. Don't forget a flow of water as a dramatic sightline or a divisional device. It can be easier to do than a pond and cheaper than a bought fountain.

Desire path: This is the preferred path, not necessarily the desired walkway put in place by the garden designer. It sometimes is wise to let your children, dogs, and your own feet show you the proper placement of paths. You can subvert desire paths, of course, with hedges, shrubs, and fences, but there is no perennial bed I know that will keep pets and children and meter readers on the straight and narrow. Be aware if you don't want to be unhappy. (And see "Hazard" below.)

Drift: An irregular and large mass or sweep of plants is a drift. It gives stability and importance to a garden in a way that lots of different plants grouped together never do. A ten-foot drift of plumbago backed by an eight-foot zigzag of yarrow and anchored by five big clumps of daylilies often is more effective than a ten-foot-long border composed of a dozen different flowers.

Face planting: Small shrubs and ground covers are planted at the foot of and underneath trees and tall shrubs to face them off or hide the bare lower legs.

Forthright: This is the broad and simple path that approaches a house directly, without curves.

Good neighbor fence: A fence constructed to look nice from both sides makes good neighbors.

Hazard: A steep bank, pool, or other "natural" barrier placed to quietly direct pedestrians and traffic. It is a way of excluding people without building a fence.

Mount: An old-fashioned term for a small hill in the garden constructed for the purpose of having an elevated view of the garden and, coincidentally, a destination. It also acts as a visual and physical barrier. The modern equivalent is the berm, which can be a fine element if allowed to be large enough, like a sculptural earthwork or embankment, but often devolves into what a photographer friend calls landscape pimples. These are sometimes justified by the need to provide drainage or, I suspect, the gardener's wish to avoid digging.

Mowing strip: A paved area beside a border or change in grade will greatly reduce hand-trimming and produce a crisp look even in winter.

Perrons: Steps in the lawn created without flanking retaining walls are a gentle reminder of human intervention in a hilly garden that you don't want to look terribly formal. They are a way of suggesting terraces without terracing.

Roundabout: A traffic circle in automobile terms, it is useful in garden traffic control as well. Put a roundabout at the center of the herb garden or where several paths meet.

Secret space: An unexpected, semi-hidden place. It can be an open space inside a bamboo grove, a close-mown clearing in a meadow, a small patio ringed with tall hedges, a sunken garden.

Sitting walls: Free-standing masonry walls just the right height for perching. These walls, which might be a visual stop, part of a retaining wall, or part of a pool, are people-friendly walls, the kind kids love. They are not soaring English estate walls, but friendly intergarden checkpoints, visual stops that signal a change in garden pace.

Terminus: From the name of the Roman god of gardens and boundaries, this word now means the visual end point of an axis, a great place to place a sculpture, bench, column, or special shrub or tree.

Zigzag walks: A Z-shaped walk or bridge slows the pace, requesting a half-halt of the stroller. This is a Japanese device often used to nudge one into awareness of a well-set scene or a special plant.

3 *Plants as Partners*

ONCE UPON A TIME I harbored hopes of growing every plant in existence, a sure sign of a youthful personality weak on the design side. I am older now, and reconciled to the sad truth that I cannot. I am simply outnumbered.

Hortus Third lists 20,397 species and notes that's an incomplete list, with "only a selection of the enormous number of fancy-named cultivars. . . . The constantly changing offerings of plants listed by specialized plant societies that are served by their own journals, newsletters and registration authorities may not always be included since they are often transient in American horticulture" (p. ix).

Here today, gone tomorrow. There is some satisfaction in knowing that the plants and I share at least this, but it also helps explain why my list of favorite plants will inevitably exclude some you can't imagine living without. All I can say is, there are many plants I have not grown and many more that I don't even know I have missed.

Then there are plants that may grow a bit but never thrive in our zones, despite songs of praise from British gardeners and their climatic cohorts in the Pacific Northwest. I am thinking of delphiniums, which are best replaced by the giant annual larkspur. Some wonderful shrubs, such as the hebes, are not possible here; and even box, which can be grown in Zone 6, sometimes succumbs to a brutal winter—just when it is at its biggest and best, of course.

My list of plants as partners is simple-minded: it includes my favorites and why, plus any problems or tips I can think of. Some of these plants are as common as footsteps. Others are hard to find, but have stood the test of my time and and that of other gardeners whose work I value.

Ground Covers

Garden writers' quest for the ultimate ground cover has reached nonsensical proportions. They will define any short plant as a ground cover, regardless of how much labor or money is needed to cover a patch the size of a sofa with it. They will claim that plants like iris, daylilies, and roses make fine ground covers, even though any second-year gardener knows they are a weeder's hell. They will contemptuously reject as hackneyed and overused the Big Three—euonymus, ivy, and vinca.

Like everybody else, I have some strong opinions about ground covers. My definition of a good one is any plant a foot tall or less that is vigorous without being invasive. If it leaps out of bounds and visits the neighbors in the second or third year, beware! I am thinking of bad beauties like the glossy yellow creeping buttercup and the poor man's cypress, *Euphorbia cyparissias.* I found both and pounced upon them—one in a meadow and the other in a cemetery—in my eager youth and regretted both in sober middle age. (I have them still, of course. I just keep them subdued by mower and uncongenial planting sites, leaving the limelight for the horticultural thoroughbreds.) I have also encountered a few ground covers that aren't: slow starters too lovely to toss once you have them, but not much good at covering ground—things like *Mahonia repens, Cornus canadensis,* and the heaths and heathers—that merely struggle and straggle in the Zombie Zones.

I look for plants that are attractive from frost to frost and beyond, if possible. That's why I have eliminated bishop's weed, with its variegated leaves that invariably turn brown and tatty around the edges before it disappears early, leaving vast bare spots in your landscape. That old favorite, pachysandra, does not grow well for me, sulking and turning brown, dying out in the center, and just generally taking too much work and never looking lush. So it's not on my list.

Ivy, euonymus, and vinca meet all my requirements; plus, they are evergreen, almost pest-free, and, best of all, common enough that you don't have to take out a second mortgage to have a planting. I am not afraid to say that they are very much on my list.

Here, then, are my favorite ground covers for Zones 5 and 6.

Ajuga reptans (bugle)

Ajuga is a lovable, ground-hugging rosette of dark green leaves, sometimes variegated, that take on a rosy or maroon hue in winter. The leaves, which smother all weeds except the immortal violets and maple seedlings, are the backdrop in spring for a multitude of dense spires of brilliant blue flowers. If the blue is too much, look for *A. genevensis* 'Pink Beauty' or *A. reptans* 'Alba', a white.

Ajuga is a "jumper." It spreads by runners and sometimes dies out in the middle so you have to repopulate the inside of a patch from the outriders. I use it under maple trees, where it has to be fiddled with every other year to stay in place. As it roots readily almost any time of year, this is not too pesky a task.

Antennaria dioica (pussytoes)

Short, cute, and tough. The little felted gray leaves tightly hug the ground, producing each spring a surprising but charming array of three-lobed "pussytoes" of flowers. Very useful for dry, sunny to semishaded areas. I think the best use is in patches, among stepping-stones.

Arabis species (rock cress)

This is for growing among stepping-stones and in rock crannies rather than as a sweep of low cover. It blooms very early in spring with white flowers from a low spiral of lettuce-green leaves. I am always amazed at how cold-hardy it is. Rock cress is one of my personal indicators that spring has actually sprung. Look for *A. caucasica*. The fringe-leaved California rock cress is not hardy to Zone 5.

Asarum canadense (wild ginger)

The glossy, heart-shaped leaves form a neat-looking, almost evergreen carpet. A fine summer companion for deep-rooted deciduous trees, but it will not compete with shallow-rooted trees like beeches and maples. Wild ginger needs the shade of trees and the rich, leaf-mold soil of the woods. As a ground cover it can be slow to cover, a bit open, in which case let fallen leaves lie among it, cultivating a woodsy look. The flowers, seldom noticed, hide under the leaves.

Ceratostigma plumbaginoides (plumbago or leadwort)

Once you have fallen under the spell of plumbago, you will never garden without it. Its summer-to-frost flowers are a heart-piercing in-digo. The foliage is nice, too. It turns a pretty red as days cool and then disappears, leaving a network of brushy, brown flower heads for winter interest. Plumbago grows almost anywhere but needs a bit of shade with adequate drainage.

Cotoneaster (rockspray)

The low cotoneasters like *C. horizontalis* have a striking sculptural quality seldom seen in ground covers. The skeleton of branching woody stems, often described as a fishbone or herringbone pattern, carries the day in winter when the glossy, leathery leaves may have darkened or even dropped. They aren't fully evergreen some winters. But, add brilliant orange-red pomes or berries, a red fall color, and it's close to a four-season winner. Watch it closely the first year or so and water when rain is scanty. I've killed cotoneaster with too much shade and dryness.

Dianthus (pinks or carnations)

The gray strings of leaves form cushions of color all year round. The spice-scented flowers in spring on tall stems are elegant icing on the cake. Indispensable in rockeries and for dry banks, it gets old and woody and must be cut back and/or transplanted for renewal. Let me put that more strongly: If you ignore dianthus, it will eventually die out.

Epimedium (bishop's hat, barrenwort)

Epimediums are the steel magnolias of the shade border. They look shy, with thin wiry stems, delicate, fluttering leaves, and fey pink or yellow flowers, but can handle the toughest competition. They grow out of an ivy bed where even my dogs can't kill them by lying on them. They are clumpers rather than spreaders for me.

Euonymus fortunei (wintercreeper)

So hardy, so easy, so evergreen. It is the ground cover of last resort and least resistance. It can be a sprawler, a climber, a near-shrub, and it's almost free, as it seems to appear in every garden, a gift of the birds. After wintercreeper blooms, attractive, papery capsules form, each of which splits to reveal a trio of red-orange berries. (*Note:* The shrub called burning bush is *E. alata* or *E. europaea.*)

Euphorbia cyparissias (poor man's cypress or spurge)

I've already badmouthed this takeover artist, but it is too nice to ban entirely. Few plants are strong and tall enough to rise above its stranglehold, although the tall bearded iris and Siberian iris seem to. In fact, that's why I keep the stuff. There's nothing prettier than the chartreuse of this spurge's long-lasting flowers in spring with the purple of the iris.

Other low, mounding euphorbias are also good, but tend to be more front-of-the-border plants, and some are rather tender for the northern parts of Zone 5.

Fragaria vesca (alpine strawberry)

Its common name should tell you something of its hardiness. The alpine strawberry is not fazed by Midwest winters or summers. It holds its pretty rosette of serrated leaves for most of the winter, when they deepen to a dark green with reddish tones, and it unfurls a new batch of lime-green leaves in early, early spring. It has pretty white flowers and tiny, delicious berries, from early spring to a few in a mild December, too! Grow in your kitchen garden or in any semi-shaded or sunny spot. Sowbugs travel for miles to find the berries and chomp big holes in them, so keep garden litter—sowbug hiding places—picked up.

This is NOT *F. virginiana,* the wild strawberry that runs rampant with long runners. The alpine variety is more of a clumper, although it tends to sulk in the middle as the clump expands and needs attention every few years to tease apart and replant the clumps. It's also easy to start from seed.

Geranium (cranesbill)

Perennial geraniums are ramblers. Called cranesbill for the look of the seed capsules, they have distinctive round, almost fringed leaves that turn red in cold weather, and a seemingly endless crop of flowers in pinks and lavenders and a few blues. You can keep a plant slow-growing in heavy soil and lots of sun, or let it fling itself to the four corners in light, rich soil in a semi-shaded border.

Hedera species (ivy)

The issue with ivies is winter burn, or browning, and subsequent die-back. Usually, ivy on the ground fares better than ivy on walls. Gardeners in the northern reaches have to be clever at what they buy, but I think the ivies are like the bamboos. They are undertried rather than underused.

Do yourself a favor and try something besides Baltic ivy. I have *H. cochina,* which has gorgeous deltoid-shaped leaves as big as salad plates, growing as both ground cover and upright cover for a chain-link fence. It's gorgeous. Others that are fine outdoors but not quite as vigorous as conventional ivy include 'Woerner', 'Wilson', white variegated 'Ivy Lace', and the self-descriptive 'Buttercup'. This last is a soft yellow that tends to revert to green. When it is allowed to climb, it seems to keep the yellow best.

Remember the old adage about ivy: The first year it sleeps, the second it creeps, the third it leaps. When it leaps, be ready to keep it edged.

Hypericum calycinum (creeping St. John's wort)

If you know the bush form, you'll love the running form. The plant has cinnamon-colored woody stems, attractive all winter, and a late spring and early summer crop of bright yellow chalices of petals cupping a distinctive cross of stamens. I like the globe-shaped buds, too. I've grown it in semi-shade, but it seems unfazed by sun. Creeping St. John's wort or Aaron's beard is a hardy ground cover into Zone 5. Although it can suffer bud damage there and in Zone 6 cold blasts, the roots are very vigorous and spring growth is rapid. A little occasional pruning early in the spring usually is in order anyway to promote bushiness.

Juniperus (junipers)

The creeping junipers—the 'Blue Rugs' and their ilk—may be boring, but they can't be beat as impenetrable evergreen cover for slopes. They will grow even in gravel. They are cheap if you buy them very early at the temporary garden shops set up at discount department stores each spring while they are numerous and still in good shape. Encourage new roots when you plant them by teasing out or slicing into the root ball.

Lamium and *Lamiastrum* (the dead nettles)

These guys are engaging shade plants, with variegated leaves that hold most of the year. The lamiums have white or pink flowers off and on, and rounded leaves that tend to sparkle. The lamiastrums have pointed leaves and yellow flowers clustered along a short spike in spring. They are nice as a woodland carpet and happy anywhere, from gravel in sun to moist clay in half-shade. In winter, don't let them get totally covered by mulch, but they can handle some leaf cover; when it is removed in the spring, they spring forth with fresh growth.

Liriope (lily-turf)

It is seldom grown well, is too tufty and too dark, disappears in winter, and is widely mispronounced (it's la-RYE-o-pee). But it *is* an attractive edger. It will bloom in rather dense shade. And I have seen it used imaginatively and well in a formal scheme with hostas under the high canopy of shade trees. My real objection to lily-turf, which has a pretty lilac or white spike of flowers in late summer, is that it is readily infested with grass and you can't tell the weeds for the liriope. It's one ground cover that you must start with a lot of plants in hand, closely spaced.

Sedum (stonecrop, dragon's blood, and many other common names)

This is a large group of tender and hardy succulents. The hardy sedums range from tight-napped ground covers like *S. spurium* or

'Dragon's Blood' to those stalwarts of the later perennial border, *S. spectabile,* with pink or coppery-red flowers at knee height.

It is important with the smaller, lower sedums to pick the right spot, somewhere dry, sunny, gravelly. You will fall in love with them as energetic trailers and clumpers for the front of the border, banks, or containers. Pick the wrong spot, where the soil is rich and other plants want to horn in, and you will hate the sedums for being such wimps that anything can roll over them. Slightly succulent, these are creeping mat-formers that root readily from the smallest piece. There is a stunning variety of leaf colors from yellow to blue and even variegated. Flowers, which tend to be clusters of tiny starry blooms with dots of stamens, range from yellow to white, pink, and red. Keep sedums well weeded as they are getting established.

Veronica repens (creeping speedwell)

An easy grower, this mat-forming veronica can leap about a bit if given ideal conditions of deep, rich soil and adequate moisture, but who cares? The flowers are an unusually intense and pleasing blue, which is great anytime, especially in early spring when you get a little tired of the predominating yellows. It has not been invasive for me in heavy soils and dry soils.

Vinca minor (periwinkle)

A trailer rather than a creeper, vinca has small, glossy green oval leaves and charming square-edged light blue flowers. Good for shade, it's a tad slow, but once it's there, it's there for life and nothing bothers it.

Perennials, Bulbs, and Corms

One of the themes of this book is that there's no use pining for what won't grow for you; but there's also no point in settling for plants rather than selecting them. The problem with perennials is that there are so many of them. It's easy to get sidetracked, trying something novel all the time and despising the classics. And it's easy to get bored, growing the same old thing just because you have it, rather than trying something new.

The following list gives my current favorites.

Achillea (yarrow)

Tolerant plants, the yarrows come in several useful versions, all of which have ferny, aromatic foliage and flat, almost platelike clusters of flowers that stand above the leaves, sometimes at a great distance. Increasingly, I find the yarrows coarse and a bit irksome in all but the herb border and maybe among rocks; however, they are sturdy and useful plants, wonderfully drought-tolerant and long-flowering—an excellent beginner's choice.

A. *millefolium* is more meadow player than border star, but there are garden varieties with pastel and deeper colors, with 'The Pearl' and its white pompon flowers in pride of place. The flowers dry easily, as do those of the even more common yarrow, A. *filipendulina,* the fernleaf yarrow, with its distinctive tall stems topped by deep-yellow saucer-sized flowers.

Alcea (hollyhock)

Actually a biennial that you sow or allow to self-sow in late summer so it makes top growth before winter, the hollyhock is an old favorite. It can use a little updating, I think. If there have been breakthroughs in breeding for tolerance to rust or resistance to defoliation by the caterpillar of the Painted Lady butterfly, I don't know about them. I grow hollyhocks anyway, even though I know that some or all will look just awful and must be hidden behind other plants.

I could kill the caterpillars. Or I could quit with hollyhocks for a few years until they go elsewhere. I can't bear either alternative and so I struggle along with seven-foot-tall, tattered hollyhocks and very happy butterflies.

Alchemilla (lady's mantle)

A beautiful plant, with silvery-green, pleated leaves and small green-yellow flowers in late spring. It's so easy and spreads so quickly that lots of people use it as a sort of ground cover and can't believe that I keep killing my new plants. I think it's too much shade and moisture, although it's said to need a bit of both.

Allium (onions and chives)

My introduction to the ornamental nature of this family came after leaving vegetable garden onions in the ground over winter in a flower bed and watching them bloom year after year. The perfectly round balls of tiny flowers atop tall hollow stems are a wonderful shape in the border. Alliums are a large family of culinary and ornamental wonders, from four-inchers to five-footers. Most bloom either white or magenta-pink. One to try is the delightful lily leek or golden garlic, *A. moly,* with starry yellow flowers in three-inch-wide clusters and big gray strappy leaves, that is wonderful as an edger. Deadhead if you don't want seed and seedlings scattered about. Grow on the dry side.

Anemone (Japanese anemone)

A choice fall-bloomer, this member of the buttercup family is a showy and fresh alternative to asters and mums. The open-faced flowers rise up at least two feet and reveal the large, plush yellow center. I prefer the clean, sharp white of all the colors, which range to purplish red and rose. There are other anemones besides the Japanese, and many of them, such as *A. canadensis,* the meadow anemone native to our region, are shorter and bloom in spring or early summer.

Aquilegia (columbine)

Dainty and fey, the columbines are spring heralds with pretty lobed leaves and flowers of such an odd shape, all lipped and spurred, that you simply must pause and dissect the first one you see. The columbines have been much bred to produce many colors and color combinations. They can be pretty spectacular. If you want to keep them that way, you must grow only one kind in one border or you will find them hybridizing behind your back and producing mongrel seedlings.

Biennials, they produce a pretty clump of leaves the first year and airy stalks of flowers the next. It is easier to start the seed than to transplant a mature plant, although tiny babies move all right. Cut off seed heads before they shatter, or harvest the tiny black seeds and toss them about in sunny places.

Armeria maritima (sea thrift)

Tiny gray-green leaves and equally exquisite white flowers a scant inch above the ground make thrift a delight. It must have sharp drainage and an airy winter mulch if any. Mine grows in humusy gravel, which rock gardeners call scree.

Aster

Asters are a must for fall bloom. You get hundreds of tiny, daisylike flowers on each plant, which are long-lasting and carefree, but they must live on the dry side. I prefer the tall ones like *A. novae-angliae,* the New England aster, that can stand rather more moisture than most. It is usually purple with a yellow center, but it's worth looking for the named variety 'Harrington's Pink', which is not just a nice color but good for cutting as the flowers won't close up on you.

I also let the native white heath aster, *A. ericoides,* with its gadzillion tiny white flowers, have its way wherever it's not in my way.

Astilbe (false spirea)

There's no such thing as a bad astilbe or too many astilbes. A distinctive plant, with handsome pinnate leaves and tall plumes of tiny florets in shades from white and cream to rose and bronze, it must have adequate soil moisture and half-shade. It will not tolerate noonday sun. Astilbes are garden gems, part workhorse and part pure beauty. Also, they are one of the easiest perennials to dig up, pot, and bring indoors in January for early forced bloom.

Baptisia (false indigo)

When you need something big and bold, try baptisia. In the blue or white version with very showy pea-like flowers, it is around three to four feet tall, is amenable to sun or dappled shade, thrives on average soil, attracts butterflies, and is drought-tolerant and long-lived. Striking, it is what I call a subshrub. Leave the dead stalks all winter or trim them out in the fall; it comes anew each year from its roots.

Belamcanda chinensis (blackberry lily)

The best use I've ever seen is atop a limestone ledge, where a long colony of these iris-lily-looking plants send up their strappy leaves and then tall stalks of small orange mottled brown flowers. As if that weren't enough, they are followed by seed pods, which split open to show a tight cluster of shiny black "berries" that hold well until winter rains beat them down. Don't try them in your deep-soiled perennial beds, where they linger rather than live, but they revel when you let them bake in the rockery.

Bergenia

The big, bold, burnished green leaves with a maroon reverse are nice. They spread in a spiral, creating a dense cluster of leaves that you just want to ruffle with your hand as you pass. Flowering, which has been sparse for me, produces a stalk of pink flowers in spring. Bergenia looks good for most of the winter, but needs a protected spot. That's why I call it an edger or accent rather than a ground cover. It's tough, but can be tattered by wind and too much adjacent foot and dog traffic. It likes good drainage. If it's not growing for you, that's a sign it should be moved or the soil improved with grit.

Boltonia asteroides

A bushy, big perennial with asterlike flowers, boltonia is a nineties kind of plant—an undemanding, drought-tolerant full-performer for late summer. It takes this subshrub several years to build up to size, which is perhaps waist-high, but when it does, one boltonia can dominate a small border. The white version, 'Snowbank', seems to be more reliable in the North than the pink- to purple-flowered varieties.

Brunnera macrophylla (Siberian bugloss)

This comes with so many recommendations I am ashamed to say I've never grown it. Up to five feet tall, it's also known as summer forget-me-not. My correspondents like its big, heart-shaped leaves and showy, loose racemes of blue flowers in early summer. It thrives in rich, moist soil and self-sows like foxglove, although some northerners treat the biennial as an annual.

Buddleia (butterfly bush or summer lilac)

I count the buddleias among perennials because they grow best as a subshrub in the border. Cut them all the way back to the ground every spring if they don't die back naturally. I find them a little graceless and top-heavy standing all alone and, with the dieback potential, a waste of space in the shrubbery.

The fragrant, large panicles of bloom in white, purple, blue, and pink weight down the stems, bending them over like commas. The buddleias can dominate a late summer border and, if winters are mild, give a sense of life to the dormant border, as small pale gray-green leaves can be persistent. They are wonderful cut flowers. My varieties are both *B. davidii.* The spring-blooming buddleia is *B. alternifolia,* which tends to hold its stems over winter and be hardier.

Calamintha nepeta (calamint)

A delicate and airy wealth of pale lilac blossoms all summer long makes this little-used cloudlike plant a treasure. It resembles catnip, which you might guess from "nepeta" in the name, and has a minty aroma. All in all, it deserves a common name, and I suggest Cloud Nine. It likes sunny, well-drained sites.

Caryopteris clandonensis (blue mist, bluebeard)

A shrub I also classify as a perennial, it's treated just like buddleias and blooms even later than they do, in August. The leaves are silvery and the flowers heavenly sky-blue. It's tidy and easy as long as it has sun and excellent drainage. I always root a half-dozen cuttings right out in the garden in early fall as insurance in case winter moisture gets the main planting.

Chrysanthemum

Mother's Day daisy is what we call *C. maximum,* the Shasta daisy, because that's when this so-familiar, so-willing, white-rayed daisy blooms. I am not a big daisy fan, thinking it a family easily overdone; but the Shastas are good fillers just when the garden makes its awkward turn from spring to summer. Keep the flowers cut and it keeps on coming a bit. When they are all done, the foliage will be a rewarding mat of bright green. You pay for all this garden help in the fall. The Shasta daisy should be dug and divided every other year at the least.

Fall chrysanthemums are a confused field. There's been some recent renaming and I never do get it straight, so I just buy the colors and forms I like without worrying over labels and then propagate as necessary each spring to keep them from going all woody in the center and dying. All need good drainage, especially over winter.

I've been disappointed in the variegated *C. pacificum* so highly touted. It grows well enough, if not vigorously, but it takes it so long to do anything that it's frost before you see a noticeable clump, much less the tight little yellow buns that pass for flowers.

Coreopsis

The only coreopsis worth having is the threadleaf one called 'Moonbeam'. It's ferny, delicate, and compact, and the pale yellow flowers blend well with almost anything else and do not require deadheading. In short, this coreopsis is the opposite of the older members of its family. I have not had much success with the pink coreopsis that came on the market in the last few years, but I hear good reports from other gardeners.

Crocus

You've got to have a few, either the big Dutch hybrids or the pretty little species that bloom in spring. I like them in the lawn, dotted about like stars. The thin leaves die back before you begin to cut grass, and so the bulbs have a chance to mature. The autumn crocus, *Colchicum,* which produces leaves in the spring and flowers without leaves in the fall, has to be planted where the fairly big and unattractive leaves can mature and turn yellow. I grow mine in an open clearing in the woods, but they also are good in rocky areas.

Digitalis (foxglove)

Every border should have this; the long bells carried in groups on tall stalks lend a look like no other. If you are a casual gardener, you will love the way it self-seeds. It's a biennial, so don't get impatient.

Echinacea purpurea (coneflower)

A prairie find, the coneflower is another good beginner plant. The daisylike flowers are either rose-purple or white and have a typical droop, with the petals reflexed down from a big orange pincushion center. It's dramatic and worth growing despite a fairly coarse and weedy look. It blooms all season. It is a cinch to grow from seed, but takes two years to flower.

Eupatorium

Mistflower and Joe-Pye weed are both eupatoriums, but they could hardly be more different. Native plants of our dry and moist woodland edges, they have great utility, vigor, and good looks. Too often passed over as "mere" wildflowers, the eupatorium family is part of the huge influx of native plants into flower borders that is a hallmark of late-twentieth-century American gardening.

Mistflower at the edge of my woods always occasions a comment from visitors who seem to see its sky-blue powderpuff flowers for the first time and ask, "Is that a wildflower? Can I get that somewhere?" It's not too tall, perhaps knee-high, and tolerates some shade. Mistflower most resembles a grown-up annual ageratum.

Joe-Pye weed is a magnificent giant, soaring in one season taller than a basketball player and topped in late summer with stately clusters of mauve flowers. It likes lowland meadow conditions, which means a bit rich and moist, like the back of your best flower border. It takes a half-dozen plants to look right.

Ferns

I am still in the process of getting an education in this vast horde, and won't distress fern-fanciers with the names of the ones I have killed. So far, I am the happy caretaker of lady ferns, which any idiot can grow as they are almost pestiferous; the couldn't-be-tougher, leathery evergreen Christmas fern that I have moved in a snowstorm without harm; and the pretty, silvery Japanese painted fern. All are planted in a small woods where they and some hostas help hide the maturing foliage of a mass of spring-flowering bulbs.

Gaura lindheimeri

A recent find from Texas, this plant has been a bit of a buzzword in the perennial gardener's pipeline in the past few years. I like the way it carries large pinky-white flowers on tall stems like a flight of butterflies and blooms in late summer.

Grasses

The craze for ornamental grasses has allowed enthusiasm to bypass field tests. Not everything I thought was hardy has turned out to be so.

I have no trouble with the miscanthus family, which is one of the bolder, bigger ornamentals with five- to ten-footers like *M. sinensis* and its striped and variegated versions and its immense cousin, the ten- to twelve-foot bamboolike *M. floridulus giganticus. Phalaris,* which is available as green and white gardener's garters or as yellow ribbon grass, is also easy. It does need to have a haircut in July so it will look fresh in September, but its only predators that I know of are my dogs, who love to eat it. Another winner is feather reed grass, calamagrostis, a fan-shaped upright grass that blooms in early summer.

Don't bother with Japanese blood grass. It dies over the winter. The lovely pennisetums, with their foxtail infloresences, are marginally hardy, too. And don't let anyone talk you into pampas grass, a South American native that will not live in the Midwest.

Helleborus orientalis (Lenten rose)

I was frustrated by the hellebores until I had one more lesson in the importance of names. I had been buying the touchy *H. niger* or Christmas rose. After watching them live long enough to bloom in late fall, then die, I discovered that what I really needed was the easily transplanted *H. orientalis* or Lenten rose. These will self-sow into colonies—a nice invasion indeed—that bloom sometime in late winter or very early spring.

Hemerocallis (daylilies)

Gardener's choice. There's no way for even the advanced gardener to sort through the nearly 30,000 hybrid choices. Pick your colors—anything but blue or pure white—and pick your height—from hand-high to almost your shoulder. I like the old citron lily (*H. citrina*), a light yellow, fragrant night-blooming daylily that is an ancestor of many new yellow varieties. I like a newer, shorter red and green daylily, 'Mallard'. I have some with dark "eyes," some with unequally sized petals that droop in an almost-too-elegant manner, some that are stocky and plain, strong gold, and some maroon and orange ones that seem rather closely related to the tawny orange ditch lily (*H. fulva*) scorned by seasoned gardeners.

There's no point in paying big prices unless you are hybridizing or playing a one-up garden game. Daylilies expand rather willingly, and you can hasten the process and reduce the cost per plant by three strategies: (1) In spring, divide a clump and pull it into pieces, planting each in a sandbox that you water and fertilize all summer long.

You should be two-for-one or better by fall. (2) Look for volunteer "proliferations"—tiny plants produced by some daylilies on the scapes or bloom stems after bloom is over. Snap them off gently and set bottoms only in a bit of water until roots form, which is a week or so, and plant. (3) Finally, collect seed and plant it. It's easy, although it may be two or three years before they are big enough to bloom. Daylilies naturally cross, and usually only one out of a thousand is of greater merit than the parents, so this is not a path to fame or fortune but merely a cheap way to have lots of mostly the same daylilies.

Heuchera (coralbells)

The variety 'Palace Purple' has taken the country by storm in the past five years, and rightly so. It's wonderful. Rich, dark purple leaves all year round, and a long period of bloom in spring and early summer with airy spires of pale flowers. However, the Perennial Plant Association cautions that now everyone and his cousin is naming purple-leaved heucheras that come from seed, and purples are not all equal. Buyer beware.

The non-purple species, which has branched spikes of tiny bell-shaped red flowers, is also worth having. Plant these where you can conveniently water them, as they don't like drought, being shallow-rooted. Sun or part shade is fine. Propagate by division or midsummer cuttings of leaves with a bit of stem attached.

Hosta (plantain lily)

Let me admit that many of the hundreds and hundreds of so-called different hostas look alike to me. I am interested enough to want to grow a half-dozen that represent the range of forms and colors: something big and blue, like *H. sieboldiana elegans;* something big and yellow, like *H.* 'Sum and Substance'; something variegated; something small; and something white-flowering, sun-tolerant, and fragrant—the old classic *H. plantaginea grandiflora.* You couldn't go wrong with any of them.

Here are some more recommended by hosta experts. It's a short list but represents an overlap of favorites that is testimonial to these hostas' reliability and beauty. Try 'Antioch'; 'August Moon'; 'Blue Angel'; 'Blue Umbrellas'; 'Ellerbroek'; 'Frances Williams'; 'Fringe Benefit';

'Ginkgo Craig'; 'Gold Standard'; 'Golden Sceptre' and 'Golden Tiara'; 'Halcyon'; 'Love Pat'; 'Krossa Regal'; 'Seadrift'; 'Sun Power'; *tokudama; undulata univitatta* and *u. albo-marginata; ventricosa* and *v.* 'White Edge'; *venusta;* and 'Wide Brim'.

I keep mulch over my hostas until well into spring, as the stiff pointed shoots can be damaged by a late frost. I remove the mulch when temperate weather hits, a move that I think reduces slug habitation. So far I don't have a slug problem, but many do. Ashes, twiggy mulch, or sharp sand deters, as do strips of copper laid on the ground.

Hyssopus originalis (hyssop)

Considered an herb, but it deserves a place in the flower garden, too. A woody plant, it can be clipped to a low hedge as an edger or allowed to sprawl and show off its dense spikes of brilliant blue (sometimes pink) flowers like a subshrub. If you keep it cut back, the spikes come along all season. It tends to die out in the center and benefits from division at least every three years. Easily grown from cuttings.

Iberis sempervirens (evergreen candytuft)

A popular low plant for facing off borders. The flat clusters of white flowers bloom over a long time and are sturdy, with a pleasing ground-covering spread. Clip after the first bloom in mid-spring for a second flush. Some varieties, especially 'Autumn Snow', will naturally bloom again in the fall.

Iris

If you can grow only one kind, make it Siberian iris. This grassy-leaved clumper is a classic garden plant. Its refined white or purple-blue flowers are always appealing, which is more than can be said of the common German or bearded iris, which gets badly beat up, often felled by rain and wind. If you have room for two kinds of iris, may I also suggest a clump or two of the stately Japanese iris (*I. ensata*) with its exciting, complex flowers often described as butterflies floating atop tall, branched stems. Go for three? Try tiny crested iris (*I. cristata*), good for dry shade and a very early sign of spring.

Liatris (blazing star or gayfeather)

A prairie import, *L. spicata* produces tall wands of feathery flowers in magenta or white that have the odd habit of opening from the top down rather than the other way around. They tolerate dry conditions and poor soils. Stiff and unyielding, they should be planted as part of a mixed border, where they are nice accents. Although you are supposed to be able to grow them from seed, I cannot seem to.

Ligularia

This is a perennial with presence, as the large round or serrated leaves rise on tall stalks to subshrub height and substance in damp, dappled shade. Mine is *L. dentata* 'Desdemona', which sets starry yellow flowers in midsummer and is lovely before and after for the maroon-stemmed and -backed deep-green leaves. It will self-sow scantily, so mulch well and do not disturb.

Lilium (lilies)

Well-drained and composted soil but no manure is the rule. Plant as soon as you get them; the bulbs are delicate. Deadhead religiously to strengthen the bulbs, and cut back dead foliage in fall to keep the bed disease-free. Lilies don't cotton to interplanting and do best in a big clump or bed of their own, I think, but they are wonderful for back-of-the-border impact. When you do interplant lilies, be sure to mark them well. They appear late in spring and can be easily destroyed while weeding or transplanting.

Propagate by lifting bulbs and removing small ones at the side or by collecting the tiny bulbils that form in the axils of leaves and stems in late summer on some species and near the ground on others. Also, you can gently, carefully dig down to expose the bulb and tug off a few of the outside scales and plant these.

As to what kind to grow, it's a bit like hostas, daylilies, iris, dahlias, mums, and peonies. There are a blue million. The large trumpet-shaped lilies can be out of scale for small plantings but they are fine planted in pots or alone in cutting beds. You will probably need to stake them.

Lychnis (campion)

The gray felted leaves and bright pink or white flowers of campion are distinctive. Once you grow it, if you allow it to set seed and mature, you will have it always, popping up in spare corners you never thought of. I like it. Some folks find the pink too garish.

Lysimachia (loosestrife)

The lysimachia family contains the wonderful *L. clethroides* or goose-necked loosestrife, so named for the bent shape of the white flower spikes. Some say it is viciously rampant. I don't find it so. Here's a fun trick: plant your gooseneck with a hedge or wall behind it so all the little crooks will point in the same direction. They really are zingers growing like this. (*Note:* The despised and sometimes banned purple loosestrife is in the lythrum family, so not to worry.)

Macleaya cordata (plume poppy)

This is for the courageous. It can easily go up ten feet in a year in rich soil and is utterly elegant with big, poppy-shaped leaves of silvery green backed in glowing, felty ivory with—the *coup de grâce*—immense and airy plumes of buff flowers that last and last and last. It is hollow-stemmed like the poppies and does not need staking so much as remedial trimming when summer storms, dogs, or children leap upon it and bend the stalks. A caution: It will run and self-sow, too, so you can be ruthless in pulling it or mowing it. Plume poppies are magnificent in arrangements, but you must sear the cut stem immediately with a lighter to seal it.

Mertensia virginica (Virginia bluebells)

Everyone's spring favorite. My mother gave it pride of place and you could see why. Pink buds opening to sky-blue, pendulous bells of flowers and silvery, soft oval leaves. Ideal in woodlands. It will spread nicely.

Monarda (bee balm)

The mopheads of ruddy red or pink or lavender are welcome, long-lasting shape variations for the summer border. It can handle dry con-

ditions, slightly moist ones too. The aromatic foliage is a bit of a pill, as
it always gets white mildew as the flowers fade. Just cut it back then
and don't fret. It's not terminal. In fact, this is a stoloniferous or spreading plant, so be prepared to keep it in bounds by burying it in tin cans
in the ground.

Narcissus (daffodils)

Again, gardener's choice. Lots of choice, too. May I suggest a bushel
basket of the inexpensive, no-name big yellow trumpets for scattering
about the lawn or under trees and some of the later-blooming pheas-
ant's eye narcissus (*N. poeticus*) for the border, wild garden, or lawn?

Nepeta (catmint)

If you want an airy cloud of blue blooms to enjoy under roses or in the
front of the border, get *N.* x *faassenii* 'Six Hills Giant'. If it's the cats
you're thinking of, they will be pleased with the less spectacular *N.
cataria,* the real catnip, with tiny white flowers held tight to the stems.
Both enjoy being trimmed and grow all the stronger for it.

Oenothera (sundrops, evening primrose)

There are two sides to this family. The day-blooming sundrops are
small safety-yellow flowers borne atop wiry stems arising out of a flat
rosette of dusky green leaves that turn maroon in the winter. The
night-blooming primroses, which come in both yellow and pink, are
stars of garden parties, as it takes almost exactly fifteen minutes for
one to open, which it does with a visible snap. Nothing fusses with
sundrops, but the primroses, alas, are favorite Japanese beetle food,
and some of the varieties are a bit weedy and big.

Paeonia (peony)

You have to plant the fleshy root just right—precisely 1½ inches below
the soil surface—or they sulk and won't bloom, but wow, when they
do! Heavy, round, petal-packed, stamen-choked, fragrant balls of lux-
ury, peonies enrich any garden. They must be staked or storms will
shatter the beauty. Your collection should include both the ball types
and the open-faced singles with stand-up yellow anthers, much loved

by bees. A good point made by Lisa Burnham of the Bloomington, Indiana, nursery Burnham Woods is that the single peonies hold up to weather much better than the lush doubles. So if you have room for only one, maybe a single is the best selection.

Peonies are forever. Spend a little money. Buy field-dug roots from a specialist in fall and plant as soon as possible. If you buy the pre-packaged, often already sprouted roots living in stifling little boxes on the shelves of garden centers, at least let them soak over-night before you plant. Feed lightly in early summer after blooms fade. Don't use manure.

No blooms? You've got to move the peonies. They are planted too deep or too shaded or have too much competition.

Perovskia (Russian sage)

Silvery stems, tiny aromatic leaves, and shimmery blue-violet flowers packed in knobby spires create an alluring mass effect of the subshrub type at the back of a border or along a driveway in full sun. Make sure the soil is poor and dry or Russian sage will flop over and you'll be disappointed.

Phlox

Phlox comes three ways. One type blooms early as a creeper. Another blooms as a slightly taller summer phlox, and that is pretty. But the one I like best is the late, tall garden phlox, *P. paniculata,* because that's when I don't have enough going on flower-wise. I prefer 'Mt. Fuji', a good strong white that resists flopover from summer storms and blends well with almost all late summer flowers.

Phlox has only two problems. First, it gets mildew, which is un-sightly but controllable by wide-spacing. (A lot of midwestern garden-ers swear by 'Miss Lingard', which is not supposed to be as mildew-prone as other summer garden phlox.) Second, it needs to be divided every three years to stay vigorous, but that's fine as you want to space them widely anyway!

A tip for all the clumping phloxes is to pinch back the front shoots in order to have lower flowers in front, or a tier effect.

The eye-catching pinks and purples of early spring phlox seen frequently on banks and in rock gardens are usually *P. subulata,* creeping phlox. I don't grow it because, lazy weeder that I am, I find it a pain in the neck, too slow to establish for much more than a patchy effect.

Polygonatum (Solomon's seal)

For the woodlands, this waist-high plant with its arching leaf stems from which dangle little bells of white flowers will form airy open colonies if kept well weeded.

Saponaria (soapwort)

Getting the right soapwort makes all the difference. I am still plagued with the species, which is loaded with pretty, pale pink flowers but is way too vigorous, which is why it's called Bouncing Bet, I guess. The one you want is *S. ocymoides* or *S.* x 'Max Frei'. Both are mounding rather than bouncing.

Sedum spectabile (showy sedum)

A favorite with old and new gardeners, this big succulent produces mounds of gray-green leaves in early spring and flat flower clusters of rosy little blooms on tall stems in the fall. Don't hesitate to divide this plant in the spring. If you don't, it will just sit there slowly getting moundier rather than actually wider each year. Large sweeps or colonies look better than single specimens. *Sedum spectabile* seems to grow almost anywhere except deep shade and damp spots.

Solidago (goldenrod)

The showiest player in the fall garden or meadow, goldenrod has a bad reputation as the source of hay fever. Not true! Blame ragweed, which often grows alongside goldenrod in fields. I grow the tall volunteer species in my "weed borders," and am tempted by newer dwarf selections.

Stachys (lamb's ears, betony)

Stachys byzantina is the fuzzy, gray lamb's ears that make perfect edging plants. The spires of soft purple flowers beloved by bees don't bother me, but some folks cut them off in order to just have the foliage. *S. byzantina* can't stand being wet. Do not leave mulch on them over winter but do allow the natural decayed leaves, what I call the "lint," to remain. It helps the plants weather the cold. Rake it off in early spring. They are vigorous, and must be divided every few years to stay healthy, so don't go overboard buying them.

Betony, *S. grandiflora,* has dark green mounding leaves with slender spikes of lilac flowers in late spring. I hear there is a white one, too, but I've never seen it. Betony requires an axe when it comes to division time, which need never happen unless you want to move it or give a piece away. It's one of those plants that are happy to be divided and happy not to be divided.

Stylophorum diphyllum (celandine poppy)

Blue-green oak-leaf foliage gives it the name I know it by, Welsh poppy. Best in loose soil in loamy woods in a half-day of sun, this is a splendid woodsy denizen. The bright-yellow simple blooms in spring are followed by attractive, plump, and hairy seed capsules. It self-sows when happy, which usually means lots of undisturbed mulch.

Thalictrum (meadow rue)

Everyone who sees this loves it. I grew it from seed and it has been a treat all along. The plant is a shin-high mound of very delicate lobed leaves and wiry stems, a bit like a cross between a columbine and a maidenhair fern. The leaves are pretty all by themselves, but this dandy plant also produces a hip-high, much-branched flower stalk that holds many rosy flowers for a good month in late spring and early summer. Said to need moisture, mine grows in the humusy gravel beds, where it gets a half to a full day of sun.

Tiarella cordifolia (foamflower)

A delicate-looking but tough wildflower from the Allegheny Mountains. The plants form a low whorl of reddish-brown leaves carried almost all winter. In spring, clusters of long-lasting, airy white racemes shoot up from the leaves. The effect is charming. I like them as low front border clumps, but some people swear they make a good ground cover.

Tradescantia (spiderwort)

For some reason, people are leery of this plant because it is related to a weed that has similar, but much miniaturized, bright blue flowers on a jointed, sappy stalk. The weed drapes itself over the ground and your plants, but the garden types are tall, strong, and long-blooming and come in shades of bright blue, pure purple, rose, and white. It is excellent in light shade or in sun.

Tulipa (tulips)

So many of the big tulips—the Darwins and Cottages, the Earlies and the Lily-flowereds—simply do not last and have to be replanted year after year. That's just the way it is, and it's worth spending money, I think, to have one gorgeous clump. For relative permanence, you must go for the short, species tulips. These include *T. Kaufmanniana, T. tarda, T. praestans,* and *T. clusiana.* Some of the early, taller Fosteriana or Emperor tulips also tend to hold their own. Give all tulips good drainage and a dry summer.

Veronica (speedwell)

Check carefully what you are getting. Some veronicas form mats, some rosettes, and some stand up as tall as your knee, which are the ones I like. These bloom in summer with pointed blue spires and can be very free-flowering. The best is *V. teucrium* 'Crater Lake Blue'. In my experience, the whites and reds flop over.

Annuals

The Midwest is a mecca for annuals, which appreciate our fast-start springs and hot summers. The only strategy I've developed is to start them at staggered times, so some are coming along fresh just as the first batch is looking shopworn.

Here are some I especially like.

Cleome

Cleome is stately and dramatic, with ever-expanding stalks of distinctive spidery pink flowers. They take a bit to get going and then never stop. If happy, they make a late-summer border and will self-sow like a banshee.

Four o'clocks

These thrive in the gravelly beds by the garage, where they self-sow into bushy hip-high hedges. Mine are variations on pink and white, which I prefer to the hot pinks, yellows, and oranges. Four o'clocks open in the afternoon, of course, and have a light, fresh scent that means summer to me.

Geraniums

Geraniums (or pelargoniums, which is their proper name) can't be beat as pot and barrel specimens. I favor pink. The white grows slowly for me; so do the ones with white and green foliage; ditto the ivy-leaved hanging types. It's easy to raise them from seed started in January. Also, they are easy to overwinter as cuttings taken in late summer and potted up for indoors.

Morning glories

These are musts. They climb the kennel fence, cross-pollinating in pink, white, and purple-blue. There are fancier ones to buy, but I like this riot of casual nature.

Nicotiana or flowering tobacco

This annual has a permanent home because of the night-blooming, green-white flowering types. The others are very nice, too, with richer colors, but that's the one I like best.

Salvias

Salvias are a new favorite, and I don't mean the too-tight, too-red bedding plants. Try *S.* x 'Superba', a deep-blue hardy, bushy sage that blooms in sun in summer. Try that old standby, *S. farinacea* or mealycup sage, too, with its deep-blue spires of flowers all summer. It sometimes lives through our winters if the ground is not too wet. Less hardy ones, which are also useful—but you must take cuttings to save indoors—include blue bog sage, purple Mexican sage, and blue Brazilian sage, as well as that herb garden standout, the red-flowering, shrubby pineapple sage. These are tropical plants, and tend to collapse at the first breath of frost. They also are gorgeous and worth the trouble of staking, as they give vibrancy to the late border.

Zinnias

Zinnias are a given, grown mostly for the butterflies, which love them. I wait to sow mine until May, which means they come along late and escape the mildew disaster.

Tender and Summer Bulbs

I am a restless gardener in this area, eliminating things like dahlias and hardy gladiolas, which flop too much for me, but always finding new loves. Here are some that have taken.

Acidanthera

The magpie gladiolus or peacock orchid is heady with fragrance. It grows shoulder-tall, with slender, grassy leaves and white flowers flared open to show a maroon center. I pack them a dozen at a time into a pot, which I water only when I remember to. I place this where I go in and out to the car. It looks beautiful and smells even better. Over winter, just set the pot indoors and let it dry out until around April, when you get them going again; set out after frost danger is over. Shake out the pots every other year and separate the little cormels that develop. Repot the big ones and grow on the little ones in other pots. They should flower in two years.

Canna

They've been overdone and overbred, but are still underused as part of a mixed border. Try them with hostas, yuccas, grasses, and gaura. The tropical, big-leaved tall rhizomatous plant is perennial in a sheltered spot at my house, near the wide eaves on the south side where things stay dry. (Don't count on this effect in Zone 5.) Store them over the winter in a cool, dry place. My stand is tall and old-fashioned, with smallish red flowers on ten-foot stalks. I don't like the shorter, plumper hybrids in apricot and yellow.

Clivia

Handsome pot plants even if they never bloomed, clivia have big dark-green straps of leaves that give way in winter—after Christmas—to big primrose-looking flower heads in orange or yellow. Clivia like to be rootbound and should be given a short rest from autumn to Christmas with limited water and warmth. Keep them outdoors in the summer.

Oxalis

The way they open in the morning at first light like an unfurling parasol is reason enough to have a pot of them on the breakfast-room table. There is one hardy type, *O. adenophylla,* but it's the blooming shamrocks in pots I like. Try striped 'Candy Cane'. The key to success is a long dormant period after blooming. Pull off the leaves and let it rest bone-dry all summer, starting it up in autumn with a drink. The way to be sure you don't water it is to tip the pot on its side. Very important, or you will kill the things.

Vines

Vines and trees are short lists for me. What can I say? Many are called, few are chosen.

Clematis

You've got to grow at least one, and that's the free-flowering, vanilla-smelling autumn clematis. It's a riot of small flowers followed by the distinctive wispy cotton of a clematis seed head. It's indestructible, I think, unlike its sometimes picky relatives. Buy one if you must, but most gardeners will have lots of self-sown seedlings to give away for the asking. Don't be shy. I can't tell you how many times my autumn clematis has been mowed down accidentally or broken off by the dogs and kids and come back strong. Actually, many clematis like being pruned. It strengthens the root ball and gives the vine vigor.

A good pink clematis for starters is 'Nelly Moser'. Once you've been successful with these two, move on to the rest. They must have sun and a good mulch to succeed.

Climbing hydrangea

H. petiolaris is a heel-dragger. It's taken me two moves to get it right, as it seems to need a bit more sun than the literature suggests. Other than that, it's no problem and is really pretty.

Honeysuckle

Avoid the Japanese type like the plague. It kills other plants. But do seek out the non-threatening types like *Lonicera brownii,* which has red flowers and blooms from March to December for me, with the biggest flush in spring. It's very hardy and uncomplaining and will not tear down arbors as wisteria does.

Hops

I grow it for the inch-long upside-down soft green "pine cones" of flowers, used to give beer its characteristic flavor. It's also a grand and fast fence or bower cover, scrambling up with hairy stems and leaves, brooking no opposition. Buy a plant. The seeds are hard to germinate.

Wisteria

I grow two wisteria plants, but the jury is still out, as I want to grow them as weeping standards or trees rather than vines and they are taking their own sweet time about it. They are pretty, but there is a price to pay. Wisteria is known to drag down bowers built without I-beams and to strangle nearby trees—both reasons why I want them as standards, not vines. Also, some gardeners have terrible problems with self-sown seedlings.

Shrubs and Small Trees

While the line between a shrub and a tree is clear enough in botanical definition, it may be fuzzy in garden practice. Conventionally, a shrub is a plant with multiple stems that does not grow more than twenty feet high. A tree is a plant with a single main stem. However, you can turn a tree into a shrub by cutting it back every year or so, forcing it to produce a bristle of stems, or arborize a shrub, trimming off all but one main stem and asking it to form a treelike canopy.

You will sometimes find shrublike woody and herbaceous perennials, such as baptisia, potentilla, angelica, rosemary, buddleia, and caryopteris, listed among shrubs, and you will find distinctly shrublike bushes, such as roses, listed as flowers.

In the belief that gardeners are flexible and practical, my list of favorite shrubs and small trees includes plants I like to use for screens and hedges, lawn specimens, border fillers, and accents.

Abelia

Bees love it. Gardeners, too, because this shoulder-high shrub blooms with clusters of plumy-pink trumpet-shaped flowers in that off period of shrub bloom, summer. Somewhat rounded and lax, the small-leaved, glossy-leaved abelias are not quite evergreen but are workhorses of borders and hedges. Abelias are often grown in full sun, but they handle a bit of shade just fine.

A. x *grandiflora* or glossy abelia is the most frequently seen. The leaves turn bronze in the fall and, if the winter is mild, may stick around until spring. As with many plants, if we get a series of cold-followed-by-warm spells, the Zombie Zones take their toll, burning the leaves and causing them to drop, but this is no big deal. The big deal about abelia is that it is a fast grower. Abelias will grow back readily in one season and so can be recommended for small spaces or large estates.

Acer ginnala (Amur maple)

The Amur maple is unkillable. That, its low height at twenty feet, and, if you like it, a bright red fall color make it as indispensable as the despised box elder for problem places. Don't go looking for it, but remember it when you've got a wind-scoured site on a hillside in clay.

Aesculus parviflora (bottlebrush buckeye)

The bottlebrush buckeye is quietly breathtaking. Don't buy the notion that only big estates can grow it. I concede that this eight-to-twelve-foot-tall suckering shrub spreads too much to be placed right up by the foundation next to the front door. But you will wish you could.

A clumping shrub with a rangy, horizontal habit, it has long palmate leaves that turn a perfect yellow in the fall and upright brushy inflorescences that can get close to a foot long. It blooms after the Fourth of July. It will flower in shade, but I think it looks skimpy there and grow mine in sun.

Amelanchier laevis, A. canadensis (nannyberry, serviceberry, or shadblow)

A small multiple-stemmed tree with gray bark, this blooms early, with a rush of white flowers that are a standout in naturalized plantings or even damp areas. The serviceberry also has knockout yellow and red fall color. Its reddish-black berries, which are edible, are seldom left alone long enough by the birds to be much of a decorative accent.

Serviceberries have few problems, although some can be too clumpy and stoloniferous for tidy, tiny yards. The most desirable members of the genus are *A. canadensis, A. laevis,* and a cross between them called x *grandiflora.*

Incidentally, this is one of gardening's pronunciation foolers. The "ch" is hard. It's am-el-ANK-ier.

Aronia (chokeberry)

A. arbutifolia, the red chokeberry, is the most commonly grown. It is valuable as a thicket-former in difficult damp sites but will grow almost anywhere. The smaller black chokeberry (*A. melanocarpa*) is less well known but just as nice. The berries of both are very attractive in the fall. Berries are the reason to grow the aronias. They last until the birds find them.

Aronias are easy to root in June from softwood cuttings, so this is one to underbuy and propagate on if you want an informal hedge.

Clethra (sweet pepperbush)

An accommodating shrub, the sweetspire or sweet pepperbush takes the gardener's worst nightmare—dry shade—and blooms and blooms with fragrant, cream-colored flowers just when you need bloom the most, at midsummer. It is a paragon among shrubs, with a fairly neat

Three seasons at the urban Louisville home of an amateur arborist show careful selection for visual interest and cultural suitability. The American cranberry bush (*Viburnum trilobum* 'Compactum') is a good choice for small yards like this, as is the short-statured 'Stella de Oro' daylily at its feet. *Photo by Michael Hayman*.

Deciduous holly pioneer, nurseryman Bob Simpson of Vincennes, Indiana, cuts some berry-laden branches of 'Sunset'. *Photo by Michael Hayman.*

Here the deciduous holly is 'Council Fire' at Bernheim Forest and Arboretum near Clermont, Kentucky. The arboretum, open to the public, is internationally noted for its collection of hollies. *Photo by Michael Hayman.*

The sulfur yellow blooms of cornelian cherry (*Cornus mas*) are like trumpet calls in the stark winter landscape. *Photo by Michael Hayman.*

Straw is one of the finest mulches, light and airy enough to allow delicate plants like these primroses to emerge in early spring. *Photo by Diane Heilenman.*

Daffodil hybridizer Helen Link at her home south of Indianapolis in Brooklyn, Indiana. *Photo by Maggie Oster.*

Some of the host of daffodils that greet visitors to Helen Link's grounds in April. *Photo by Paul Lightfoot.*

A rare weeping serviceberry or Amelanchier, developed from a seedling found in the wild at the Shelby–Oldham County line by Kentucky plantsman Theodore Klein of Crestwood. *Photo by Michael Hayman.*

A happy family of ajuga, rock cress, and young lamb's ears lives in the crevices of a limestone walk at the author's garden. *Photo by Diane Heilenman.*

Bridges can consist of simple affairs like a plank span or more elaborate home carpentry. *Photo by Diane Heilenman.*

Deep blue Siberian iris and multicolored German bearded iris—all hand-me-down plants with no names—mix with the chartreuse flower heads of false cypress (*Euphorbia cyparissias*). *Photo by Diane Heilenman.*

A mixed border at high summer sports complementary colors of yellow and purple. There's purple coneflower, black-eyed Susan, yellow daylily 'Sunflare', purple liatris, and white-striped gardener's garters seen against the developing seedheads of the tall and dramatic Queen of the Prairie or *Filipendula ulmaria*. *Photo by Diane Heilenman.*

Alliums are decorative relatives of the pungent onion but, unlike it, thrive in semi-shade. *Photo by Diane Heilenman.*

Cardoon, cousin of the artichoke, is a bold foliage plant with an immense vase of prickly silver leaves (with edible stems at the crown) that may overwinter if draining is perfect and mulch deep. The second year it puts forth a crop of incredible, saucer-sized blue thistles. *Photo by Diane Heilenman.*

Cleome is a good old-fashioned garden annual that suits the cutting bed, the mixed border, and formal, annual bedding-out plans. *Photo by Diane Heilenman.*

habit of growth and yet a tendency to sucker that makes it a candidate for an informal hedge. Buy a few and let them grow for a few years and you will find when you dig them up that you have tripled or quadrupled your supply. You will have to fend off Japanese beetles, which munch the blooms as they open.

Clethra is claimed to require acid soil, but mine are planted next to a limestone foundation.

Cornus (dogwood)

What a family! *Cornus florida,* the beautiful American dogwood, is justly famous, but is not hardy much north of Chicago. Although it is an icon of the Ohio River Valley and points south, there it is threatened by anthracnose. Another outstanding small tree is the Japanese dogwood, *C. kousa,* with its big pointed petals and red raspberry fruit. The related but very different cornelian cherry (*C. mas*), a big, spreading multiple-stemmed shrub, lights up the yard in early spring with a universe of tiny, starry pale yellow flowers. And it has red fruit in the summer and fall and attractive peeling bark in winter.

Cornus sericea, the shrub dogwoods—the red twig and the yellow twig—are showy for four seasons, with early foliage, flowers, berries, and, in the winter, colorful stems. Cut them back hard near the ground every few years to encourage lots of young growth, which has the best color. Again, they are easy to start from cuttings, so you can readily produce dozens from some minor trimming in late winter. Remember these plants if you want to have a hedge but are short on capital. Both shrubs have a showy variegated form, with the variegated-foliage red twig dogwood far more common than the 'Silver & Gold' variegated yellow twig. Much more expensive and rare are the variegated giant dogwood, *C. controversa,* and the tricolor *C. florida* dogwood with a rose, white, and green leaf.

Cotinus (smoke tree)

There are two types of smoke trees: the gaudy purple and the plain green, which I prefer. Even the latter is pretty darned dramatic in early summer with its long-lasting airy plumes of "smoke" or flowers. It's small, interestingly irregular in branching in the winter, and probably best as an accent or single plant, although I've never seen a grove of them; it just might be stunning.

Cydonia (quince)

This is not the spring-flowering Japanese quince but the quince tree, a fine but underused ornamental. I have six grown from seed because I was fortunate enough to meet the late Adolphe Vogt, a Louisville breeder of peonies and Japanese iris and torchbearer for the cydonia. The tree is small; it blooms as pretty as any apple, bears large golden, astringent fruits tasty in pies, holds its superb mahogany fall color well into winter, has no pests that I know of, and is easily hardy to −20 degrees.

Enkianthus campanulatus

All you ever see are pictures of the tiny clusters of lily-of-the-valley look-alike flowers in cream and red. These are rather small, and significant only at close range. You should grow it also for its neat, upright habit with spiraling branches, bright red stems, and a rich, red fall leaf color.

It is not common, but is a paragon. I grow mine in absolutely the wrong place, on the west side of my house, in average rather than acid soil, and have had no problems of any sort with it.

Forsythia

Why don't we ever call this by its pretty common name, golden bells? Why do we grow only one common garden variety, the all-too-showy, all-too-vigorous spring-bloomer? There are nearly a dozen varieties, of which I like best the white and green variegated *F. intermedia* 'Spring Glory'. Most of the others, notably a cutleaf forsythia and a knee-high 'Arnold's Dwarf', which seldom flowers, have been slow for me. A note to northern gardeners, who think any forsythia is great, since they don't grow easily up there: *F. mandschurica* 'Vermont Sun' is said to be hardy to −30 degrees F and, to boot, blooms weeks earlier than any other forsythia. Also keep your eyes open for *F.* x *intermedia* 'Meadowlark', developed in North and South Dakota, with a flower bud tolerance for cold down to −35 degrees.

Fothergilla

If you married a witch hazel to a bottlebrush buckeye, this is what you would get. The leaves are squarish and leathery like those of witch hazel and turn a similar sunset shade in fall. The spring flowers are creamy, sweet brushes with a distinctive honey scent. It is a prince for soils with less than adequate oxygen content, but why make it work hard if you don't have to? Give it well-drained, rich, acid soil.

Fothergilla is one of those expensive, uncommon shrubs that you will kick yourself for not getting early on and more of and planting them in prominent places. It comes in tall (*F. monticola,* a.k.a. *F. major*) and dwarf (*F. gardenii*) versions; both are basically small shrubs not much taller than waist- to head-high. The short guys bloom with the dogwoods and the tall guys a bit later.

Halesia carolina (silverbell)

The Carolina silverbell can be a shrub growing up to twenty feet high or a medium-sized tree, forty feet tall. Both look best at woodland edges and along paths—the bell-like flowers in early spring are small and need a little up-close viewing. They are not showy enough to compete with a dogwood or viburnum. Be sensitive; plant your silverbell where it can shine without showoff neighbors.

Hamamelis (witch hazel)

The witch hazels, promise of spring, promise of winter. Mopheads of flowers, yellow petals tangled in glowing disarray, appear as early as January some years and have the charming habit of rolling up their ribbons if it gets too cold. My 'Arnold's Promise' begins to bud out with bright red dots against the stems before Christmas, and bursts into bunches of yellow ribbon as soon as there is a warm spell. *H. mollis* or Chinese witch hazel is on my wish list as more floriferous and fragrant, along with various crosses that bloom red and copper-colored.

All the varieties from the Ozark to the Virginia to the Chinese like woodsy places, but need a good patch of sun each day. The fall leaves are a good yellow, and light up the autumn woods. Admittedly, witch hazels are just there most of the summer, but are valuable as fillers in dampish, woodsy borders where they tend to round up and spread as they age. (Not too dampish, however. I killed a young one by letting its feet get wet over winter.)

Hibiscus (rose of Sharon)

What a good old standby! Every midwestern yard should have one of these, along with a spirea and a snowball bush, either the hydrangea type or the viburnum type.

Rose of Sharon comes out so late in the spring you think it's dead, then makes up for it by sporting fat, tropical-looking blooms from midsummer to frost in sun or even fairly dark shade. I have one that blooms under a maple, the real test of unflappable bloom. They are a cinch to train as a single-trunk, lollipopped standard; I like this look much more than the flat-topped trimmed hibiscus hedge. Problems include rampant self-sowing, unless you get one of the new sterile types, such as the all-white-flowering 'Diana'. Japanese beetles are a horrid if controllable pest.

Hydrangea

I grew up with a huge snowball bush in the turnaround circle of the drive, presumably *Hydrangea arborescens* 'Grandiflora'. It was the backdrop for many a family photograph because it held its dried globes of flowers all winter and freshened up nicely in the spring. These are midwestern icons, deservedly so (it is said all *H. arborescens* are descended from one found wild in Ohio at the turn of the century), but try a few others.

Perhaps the best is the oakleaf hydrangea, *H. quercifolia*. The leaves are leathery and large, the flowers great pyramids of creamy, greenish white. It blooms in the shade, and the leaves turn a rich mahogany in the fall. Buy this in groups of three. Do not skimp.

Another hydrangea I like a lot is the lacecap, named for the look of its flat flower cluster. Mine is the variegated type, *H. macrophylla* 'Mariesii Variegata', and it is hardier than most of the French or big-leafed hydrangeas. Use it cautiously in Zone 5 and mulch well over winter. With its white-edged leaves, the shrub is interesting most of the year, not just in late summer when it blooms.

Ilex (holly)

More midwesterners should grow the deciduous hollies—the possum haws, the winterberries, *I. decidua* and *I. verticillata*. They are gorgeous, locally bred (in Illinois and Indiana), and provide colored berries almost all winter on bare branches. Like all hollies, they need a male for every five to ten plants to pollinate and produce berries on the females. Use them in groups. They can handle dampish spots, too.

Another holly recommended by Zone 5 gardeners is *Ilex glabra,* the inkberry. It is an evergreen native resembling boxwood which, unlike boxwood—which is marginal even in Zone 6—is hardy well north of Zone 5. That's why I'm trying a few inkberries instead of boxwood for winter structure in my herb garden. Although inkberries can grow up to nine feet tall, my variety, 'Compacta', is supposed to make a mound no taller than three feet and much lower if I prune. It berries precociously; even my six-inch-tall youngsters have some tiny black fruits. *I. glabra,* like the deciduous hollies, is a native of moist lands but also grows happily in drier circumstances.

Many of the evergreen holly shrubs and trees developed from English and Chinese hollies are not suited for the hot, dry summers of the Midwest, or our winters, either. Look for 'China Girl' and 'China Boy', 'Blue Boy' and 'Blue Girl'.

Itea virginica (sweetspire)

Why itea, which no one has heard of? It's the summer flowers—long spires of densely packed, scented flowers. . . . No, it's the affinity for moist soil and shade. . . . Or is it the ruby red fall leaves? There are so many reasons to like this shrub, and yet so few of them are grown. Itea also suckers, a boon for impatient gardeners and no big deal for the patient, as it is amenable to pruning.

I have *I. virginica* and *I. virginica* 'Henry's Garnet'. The former grows in heavy clay with about three hours of morning sun. The latter is in gravelly humus (a former driveway) with sun off and on all day. Both are doing well. I expect the species to grow over my head, the named variety to get shoulder-high.

Kalmia latifolia (mountain laurel)

This is a beautiful, broad-leafed evergreen of the acid-soiled woods. The blooms are mostly pink, although there are many variations. It will winter burn in wind, so site it in a sheltered spot. It grows in shade but can tolerate sun, too. There are two keys to growing mountain laurel and the closely related rhododendrons and azaleas. Plant high, on a mound if necessary, in well-drained humusy soil—an old rotten tree stump works—and water like crazy the first year.

Kerria japonica (Japanese kerria or gypsy rose)

This has made the list on the strong recommendation of fellow gardeners. I've not yet grown it. They like the yellow spring flowers on arching stems, bright green all year, with the double 'Pleniflora' preferred to the single-flowering types.

Leucothoe

A mounding low evergreen, leucothoe has arching branches with shiny, dark-green lance-shaped leaves. It sets graceful bunches of bell-shaped flowers in the spring. It's evergreen at my house, but some types are not hardy in Zone 5. If you want hardy, get *L. axillaris* or coast leucothoe. The variegated "rainbow" type is not suitable for winter in the upper Zombie Zones.

Lonicera fragrantissima (winter honeysuckle)

A grand gardener's companion, this is a late-winter- or early-spring-flowering fragrant shrub that needs a bit of pruning to keep its shape but is virtually evergreen in our zones.

Magnolia stellata (star magnolia)

This small tree is the smallest magnolia and one of the most floriferous. It can handle our spring frosts and bounce back and it sets flowers late, yet before leafing out. Buy as big as you can afford. It's a slow-goer in early life.

Nandina (heavenly bamboo)

The nandinas (which are indeed heavenly but are not even distant cousins to bamboo) are not for Zone 5, but if you garden in Zone 6 take advantage of these decorative, airy, and elegant evergreens with stalwart, pendulous clusters of orange-red berries all winter. The leaves are reddish over winter. I use nandina as an untrimmed hedge for places where I want a barrier but not total sight-blockage. They self-sow and sucker moderately and are simply terrific for cutting at Christmas. When you must trim or prune them, do so by taking off entire, alternate branches to the stem. Do not give them a formal overall hedge buzz, which ruins the nandinas' good looks, although you often see it done that way in cemeteries.

Philadelphus (mock orange)

I have the oldest of the old-fashioned mock oranges, I'm sure, as my gigantic shrub probably is of an age with my 1910 house. The single white blossoms with yellow centers are eagerly awaited each spring. They look good and smell good. I love to cut them for the house. I have split the big bush off at the edges for four more bushes to make a tall screen along one side of the drive. Mock orange does get dense and requires an energetic pruning of selected older stems all the way to the ground every other year, at the least, to look right.

Rhododendron (rhododendrons and azaleas)

We midwesterners can't grow these shrubs without a few disasters. But we should keep trying. Some are good for us, and a fair amount of research and breeding is being done by regional nurseries, as well as some researchers in Germany (!), to find cultivars tolerant of quite alkaline soil.

Most of us need rhododendrons that tolerate wind, sun, drought, and soils on the limey side of acid. These include the following so-called "ironclad" varieties: 'Aglo', 'Goldsworth Yellow', 'PJM', 'Olga Mezitt', the red 'America' and 'Nova Zembla', and the aptly named rosy-lilac 'Roseum Elegans', said to be the test rhodie. Try that first, and if you fail, give up.

Among azaleas, look for the Exbury hybrids and for the plumleaf azalea, *R. prunifolium,* an odd late-summer-bloomer you will like. The hardiest azaleas are the mostly purple-flowered Gables, from a Pennsylvania nursery. Many of the Girard nursery-bred hybrids have "Gable blood" and are hardy for us, too. Also ask about the Shammer-ello hybrids of northern Ohio, bred from and with Gable and Girard for increased cold tolerance and yet still some choice in colors. One nursery in our region that specializes in such azaleas is Holly Hills in Evansville, Indiana.

I know this is a short list, considering the hundreds of varieties available, but it's one you can trust, assuming you plant them in well-drained, aerated soil. The reason so many are planted on mounds or on hillsides is that they have shallow roots. Another tip: disbud immediately after flowering to encourage more branching and, because they bloom on new growth, thus more flowers.

It is perhaps worth noting that florists' azaleas and the no-name azaleas available around Easter and Mother's Day are unlikely to live in our gardens.

Rhus (sumac)

Too often dismissed as a hedgerow pest, the sumacs are a varied family, with two that I particularly like. *R. typhina,* staghorn sumac, is a statuesque clump-former with interest all year, from the sculptural stems to the staghorns of ruddy fruit and brilliant pinnate leaves in the fall. *R. aromatica,* fragrant sumac, also draws me to it each season. In winter I like to inspect the pointed buds, a light brown criss-crossed with dark bands. In early spring these break into yellow catkins and scented flowers. The leaves are small and lobed and pretty, aromatic, too. They turn an unrivaled purple and burnt orange in the fall. Mine grow as erosion control in a gravelly spot near the drive.

Rosa (roses)

The problem with roses is that you get lost in admiration and greed and suddenly you have too many. I grow roses on a pergola and now specialize in the so-called old or shrub roses with an emphasis on climbers and ramblers, but I still love them all, from the teas to the floribundas. Midwesterners can't grow and should avoid the tender roses with China and Bourbon "blood" in their ancestry.

My batch right now is limited to a dozen or so varieties, including *R. glauca,* sometimes called *R. rubrifolia* for its magnificent ruddy leaves; some David Austin English roses; a Madame Alfred Carrière, which is one of the few noisettes that are hardy in Zone 6; a wonderful shrubby 'Cerise Bouquet'; 'Rosa Mundi', the striped rose named after Henry II's mistress; a few whose names I have forgotten or can't read on the labels; the great rambler 'Bobbie James'; and I'm playing with the miniatures, which are suitable for pots as well as in-ground growing. A tall bush rose I like a lot is *R. rugosa* 'Alba'. The rugosas are cast-iron except for Japanese beetles.

I also have a favorite single, 'Kathleen', that I grow on the garage wall. Every garden that has more than one rose should make one of them a single, with its four to eight petals and prominent stamens. My 'Kathleen' is a pale apricot. Another that is vigorous and hardy is 'Dainty Bess', a well-loved hybrid tea single with big pink petals and dark red stamens which also comes in a ten-foot-tall climbing version.

If you can have only one climber, make it 'New Dawn', the standard of large-flowered fragrant repeat-bloomers with pale, pale pink flowers. It always looks nice. It's trouble-free, and its amenable nature suits it for fences, walls, arbors, and pergolas. Or you can let it arch and become a trailer if you have the room. Look for any of its progeny or relatives: rosy 'Rhonda', strongly perfumed 'White Dawn', deep-pink 'Bantry Bay', and silvery pink 'Awakening'.

Another rose recommended by gardeners in our region is a paragon called 'The Fairy', a low, shrubby polyantha with heavy crops of small seashell-pink blooms. It's grand for small gardens, as a low hedge, and to face off borders.

Midwestern gardeners from Illinois to Kansas rave over the roses bred by Griffith Buck, a former horticulture professor at Iowa State University in Ames. His work from the 1970s and 1980s focused on vigorous, disease-free, floriferous, shrubby bushes that can take the summer heat and the winter cold. His roses include 'Hawkeye Belle', a blush-pink shrub; 'Music Maker', a low floribunda with pink flowers; 'Prairie Flower', a single, deep pink with white at the center and prominent yellow stamens, that grows about waist-high; 'Prairie Harvest', a soft yellow hybrid tea with long stems suitable for cutting; and 'Carefree Wonder', a three-by-three-foot lush, floriferous shrub rose with double pink flowers that have a distinctly tea rose look. 'Carefree Wonder' is touted as both a specimen rose and a "living fence."

Two trends in the rose world are ground-cover roses, which are sometimes also called patio roses, and roses for hedges. On these subjects it is good to remember that there are some wild and reckless growers in the rose family. The ground-cover roses, which tend to sprawl and cascade, are not for small spaces, but for troublesome banks and big containers. Be sure not to plant them too close to walkways. I experimented with the Meidiland ground-cover roses, but did not keep them. In the wrong place, they became as vicious as a chained dog, biting everyone who walked past them. The ones with white petals turned a dirty brown as they aged, and since the plants were not "self-cleaning" the old flowers did not fall off. And the red ones were a bit too startlingly intense. Weeding was a problem, too, but that, I think, comes with the territory.

Now, after more research, I am trying the rose-pink 'Blooming Carpet', which is a foot and a half tall by four feet wide and which everyone says is the best, and 'Snow on the Heather', a white rose supposedly impenetrable to weeds that runs up to eight feet wide.

If you don't want to play with unknown roses, you can achieve much the same effect, only in increments of ten feet or more, by pegging down old ramblers like the beautiful 'White Gardenia', a one-time bloomer with attractive bronzed foliage.

Back to the widely promoted Meidiland family. I do think the pale pink 'Bonica' is a good doer if you have the room for a hedge five feet square. The hedge rose I value is 'Gruss an Aachen', a repeat-blooming, pale blush pink, fully double beauty that tolerates some shade. It is a good hedge or face-off plant for the front of the border as it grows about two feet tall by three feet wide and does not throw up wild, long canes out of the sides and tops.

Hybrid tea roses are a vast ocean of indecision for me. I do have a few whose names are long lost, but pass along two that have proved themselves in a fellow gardener's beds. One is 'Double Delight', a fragrant three- to four-footer with double flowers that are carmine on the outer half of the petals and creamy yellow on the lower half—very dramatic and looking rather like ornamental cabbage in miniature. The other is a classic pink, 'Queen Elizabeth', a long-time favorite from the 1950s. Very tall, it is a grandiflora that can romp to six feet or so, and can be too vigorous for small spaces. The solution is to let it go up, turning it into a short climber, wall rose, or pillar candidate.

Spiraea

An old-fashioned favorite, the bridalwreath spirea (*S. vanhouttei*) is an arching May bloomer with clusters of white flowers held closely but not tightly along the stems. Cut it back to the ground. It returns. Stick it in shade. It blooms. Grow it in gravel, grow it in clay. It will keep on trying. If you have the space, you can try some of the newer pink-flowering spireas. They are just as accommodating. The two I know are 'Pink Princess', a knee-high shrub with constant pale pink flowers just dandy for the perennial border, and *S.* x *bumalda* 'Goldflame', which some call gaudy but which I like for its constant shifts in color: twigs come out orange, leaves are chartreuse, and the flowers are sharp pink.

Viburnum

If I had to settle for just one family of shrubs, I'd pick the viburnums. They are top-drawer shrubs for the Lower Midwest. I have taken to writing "any viburnum Zone 5-6" when the order form asks for substitutions. I wish a few more of them did better in shade, but if you select carefully you can find viburnums for almost any site, any use. They all have nearly four seasons of interest, with showy, flat clusters of flowers in spring and early summer, beautiful and sometimes edible berries you'll have to fight the birds for, good fall color, and distinctive crinkly leaves that may hold for some or all of a winter.

Presently I grow four types but am familiar with a few others. My pride is the doublefile viburnum or *V. plicatum,* which sets its branches and flowers in horizontal layers. I have *V. acerifolium,* the maple-leaf viburnum, naturalizing in the woods, as it is good for shade. Ditto for *V.* x *rhytidophylloides,* with its long, crinkly, leathery leaves backed in soft buff in the spring. I have a large clump of *V. carlesii,* Korean viburnum, where it gets a half-day of sun, near the back door, which is, anyway, the requisite spot for this early spring bloomer with its incomparable scent of sugar and spice.

It's important to know that the coveted spring-scented viburnum comes in three types. *V. carlesii,* the oldster of the group, has been superseded in most nurseries by the leafier, glossier, and less blight-prone *V. burkwoodii* and *V. juddii.* I, of course, managed to get the oldster before I knew what I was doing, but so far it is healthy.

V. trilobum, the American cranberry bush, is a terrific hedge plant that does not require pruning and grows shoulder-tall. It does not flower easily. Another, *V. dentatum,* does, but it is a very tall shrub, suckering and sometimes getting a bit dark and overbearing.

Here's one to look for: 'Summer Stars', a doublefile viburnum from Canada said to bloom *all summer long* and to be very hardy in the top of Zone 5.

Trees

Here are a few trees that are simply very, very fine and worth spending time, money, and space on. Because they live so long, the placement and choice of trees are critical decisions. Certainly, there are times when any tree is better than no tree, but that's hardly what gardening is about. Some of these recommended trees will take a little sleuthing to find. They are worth it. Each has some special trait to recommend it past all others.

Acer (maples)

These need no introduction, although there are a few to avoid, such as the silver maple and Norway maple, that are weak-wooded fast-growers. Some to enjoy for generations include *A. rubrum* 'Red Sunset' and *A. palmatum* 'Bloodgood', a small-statured Japanese maple that can handle midwestern heat. Also consider *A. pensylvanicum,* moose-wood or striped bark maple. It has bright red new stems, white-striped bark on young branches, and pretty pink leaves budding out in the spring. It's an understory type, heading out at around twenty feet. If you grow it in a lawn, be sure to mulch it well and try to place it out of the wind.

Aesculus (buckeye)

A big, sprawling tree, the buckeye is a Midwest icon from the days of wide open spaces. It is not for small city gardens but can be a splendid punctuation mark on larger lawns with its dramatic trusses of red flowers in spring and distinctive shiny brown buckeyes in the fall.

Carpinus caroliniana (hornbeam)

This is the American hornbeam or blue beech. The European hornbeam, which also is outstanding, is *C. betulus*. (Neither should be confused with the native hop hornbeam, *Ostrya virginiana*.) Both are medium-sized trees adaptable to sunny or understory sites, and both have a wonderful thin, gray bark that has a muscular look. They sport tiny pleated leaves and catkins in the spring and a wonderful gold-to-purple fall color range. Get them little. They don't transplant easily.

Cercidiphyllum japonicum (katsura)

Katsuras have heart-shaped leaves that smell of cinnamon in the fall. Honest. They are quick in youth, running up to twenty feet and then slowing down before they move on to a reported forty to one hundred feet tall. The weeping form is stunning and stays short.

Cladrastis lutea (yellowwood)

Yellowwood grows anywhere and can handle compacted soil because it fixes nitrogen from the air. It has pinnate leaves, a muscular smooth gray bark like a hornbeam, and big, drooping panicles of fragrant white, pea-like flowers in the spring. Try it for that compacted site near the walk, drive, or street. Try it outside your bedroom window. Put it anywhere. It's a terrific native American.

Cupressocyparis leylandii (Leyland cypress)

This intergeneric hybrid from *Chamaecyparis* x *cupressus* should be used for speedy but not weedy growth. It's an evergreen that can add a foot a year to its stature, up to a conical sixty feet.

Liquidambar styraciflua (sweet gum)

The distinctive star-shaped leaves are pretty anytime but simply spectacular dressed in their fall golds, russets, and reds. A single branch in a vase is a sight to behold. Some people object to the spiny round fruits which drop over winter, so it may be a tree for a site away from sidewalks and patios. Otherwise, it has everything going for it—troublefree, fast and easy, attractive.

Maclura pomifera (Osage orange)

Trash tree, you sniff. It is not popular to like Osage oranges. You've been sold a bill of goods on this wonderful, indomitable tree of the plains, a native of Kansas that the Osage Indians used for bow wood. In youth, it's a bit thorny and impetuous, with glossy green leaves and huge crops of the bizarre hedge apples that resemble alien brains. It's called "orange" for the color of the wood and a dye that can be extracted from it.

The Osage orange, officially called *Maclura pomifera* after geologist William Maclure (1786-1840), who discovered it for the white folks, roots readily and was often planted as hedgerows and cattle fencing in the Midwest. Kansas researchers have selected now for a mostly thornless, fruitless male that is highly recommended for city lots as it tolerates compacted, airless soils. In maturity, it is a tree with an idiosyncratic profile and immense personality.

Magnolia virginiana var. *australis* (sweet bay magnolia)

This is the best big magnolia for us. It flowers late enough to miss frost damage, and its handsome, slightly droopy leaves are evergreen.

Nyssa sylvatica (tupelo)

The stately tupelo is arrow-straight with a dramatic black trunk, wonderful mahogany fall color, and an ability to live in normal to swampish conditions. I grew up watching our tupelo change color outside the breakfast-room window. If you have a larger than average yard, I recommend it.

Oxydendrum arboreum (sorrel or sourwood)

This is a lovely specimen tree with drooping, scented racemes of flowers at the tips of the branches and a superb red fall color. Don't be alarmed if your young tree dies and then suckers back up. This happened to me and a friend, with no loss to either tree's perfect symmetry. I guess the moral is, buy your sorrel young.

Picea omorika (Serbian spruce)

A dark evergreen that keeps its lower branches, a nice habit for privacy. It is, like many spruces, a slow grower.

Pinus cembra (Swiss stone pine)

This is a hard sell for some reason, possibly because it is slow compared to the white pine. However, Swiss stone pine is to the white pine as a diamond is to a Cracker Jack ring. It is compact without being dense. The needles are always a bit stiff, the tree neat and trim in outline, almost formal-looking. Try it for small spaces.

Sophora japonica (pagoda tree)

I fell under the spell of *Sophora japonica* once during an al fresco lunch. It is the best tree ever for sitting under. The high branches spread like a ceiling over you, the leaves are airy like a locust's but without thorns. The pagoda tree blooms with yellow pea-blossoms in summer and can stand city pollution and Midwest cold, although some of my saplings were killed to the ground during an intemperate cold spell one fall before things had gone fully dormant.

Taxodium distichum (bald cypress)

The bald cypress is a distinguished-looking large lawn tree often seen planted at lake edges in public parks. On home grounds, too, it is beloved for its fast growth and soft green lax needles that turn a cinnamon-brown in the fall. Like many deciduous conifers, it has a beautiful scaling bark visible in the winter.

One slight caution. It is called a bald cypress because it will continue to thrive even if it loses its "head" to high winds.

Tsuga canadensis (Canadian hemlock)

All the hemlocks from prostrate dwarfs to forest giants are graceful evergreens. They have a reputation as somewhat slow, but if kept mulched, I find they grow as fast as the supposedly zippier Leyland cypress. They will put up with almost anything, even a bit of shade, but damp feet do them in.

Companionable Combos

It is helpful to think in pairs or threes when planting. That way you create harmonies and deliberate contrasts rather than chaos. Refer to this list when you need a jump start in planning perennial beds.

Candytuft and tulips
Tulips and bugle
Bugle and coralbells
Bearded iris and spurge or poor man's cypress
Spurge, hardy geranium, and bergenia
Bergenia, bearded iris, and peonies
Peonies and columbine
Columbine and Shasta daisies
Shasta daisies and almost anything
Narcissus and Solomon's seal

Solomon's seal and Siberian iris
Siberian iris and bearded iris
Bearded iris and pinks, or dianthus
Pinks and lamb's ears
Lamb's ears and yarrow
Yarrow and lilies
Lilies and daylilies
Coneflowers and hardy geranium
Hardy geranium and hosta
Hosta and ferns
Ferns, foxglove, and lamium or dead nettle
Lamium and ivy
Ivy and roses
Roses, foxglove, and catmint
Roses, rue, and rose campion
Roses, thyme, and annual alyssum
Phlox and daylilies
Daylilies and helenium or Helen's flower
Helen's flower and yarrow
Yarrow, Russian sage, and artemisia
Artemisia and anything
Fall sedum, rosemary, and annual cleome
Monkshood and asters
Asters and veronica
Asters and chrysanthemums
Chrysanthemums and anemones

Graceful Successors

While you can extrapolate a sort of succession of bloom from the roughly sequential list above, here's a longer look at what the great East Coast gardener Helen Van Pelt Wilson thought of as the five "waves" of bloom. Using her notion, I divide the Lower Midwest growing season into five segments, listing what tends to bloom in each. Of course, with daylilies and phlox, chrysanthemums and iris, even peonies and tulips, you can have a succession of bloom within the division by selection of early-, mid-, and late-blooming varieties. The more familiar you become with plants, the easier it is to do. It all takes time, of course, not to mention money and energy, so don't be impatient with yourself.

If you do something wonderful, take a picture or write it down. If you do something stupid, move the plants or cut off the offending flowers to avoid color clashes until you can make a move.

Early Spring—April and May

Spring bulbs such as crocus, trout lilies, snowdrops, grape hyacinth, and daffodils come on strong. Try rock cress, too, for bloom unfazed by early spring chills. Tulips can be dicey, springing into life with early warmth only to be blackened by a return to winter. Unfurling foliage of bergenia, spurges, iris, and some herbs is also a visual delight.

Spring—May and June

Look for shows from iris, primroses, coralbells, columbine, peonies, poppies, and Shasta daisy, which is sometimes called the Mother's Day daisy around here because it blooms so dependably on that day in early May.

Early Summer—June and July

Now is when most gardens peak, with foxgloves and roses, pinks, coneflowers, betony, baptisia, astilbe, valerian, meadow rue, hollyhocks, lilies, and sunflowers coming along. Annual larkspur, a good substitute for delphinium in the Lower Midwest, is at its best, and most annuals are looking fresh and young. Daylilies begin their long and faithful role in the garden, and Japanese iris do a star turn in July.

Late Summer—July and August

Summer heat and drought have taken their toll, but daylilies remain strong, also bee balm, sea lavender, black-eyed Susans, yarrow, hibiscus, hosta, and phlox.

Fall—August and September

Let wildflowers and prairie stalwarts take over: gayfeather, Queen Anne's lace, hardy asters, hardy ageratum, boltonia, goldenrod, and the long-blooming black-eyed Susans. Also grow more refined phlox, hostas, some daylilies, veronica, and anemone. The annual salvias, half-hardy plants here, are strong now, too.

Long-Season Performers

A few perennials are companionable over a long period. Many of these good-doers from about June through September are excellent border diplomats, providing easy transition from one flush of bloom to another. In order of increasing height from front of border to back, try lamb's ears, veronica, hardy geranium, catmint, coralbells, calamint, baby's breath, phlox, maiden grass, plume poppy, and any of the artemisias, annual or perennial, which can be as short as dusty miller or as big and shrubby as wormwood.

Possible Pests

If you have a small garden, here are a few plants to use with caution. They are either rampant spreaders or rather big and ungainly: hollyhocks, mulleins, horsetail, the spring bulb called star of Bethlehem, perennial sunflower, evening primrose, Shasta daisy, rose campion, sweet rocket, soapwort, rose of Sharon shrub, and spurge or poor man's cypress.

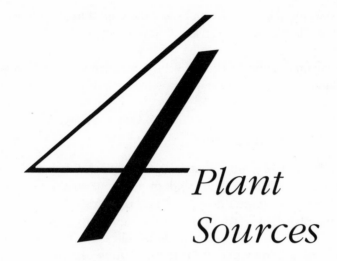

4 *Plant Sources*

IT'S EASY TO wind up with the wrong plant, especially if you have an easily aroused, adolescent gardening personality—and who doesn't? When you are eager for immediate garden satisfaction, a tomato plant is a tomato plant and who cares about varieties. Or, all you want is a flowering hedge, for Pete's sake. Forsythia is fine.

Later, you begin to separate sex from love, in a botanical sense. You have had enough of those cute salad tomato plants that produce millions of golf-ball-sized fruits. What you crave are substantial Italian plum tomatoes for making sauce. You yearn for something more than a brief fling of bright color in spring, which is about all most forsythia will provide. You want a hedge that is companionable year round—spring flowers, fall berries, evergreen foliage, tidy growth.

Of course, some of us never grow up. I *like* that retinal blast of saturated yellow from garden-variety forsythia. It's spring to me. However, I am protecting my reputation with recent purchases of dwarf forsythia and two kinds of variegated leaf forsythia, which I hope will extend the shrubs' visual interest past two weeks in April. Nice as they are, though, when I look at the new forsythia gang, all I see is the check I wrote. When I look at the plain, old-fashioned forsythia that threatens to swamp the front porch, I see the old drinking buddy who brought it to me in a garbage bag, a cull from forsythia that had overtaken her garage.

This brings us to the first great source for plants—your friends and acquaintances.

Other Gardeners

Never feel guilty about accepting a plant. Gardeners like to give plants away, but they are seldom generous to the point of stupidity. Although we won't give away rare or hard-to-grow plants, we gladly share hardy, vigorous ones that are growing us out of bed and border. Or, as North Carolina gardener Elizabeth Lawrence recalled in her classic 1942 work, *A Southern Garden: A Handbook for the Middle South:*

> I began digging up the masses of forsythia and jasmine that had overgrown the shrub border, offering them to all those new enough to gardening to be willing to take anything offered, and going about from garden to garden to see if anyone was discarding pink, I collected a purple-leaf plum . . . flowering almonds . . . and redbuds. (P. 40)

So you see, the sense of guilt, if there is one, may be on the side of the gardener who is secretly saying, "Thank goodness I got rid of those!" This hidden agenda behind the generosity is, I think, the basis for the superstition among gardeners that it's bad luck to say "thank you" for a plant. Whether it really is or not, I don't know, for I have said many a "thank you" by mistake, but I now can smoothly offer the proper response: "I won't say 'thank you,' but I will take very good care of it."

There is a fair amount of etiquette not found in any book on giving and receiving free plants.

The first step in obtaining an offer is profuse enthusiasm while walking through the potential donor's yard. "What is that lovely thing? It isn't . . . ? Yes, it *is* XYZ! I've heard about it and coveted it but never seen it. Gosh! You grow it so well."

Usually, only a dead gardener will not respond with an offer of a start, a cutting, or seeds saved. If the garden host says with regret that the plant is too young, too puny, too new to mess with, you simply ask where she got it. When she tells you, it is proper then to say "thank you."

Should your host hesitate, dampening your enthusiasm with mild or strong mentions that the desired plant is a bit rampant or wildly invasive, be advised that this can mean you will be trying to get rid of it, too, in under three years. I have been amazed at the number of gardeners visiting me who gladly carry away starts of the wild meadow buttercup, a deceitful charmer that will strangle sweet-natured ground covers like epimedium (barrenwort) and give sturdy old ivy quite a battle, too.

When you are offered plants, even take-over plants, try to give something in exchange. It is critical to assess the host garden and ask the host gardener if such-and-so would be welcome. Not everyone will want your surplus garlic chives, but they might be pleased with a bit of your choice Japanese iris. Or a bottle of wine is nice. In fact, my most memorable plant-exchange gift was a homemade gourmet casserole of artichokes and prosciutto, and my second most memorable was a loaf of fruit-nut bread, so you can see where my true interests lie.

Etiquette also suggests that the recipient bring his own spade and boxes, pots and plastic bags, as well as some means of labeling things. Do not dig unless your host suggests you do so, but you must make the offer.

If all you get is a skimpy bit and the gardener apologizes for giving you such a small start, the proper response is along the lines that small starts do better, which is true.

Do not hesitate to call and effuse about how good things look and how well everything is doing. That's also the time to describe mystery plants which somehow lost their labels, and it's the time to note if something didn't make it for you.

Plant swapping is not only an enjoyable gardening activity, it is sometimes the only way to get certain plants. Those that seem to be forgotten in modern trade are pass-along plants like that lovable garden monster, the herb angelica, the tropical night-blooming cereus, the pink-blooming hardy begonia that is a mainstay of the fall border, and what I call Chicago canna, a ten-foot-tall old-style tropical plant with smallish stalks of red flowers beloved by hummingbirds. I call it Chicago canna because that's where mine came from, and it is where the lusty grower is much in evidence as a summer privacy screen on city lots.

In time, you will find that there are many other plants on the market that you don't need to pay for: they are there in excess in other folks' yards. Here are a few: no-name yellow daffodils of the old, big trumpet variety, ivy, ajuga, lamb's ears, German iris, Shasta daisies, sedums, most herbs, lady and Christmas ferns, various daylilies, yarrow, tansy, and the striped ornamental grass called gardener's garters. And there are any number of shrubs and small trees that sucker or self-sow, in addition to the aforementioned forsythia, including rose of Sharon, privet, shrub dogwoods, mock orange, some hollies, rugosa roses, redbuds, and some viburnums. At least be aware that they are so readily multiplied by division, grown from seed, or rooted quickly from cuttings or layering that it's a shame to buy more than one.

For instance, as noted earlier, some daylilies produce tiny starter plants on the dying stem of the flower scape, which can be snapped off, rooted in shallow water for a week, and planted out. Many Asiatic lilies produce bulbils on the stem, which will grow into flowering bulbs if planted and left alone for a few years. A lot of vines will root where their stems touch the ground, producing a multitude of possible babies if you just cut them off the mother plant. Species roses can be started from cuttings of semi-ripe wood taken in late summer or early fall. You can root gooseberries, willows, forsythias, weigela, germander, hyssop, artemisias, geraniums, and many more by just sticking a twig in the ground—they are that willing. Keep your eyes open. Any stem that shows tiny bumps or actual roots at a node is a candidate for a quick-rooting cutting. A number of plants *enjoy* being dug up and divided, among them iris, yarrow, daisies, mums, and many perennial herbs. When a plant starts looking tired and woody, it may just need to be divided.

Almost all annual bedding plants, from pansies to pelargoniums, can be started at home from seed, which is relatively inexpensive. Thompson & Morgan's seed catalog is one of the best, in terms of depth of varieties offered and a system of pegging which are the easy ones, which are hard for the home gardener to start. Usually the only problem is timing, as many of these need to be germinated in January or earlier if you want big plants with flowers by May. Also, you need a place to grow them indoors with sufficient light.

Saving Seed

Saving seed is more than saving $1 a packet. It's the only way to perpetuate a special variety that has gone out of commercial production. It's the only way some heirloom varieties of vegetables have survived the hybridization and plant-improvement programs of the twentieth century. And it is at the very least a pleasant way to get to know your plants.

Start with annuals, which are usually very accommodating seed-setters. Most will come true from seed, or produce a similar rather than hybridized next generation. Some plants are rampant hybridizers, such as biennials like columbine, pansies, and violas.

Most seed matures in late summer or fall. Often it's a simple matter of keeping an eye out and wandering over one day with a pre-labeled self-closing plastic bag into which you tap the seed. Sometimes the seed pod shatters suddenly and you will want to put a little paper bag, punched with air holes, over the developing pod so it shatters at perfect ripeness into the bag. Dill does this and so does impatiens, which propels its seed outward with a fascinating spring mechanism that is the reason for its nickname "touch-me-not."

If necessary, dry seed spread out in a dish or on paper for a week and then store, sealed, in a dry, cool place. Wet is more damaging to seed than cold; I have often kept my seed on the unheated screened side porch in a moisture-proof tin without a problem.

Some plants will self-sow if you let them, including wild poppies, columbine, dogwoods, hollyhocks, chives, cleome, larkspur, foxglove, cypress vine, nicotiana, four-o'clocks, morning glories, and many other annuals, perennials, and biennials. You can also do this for them, shaking the seed pods over the place where you want them to grow. Some annual seeds, like marigolds and tomatoes and impatiens, are not really cold-tolerant, but you sometimes can get them self-sowing to a limited extent, anyway. It's worth educating your eye to the seedling stage of these things, so you don't pull them up as weeds. Most can be moved about the garden in spring.

One small word of caution. Don't get carried away as I have done and wind up with a pint of cleome seed and a gallon of cosmos, envelope after envelope of the tiny black grenade-shaped four-o'clock seeds, and so much marigold seed that I could be taken for a Burpee. Much of this seed went begging and was never planted. It was mere gardener's greed.

Local Nurseries

There is no substitute for a good neighborhood nursery, one that inspires gardens by the very fact of its existence and the scope of its holdings. It is axiomatic that if you can see a plant before you buy it, you will bypass many disappointments in terms of size and vigor. That's why you should use mail order only when you can't find a good, healthy plant locally. It's worth taking the time to learn your local resources.

My first nursery purchase was a pot of gayfeather or liatris, a half-priced special at the summer sale many greenhouses and nurseries have in late June to get rid of tag ends of spring stock. I bought it because it was in flower, and I was still in the selection stage that requires buying plants in flower so one has some idea of what they look like. It was summer, and this was a summer-bloomer. I fell for the purple bottle-brush spire of flowers and got it. That's how sophisti-cated plant selection can be. (It's my personal theory that this depen-dence on buying in bloom is why so many of us have flower gardens heavy on springtime color, since that is when most plants are sold.)

An eye-opener for me has been the annual spring seedling and plant survey I do for the newspaper that employs me. It takes at least one full day and hundreds of miles to drive to a selected cross-section of plant shops. I always find differences in plant care, prices, and di-versity; and each year I discover a new favorite outlet. If you try it, you will be amazed at how quickly you learn to spot bargains and bad plants.

Not everyone can tootle around like this, I know, but do it at least once, and when you find a nursery or garden center you like, patron-ize it. You may pay a bit more now and then, but you are cultivating a friend in the nursery business.

Ask questions. Do they propagate their own plants (very good) or truck them in just for spring (not so good, but acceptable)? Plants have to come from someplace, it's true, but I like garden centers that are real nursery-style plant places rather than warehouse holding areas.

Are the plants labeled with Latin names, or can the Latin names be determined? This is a big issue when you want a specific cultivar or want to be able to look up performance records before you buy. For instance, I just learned that the reason I have been unable to grow a lawn "carpet" of chamomile is that I kept buying the wrong plant. You need *Anthemis nobilis* or perennial Roman chamomile, not the ordi-nary German type, *Matricaria chammomilla,* a three-foot-tall plant that is used for making tea.

Is there anyone available to walk around with you and talk plants, or do they just stand behind the register and ring up sales? Can they tell you what the plant will look like in three years? Have they grown it? Is there anyplace on the grounds where you can see mature specimens? This is a terrific marketing tool and gardener service that you occasionally find. Treasure the experience. I am surprised at how few places do it.

Use your eyes. Are the plants treated right? Is shade cloth or other protection provided for sun-hating plants? Are the same types of plants displayed together or scattered around? I like a place that pays attention first to plants and second to window dressing. Is there a variety?

I love family-run businesses, even if it means a bit of a trek to get there, even if it means stepping over the resident sleeping dog or being kept waiting while someone tends to a child.

When you find a place you like in early spring, return in late June for any possible discount sales and again in the fall, a great planting time and a time when you often get big plants for small plant prices as they don't want to carry any more over the winter than necessary.

Whenever possible, go on a weekday or early on Saturday.

Groceries and Discount Stores

A lot of my early plant buys were from these enticing but dangerous plant venues. The temporary garden shop erected in spring by countless stores is not necessarily a bad resource, it's simply a little more buyer-beware than your average garden center—which is not a hazard-free shopping paradise all the time either, I might mention.

Anyway, groceries and discount department stores have probably launched many a modern gardening passion. I used to feel intimidated at local garden centers. I spent more time reading labels and being horrified at prices than actually looking at plants. At that time, I was uncommitted to spending money on plants, and hid my interest even from myself by impulse buys at the discount store. A $12 basket of pansies went in the shopping cart with motor oil, toothpaste, and paper towels. My first hostas, plucked from a card table in front of the supermarket in late spring and just about dead, were bad buys. I have nursed them along, but they will never be anything more than unexciting medium-sized, green and white whatever hostas. They put me off hosta for years. Until, that is, I chanced to make the buy of a lifetime, great big, bold, and healthy *Hosta sieboldiana* in pots for $6 each at a greenhouse that did not know what it had.

So you see, it all evens out if you just keep gardening long enough.

Eventually you get to know most of the pitfalls in buying from the occasional plant-seller who is in it more for the quick springtime income than for the love of plants. You cannot always count on these vendors to know what they have received, or assume that everything they offer for sale will thrive in your area. Be especially wary of the so-called hardy azaleas sold for Easter and Mother's Day. Nor can you trust clerks temporarily turned into horticulturalists to keep things watered enough or not too much. And when labels are missing, you are on your own to make identifications.

Varieties offered generally are the horticultural equivalent of winter tomatoes—long on looks but short on flavor. Many of these are the plants that are easiest to propagate and grow, so that it's no big loss to the store if a dozen prostrate junipers die or a half-dozen generic crabapples go unwatered and wither.

Perversely, as time goes by and your plant vocabulary increases, you will find that discount stores can be fascinating sources. There will be the occasional odd shipment of desirable, choice, and healthy-looking plants, usually perennials. To get these buys, you generally must scope out the shops very early in spring, shortly after the trucks are unloaded. It is my experience that, while a few grocers and discount merchants take very good care of plants, the later in the season you buy, the riskier it is.

Incidentally, I no longer buy bulbs from grocery or discount store displays. The hot indoor storage conditions are brutal. I am convinced that the only way to go is to order direct from a bulb merchant.

Regional Specialists

If given a choice, I'd rather buy an apple tree grafted and grown down the road than one produced in Georgia. I'd prefer a rose from a grower in Ohio rather than one in California and, if possible, I'd opt for a rose grown in central Ohio rather than one from the more temperate areas up around the lake. I try to find plants grown roughly in the same area they will be transplanted to on the theory that there's less stress for a rose or apple tree if it's been living in the Zombie Zones already and is not an involuntary import.

A little "buy locally, think globally" notion creeps in, too, but there is such an element of self-interest for the gardener in seeking out regional specialists that you can't pat yourself on the back too much. One salutary sideshoot of the notion is that you often can drive to the regional nurseries, pick out your plants, meet the owner/growers, and have a great day out of the garden.

One of the easiest ways to discover regional specialty growers is to join as many local and regional plant societies and chapters of national plant societies as you can. Dues are generally modest and the returns high. You will learn lots, even if your involvement is limited to opening and reading the newsletters and journals such societies publish, but most also have annual plant trades, sales, or auctions, and many clubs sponsor annual garden and nursery tours. All such things are invaluable perks of membership.

The list at the end of the chapter includes a number of regional specialists as well as a few farther away. Many are great destinations for a one- or two-day garden-looking, garden-buying jaunt. Some offer catalogs, and others do business by mail order only. All are excellent resources for those who garden in the Lower Midwest.

Call before you request a catalog to see if there is a charge. Call before you go. Not all these places are open to visitors, or they may not be open all the time. Many require that you make an appointment as much as a week ahead.

Mail Order

Mail order is addictive. The prices! The variety! The ease of at-home shopping! The visions that derail your common sense!

Before you get giddy with what appear to be incredibly low prices, check shipping costs and plant size. A $3 oakleaf hydrangea "bush" may be a delicate, ankle-high sprig that will be hard pressed to survive shipping, much less winter at your house. And the shipping costs for your bargain may be as much as the purchase price.

Sometimes you can save a significant amount by pooling an order, which enables several gardeners to order in bulk and pay one shipping fee. I've done this with perennials and bulbs. It was a headache keeping track of whose portion of which part of the order had arrived. It was complicated immensely by various complaints and returns, which had to be dealt with jointly, too. I would not do it again unless we were simply splitting an order of one hundred tulip bulbs of the same color and type.

None of this means I quit ordering by mail or stopped spending untold winter hours reading catalogs and marking them up in fits of fictional spending. It only means I am still learning how to mail order well. I certainly don't know it all, but here are some insights I've gained.

THINK SMALL

In my naivete I once imagined some eager gardening type—another me—avidly opening the envelope with my order in it, nodding his head with satisfaction at my sagacity, and immediately trotting forth to the fields to dig and hand-pack just what I wanted.

This may happen, but more often the plants are dug in the fall, labeled, bundled, and put into cold storage, whence they are plucked in early spring and sent along. Sometimes the biggest mail-order companies have other companies growing and shipping things, so your plants may be ordered from South Carolina or New Jersey but actually be grown in and shipped to you from Minnesota.

That is why, again, I like small, family-run mail-order operations where they put their hands on what they grow and sell. I think you tend to get better quality.

THINK BIG

As you read catalogs, remember: Yellow highlighter markers are cheap. My strategy for not getting carried away with desire is to mark up the catalog with abandon first, go through it twice and winnow out the silly impulses, go through it thrice and tally the cost, go through it a final time with realistic resignation, and make out an order. This is generally a good six inches shorter and $100 less than it might have been.

ATTEND TO DETAILS

As you fill out your order, take care to write clearly. I always request on the packing label I fill out with my address that plants be left in the shade by the UPS delivery person. They are not always left in the shade, but at least I tried. If I am especially concerned about an order or the timing, I request a collect call when the order is shipped.

Make a copy of your order and put it in the catalog. Thus, you can refer easily to order and growing instructions when the shipment arrives. Do not be afraid to call if you think your order is overdue. I've had one place just slip up and forget the second half of an order.

Open packages immediately. Do not have dinner first. Unpack and let potted plants sit in bright but indirect light for a few days before planting. You must plant any bare root material immediately, but you can soak them in water as long as overnight.

I give private bonus points to companies that send stuff packed in recycled newspaper, leaves, straw, or anything but those white plastic peanuts.

A lot of people get incensed over receiving the wrong plant, a dead plant, or no plants at all. Things happen. In a decade of mail order, I have had far more successes than failures, and each failure that I have bothered to call about has been rectified (except one, and I will never order from that company again).

My final advice for mail order is to make phone calls. It's a small cost to find out if they are out of something before you go to the fuss of ordering it. You often can chat about the suitability of the plant to your area if you call early in the season when the plant seller's life is not the pure hell of spring orders.

Roadside Finds

This is one of those taboo subjects that just about all gardeners indulge in but don't want to admit to in print. Me, either. We are all adults, and we all know that it's just as wrong to collect plants from the wild as it is to steal plants from the local branch bank's landscape.

That said, let's admit that most of us have coveted if not actually collected a plant or two, pinched a seed pod, or snapped off a twig.

What to do about this impulse?

One of my all-time favorite short stories, by John Updike (it appeared about six years ago in the *Atlantic Monthly*), was about a retired man who so coveted his neighbor's mature rhododendrons, compared to his just-started babies, that he tried to dig one up early one morning and was shot in the process.

The moral is: Ask first.

Collecting seed is generally harmless; a cutting or two seldom disfigures a plant; but wholesale removal can be not only folly but a failure if not done at the right time of year or in the right manner for success.

Don't waste your time.

Any surreptitious breaking off of branches is bound to fail as a cutting technique unless you have a knife and plastic bag in your pocket with a cooler handy in the back of the car and go straight home to prepare and stick the cutting. One exception might be sedums, and I will admit to picking up a piece found on the floor of a greenhouse once. Technically, that was trash collection and not stealing.

Never bother collecting a plant in full bloom. Instead, mark it for seed collection. If the weed in question is being bulldozed, I might not feel too many compunctions about liberating it without permission, although I did that with a cactus in South Carolina once and it bit me rather badly.

No Matter Where

SELECT, DON'T SETTLE FOR A PLANT

Determine for sure what the plant is called that you want—that it is a red-fruited 'Donald Wyman' crabapple and not yellow 'Golden Harvest'. If what you admire is a 'Winter King' hawthorn tree—incidentally a Midwest cultivar—then be sure you get that and not some generic brand that loses its red berries early in the winter.

This can sometimes take some searching. The forces that shunt a plant into commercial production and keep it there are a complex of inertia, economics, plant qualities, novelty, and plant hardiness. Generally, the newer a plant is—either in breeding or in availability to the retail market—the more expensive it will be. The reason is not necessarily price-fixing. It often has to do with limited supplies, as it takes time to propagate even the most willing subjects, and they have to be grown along for a number of years before that so that performance can be evaluated.

Some plants are expensive because they are slow to increase or difficult to get started. This includes many rhododendrons, some ferns, beech trees, bottlebrush buckeye bushes, blue or Himalayan poppy, and whatever plant it is you just fell in love with and must have. Some plants are hard to locate because, while they are choice, they are not popular. Often, this is because we don't know about them. We don't know about them because the nurseries are not offering them. The nurseries are not offering them because we don't buy them. We don't buy them because they are a few dollars more. It's not quite that simple, or circular, but gardeners do have to be aware that if we continue to settle for the lowest-common-denominator plants, that is all we will get.

DON'T BUY NAME BRANDS IF GENERIC WILL DO

There will be times when names don't matter, like when you want to naturalize daffodils or daylilies. Then, buy the cheapest, healthiest plants or bulbs you can find, or cadge some starts from a friend.

Unless you are a breeder or avid collector, it is seldom worth competing for the first, expensive offerings. Like microwaves and computers, they will get cheaper and more widely available as time goes on. Or at least they should. I have often been surprised at the long run of high prices on the popular Stella de Oro daylily.

ASSURE YOURSELF THAT THE PLANT IS HEALTHY

This means vigorous, not necessarily big. Often, this means you have to inspect the roots. If you can't remove a plant from a pot, at least look at the bottom of the pot. You'd like to see tiny white roots just beginning to sprout from the drainage holes rather than a tangle of tough brown roots spiraling about.

Plants that fail to thrive can be those that have been stressed by shipping or poor holding practices, such as too much sun and wind and not enough water, a not-uncommon event in some discount and even garden center scenarios. Even healthy-looking plants should be coddled for a few days to a week after purchase before planting. Hold in a semi-shady spot out of the wind and let them catch their breath before you throw them into new circumstances.

Bad plants are the bane of all plant growers, whether you stand on the selling or the buying side. The question is not if it will happen to you, but when it will happen and what you will do about it.

Most plant sellers want their customers to be happy. Many will provide replacements if death occurs shortly after purchase, even for the first year. Many will ask no questions. Keep receipts.

You have some obligations as a consumer, too, and I pass along a few rather obvious tips only because I am amazed at what gardeners in the throes of spring buying frenzy will accept.

Never buy a plant with bugs on it. Never buy a plant that is clearly distorted, odd-colored, puny, or living in a pot with green slime. A wilted plant is strictly off-limits. So is one that arrives with mold of any color on its leaves.

If you have the option, buy plants grown in square rather than round pots. They are less apt to be pot-bound, a condition where roots grow in a life-choking spiral. If you buy a plant with this hard mass of roots, be sure to snip it in several places or tease it open before planting to encourage the formation of new, white roots.

Select plants before they flower, even before they bud if you can. If you can't, pinch off most or all the buds as you plant. This will help your transplant spend energy on roots rather than flowers.

A Selection of Plant Sources

I'm sure this list can be expanded, and I would welcome hearing about other good area nurseries. Although it is in the nature of a busman's holiday, I always try to visit a nursery and a botanic garden when I'm traveling. I've had great experiences, and gotten great plant buys, doing this. It is heartily recommended if your family will knuckle under. I had to live through a day in the Smoky Mountains, eating cotton candy and driving little cars around little tracks, but I got my folks to spend a day with me at the nearby Holbrook Farm and Nursery in Fletcher, North Carolina, which, under the watch of owner and former Louisville native Allen Bush, is becoming one of the country's more interesting specialists in hardy, unusual, and good native perennials that very happily make the trek west over the Smokies.

Applesource
Route One, Chapin, IL 62628
(217) 245-7589

Tom Vorbeck has done for apples what vacuum-packed gourmet fresh pasta did for macaroni. An orchardist and visionary apple entrepreneur, he offers boxes of apples that come in varieties you've never heard of, but should sink your teeth into, such as Melrose and Mutsu, Arkansas Black, Fuji, Jonagold, and Prairie Spy. Three of the four vendors that supply Tom with over 100 different named apples are from Indiana, Illinois, and Michigan, giving Applesource a uniquely midwestern slant. If you are wondering what kind of apple trees to grow, buy a box of these apples first.

Bluestone Perennials
7211 Middle Ridge Rd., Madison, OH 44057
(800) 852-5423

The deal here is small but healthy plants, so you get big value for little bucks. They've got tried-and-true garden classics, and not just ordinary stuff. Irresistible. They put out a good mail-order catalog. If you visit, take the station wagon and leave the kids at home. You'll want the extra packing room.

Burnham Woods
6775 Hudoff Road, Bloomington, IN 47408
(812) 339-0616

A small family-operated business specializing in herbaceous perennial plants. All of the plants available in the nursery can be found growing on the informally landscaped grounds, where they undergo constant evaluation for their performance under midwestern climatic conditions. Those unfamiliar with the area should phone for directions. Open 9-5 Wednesday through Saturday from May through September, in April and October by appointment.

Companion Plants
7247 N. Coolville Ridge Rd., Athens, OH 45701
(614) 592-4643

I discovered this gem of an herb plant resource while scouting out an unusual but wonderful artemisia, *A. lactiflora* or ghost plant, a fall-blooming five-footer suitable for the back of the border. They've got it, plus nine other kinds of artemisias, eight kinds of yarrow, five sorts of *Agastache* or hyssop—very decorative, big, hardy perennials in yellow and blue and red—not to mention catnips, sages, and bee balms. They also carry seed.

They are open Thursday through Sunday, March to Thanksgiving. They don't answer the phone on Wednesdays or holidays or anytime in January.

Dabney Herbs
P.O. Box 22061, Louisville, KY 40252
(502) 893-5198

A one-woman operation with plants grown in northern Kentucky and the mountains of North Carolina, this mail order–only business runs to plants, seeds, dried herbs and spices, aromatic oils for aromatherapy and potpourri, miscellaneous tools, garden decorations, crafts, and books.

Glasshouse Works
Church St., P.O. Box 97, Stewart, OH 45788-0097
(614) 662-2142

The 1992 catalog runs to ninety-two pages of close-printed plant lists, including an enticing section of annuals, perennials, and hardy shrubs. Co-owners Tom Winn and Ken Frieling carry quite an array of plants; and, while their mail-order business is increasing rapidly, they anticipate visits from garden buffs and always have great gardener-insider suggestions for other stops and accommodations in the area, which is near Wayne National Forest and Athens, home of Ohio University.

Hatfield Gardens
22799 Ringgold Southern Road, Stoutsville, OH 43154
(614) 474-5719

Now in its twenty-seventh year, it specializes in hostas, daylilies, and narcissus, including some of the newest and finest varieties. The catalog lists the dozen or so "Open Garden Days" each year when the gardens can be visited without an appointment to see various species at their peak.

Heirloom Old Garden Roses
24062 Riverside Drive N.E., St. Paul, OR 97137
(503) 538-1576

A family operation based on a passionate love of roses; home-grown stock, grown on its own roots rather than budded, which makes the plants more winter-hardy; and an incredible selection, from old-fashioned ramblers to new climbers to antique minis and new minis, not to mention terrific and, as far as I know my roses, dependable descriptions and hardiness ratings. Their roses are guaranteed virus-free (virus can be a problem with some roses shipped from warmer climates). Prices are reasonable, although there is a $1.75 per plant shipping charge. The roses are container-grown, so they can be shipped anytime your weather and circumstances can handle them.

The garden, designed by owners Louise and John Clements, is open March through October, and features almost 500 varieties and a 100-foot-long pergola. My only regret is that they are not in the Midwest.

Highland Succulents
1446 Bear Run Rd., Gallipolis, OH 45631
(614) 256-1428

This has got to be the weird plant headquarters of the world. Mail order only. The collection is heavy with rare, unusual, and stunning dryland plants with specialization in bulbous-stemmed, brilliantly flowered pachypodiums, one of the most avant of the avant houseplant trends in recent years. While most of the offerings are considered houseplants, the northern hardiness limits for cacti and succulents are unknown, as many a C & S buff is busy proving with sandy, rocky, raised beds of blooming echeverias, agaves, and yuccas.

Holly Hills
1216 Hillsdale Rd., Evansville, IN 47711
(812) 867-3367

Brothers Stephen and David Schroeder carry on the work of their dad, H. R. Schroeder, with evergreen azaleas bred for our midwestern conditions. The selection includes lovely late-summer-blooming native azaleas that are regrettably little known.

Huff's Garden Mums
P.O. Box 187, 618 Juniatta, Burlington, KA 66839-0187
(316) 364-2933

A large plant list and many special group offerings make this a mail-order and nursery shopper's paradise for those who want lots of chrysanthemums at reasonable prices. The firm is noted for carrying older, hard-to-find varieties, but get 'em while you can. Owner Charles Huff told me he might have to start culling out the slow-sellers.

Klehm Nursery
Route 5, Box 197, Penny Rd., South Barrington, IL 60010-9389
(800) 553-3715

I think of this as the peony place, period. Others associate it with Japanese iris, hosta, and daylilies, which altogether form the core of this mail-order firm that also offers an eclectic and interesting selection of "companion plants." They don't have it all, but what they do have is outstanding and all home-grown. Catalog $5. The gardens are open two days each year.

Klein Nursery
4004 Glenarm Rd., Crestwood, KY 40014
(502) 241-8338

Jules Klein makes grafts and propagates unusual woody plants from shrubs and trees in the family's private arboretum, developed by his father, respected plantsman Theodore Klein. It's best to order from this wholesale operation through special request at the retail level.

McClure & Zimmerman
P.O. Box 368, 108 W. Winnebago, Friesland, WI 53935
(414) 326-4220

This Wisconsin mail-order firm offers an in-depth selection of bulbs, from common spring types to hard-to-find alliums and species tulips. You won't find color photos, but the descriptions are good and so are the prices.

Milaeger's Gardens
4838 Douglas Ave., Racine, WI 53402-2498
(414) 639-2371

This Wisconsin establishment gets rave reviews from many of my correspondents. I have not yet used this nursery, which carries shrubs, perennials, prairie wildflowers, and ornamental grasses.

Nolin River Nut Tree Nursery
797 Port Wooden Rd., Upton, KY 42784
(502) 369-8551

The production of more than a hundred varieties of grafted walnuts, pecans, heartnuts, chestnuts, butternuts, and hicans is at the heart of owners John and Lisa Brittain's homesteading on the rocky hillsides of Upton, Kentucky. They specialize in trees that bear well in this region, are more pest-resistant, and have larger, meatier nuts than ordinary types.

Pinecliffe Daylily Gardens
6604 Scottsville Rd., Floyds Knobs, IN 47119
(812) 923-8113

Energetic owner and traveler Don Smith takes pride in having the
latest hybrids. This does not mean all his offerings are inexpensive,
but the display in July is fantastic. Hostas also are available. A home-
grown operation in the hills of southern Indiana, with display gardens
open by appointment.

Prairie Nursery
P.O. Box 306, Westfield, WI 53964
(608) 296-3679

Native grasses and flowers are the specialty, as well as materials
for butterflies and birds.

Prairie Ridge Nursery/CRM Ecosystems, Inc.
9738 Overland Rd., Mt. Horeb, WI 53572
(608) 437-5245

The thrust of the company is production of native seeds and
plants for low-maintenance erosion-control plantings under various
growing conditions. Also consultation. Many pre-selected combinations are offered in collections.

Rocky Meadow Orchard and Nursery
Route 2, Box 2104, New Salisbury, IN 47161-9716
(812) 347-2213

Here's a place that will have a tree for almost any of the apple
varieties that catch your eye. Owners Ed and Pat Fackler have been
working for nearly a decade to produce apple, crabapple, pear, and
other fruit trees that live and live well in the Zombie Zones of the
Lower Midwest.

Ronninger's Seed Potatoes
Star Route, Moyie Springs, ID 83845
(208) 267-7938

They offer more types of organically grown seed potatoes than you imagined existed, but also are digging into garlic bred especially for the Midwest, like German Red.

Schott Gardens
2209 Nashville Rd., Bowling Green, KY 42101
(502) 781-0254

Daylilies only, and with eighteen pages of single-spaced listings, this retail outlet on the southern fringe of our midwestern region offers a good selection of the choice common and unusual varieties. One of the display gardens is at the home of owners Casey and Cindy Schott.

Shady Hill Gardens
821 Walnut St., Batavia, IL 60510-2999
(708) 879-5665

These mail-order geranium specialists outside Chicago offer a lot more than red and pink zonal geraniums. Among the more than 1,000 varieties are regal, cascade, ivy-leaved, miniature, floribunda, sunbelt, fancy-leaf, cactus-flowered, tulip-flowered, rosebud, stellar, bird's egg, and phlox geraniums, as well as some heirlooms from the early 1800s. If you want something different in your window boxes, but still want dependable geraniums, try Shady Hill.

Shady Oaks Nursery
112 10th Ave. S.E., Waseca, MI 56093
(507) 835-5033

True to its name, the company specializes in perennial plants, shrubs, and grasses that like shade—many of them natives. Mostly mail order except for hosta sales in spring and hosta "fairs" each Saturday in June when display gardens are open to the public. Browsers are also welcome at other times, except during the height of the shipping season, April–June.

Shooting Star Nursery
311 Bates Rd., Frankfort, KY 40601
(502) 223-1679

The specialization is native plants of eastern and midwestern North America. The operation, owned by working botanists Sherri and Marc Evans, sells only nursery-propagated, rather than collected, wild-flower and other native plants for habitats such as woodland, wet-lands, savannah, prairie, and roadside plantings, but most are sterling additions to the cultivated border, too.

Simpson Nursery Co.
P.O. Box 2065, Vincennes, IN 47591
(812) 882-2441

Robert Simpson is the man who "discovered" deciduous hollies and the award-winning Winter King hawthorn. This is a wholesale operation; Simpson's cultivars and selections are usually available by special request at your favorite retail nursery.

Soules Garden
5809 Rahke Rd., Indianapolis, IN 46217
(317) 786-7839

This is a case of a private collection that just grew and grew into one of the Midwest's largest hosta outlets. Daylilies, too. They have mail-order service, but a visit to see the thousands of hostas growing under evergreens and pick up your chosen plants, freshly dug, is worthwhile. At the nursery, owner Marge Soules also offers companion plants (epimedium, *Lamium* 'White Nancy', Japanese painted fern, etc., etc.) not available by mail. During peak bloom (roughly the first three weeks in July), the daylily beds are a sight to behold.

Springvale Farm Nursery, Avid Gardener
Mozier Hollow Rd., Hamburg, IL 62045
(618) 232-1108

Their mail-order catalog offers unusual and choice shrubs, trees, and perennials that have proved both winter-hardy and summer-hardy in the Midwest. Plants come in small sizes for coddling along, and medium sizes for planting directly into the landscape.

5

Keeping Plants and You Happy

IT IS A GIANT of a grass, fully twelve feet tall, stretching its fan-shaped seed heads up to the sun like a crowd of hands raised to wave. I know this ornamental grass only by its Latin name, *Miscanthus floridulus giganticus*. It is a plant that makes me very happy. It is the first thing visitors comment on and the first thing I long to see each spring as I search, bent over, looking for the stiff green shoots that suddenly appear out of the dry, spearlike stubble. They move up at such a rate that they soon overtake the neighboring foxglove, sprint past the night-blooming primroses, and tower over the goldenrod and salvias by August. The impulse to height is not quite countered by the strength of the reedy canes, and as it moves upward in the center, the outer edges move gently outward and down to arch over the stone wall and flirt with the driveway.

That grass has a presence that makes me feel like I'm talking to the gods of nature. I like to stand under it and watch the September bees try to work gold pollen from the long, slender fingers of the grass's flowery hands. I sometimes go out at night and nudge the stalks, just to hear them whisper to each other. By the time a wet snow in January has smashed it down, I will be content to cut the dry, brittle reeds—no larger around than a nickel—down to a rough stubble, content to know that their life force now lies underground in a tangle of roots fully as dense as concrete.

I am glad this plant is happy, as gardeners like to say of plants that are growing well. However, watching it season to season, I realize that the notion of making plants happy has a selfish motivation. Everything we do in the garden, we do for us.

My wonderful talking grass was the impetus for making what has become a prime feature of my yard, a deep border set against a dry stone wall that acts as a retaining wall from the gravel drive to the circle of lawn in front of the house. The giant grass and other ornamental grasses love it there. I am a lazy gardener, and this border was my first done with no digging. It was initiated by a winter's worth of living with strips of black plastic laid over the grass and pegged down. In late spring, the sod was pretty much dead and could be scratched out and the ground duly tilled and planted. Then, since a lot of gardening is correcting your mistakes, I had to extend the border. It was too narrow, too skimpy-looking for the big grasses and the broad driveway and the two-story, thick-bodied house.

The border was extended rather painlessly by using an herbicide as the lawn began to grow last spring, then covering the planned extension—some three feet more wide by sixty feet long—with layers of newspaper, planting through the paper, and then covering it up with deep-brown, crumbly wood chips, which are all that's left of two great beech trees.

I tell this story of grasses and border by way of preface to the notion that the essentials of making plants happy need not make the gardener miserable.

Soil Improvements

Bed Preparation

When I was young I thought you had to flail away with shovels and rakes and ache for days, but there are many ways to go about this unavoidable task. The big issue is getting rid of sod, unless you are starting at a newly constructed house, where the problem is finding any decent dirt to plant in, since many builders "finish grade" by burying plasterboard and wood scraps in the clay rather than leaving you any usable topsoil.

First outline your bed. Use stakes and twine for straight edges and a garden hose for curves. Or eyeball it. You can always fine-tune the edge later and probably will, again and again. Unless you go to the trouble to create a permanent edge of sunken brick, stone, plastic edging, poured concrete, or other material, you may as well put $50 in your budget for one of those dandy but pricey edging tools that work with a rocker motion. Then it is time to get serious about a little work.

NEWSPAPER AND WOOD CHIPS

My current favorite, this is perhaps the least laborious method. On a windless day, lay down newspaper six to twelve pages thick over the area of the proposed bed. As you do, cover it quickly with mulch to keep it in place. You plant by cutting an X-shaped hole in the paper in the case of small plants, while with trees and shrubs it's often easier to plant first and surround the shrub or tree later. Whatever way you go, the paper is a slowly disintegrating weed barrier that will not kill earthworms or keep the ground excessively dry, as plastic will. If you tackle your project in small stages, you can manage alone. Two or more workers can speed the procedure up.

SOLARIZATION, PURIST STYLE

Along about the hot days of July, dig a trench around the perimeter of the area you wish to clear of weeds and grass. Cover the area with clear plastic, laying the edges in the trench and burying them to keep them down. Run a hose in along one loose side and flood the area. Remove the hose. Seal the opening and wait a month or so. With temperatures steadily in the eighties, everything in the area should be killed by elevated daytime temperatures well over 100 degrees.

SOLARIZATION, HOME STYLE

Not as harsh, but slower, this home-devised method involves heavy black plastic and homemade "U" pegs made of wire. Mow the area you wish to turn into a border or bed and rake it clear of sticks, stones, or other debris. Lay down the plastic. Do it in overlapping strips, using the threefold thickness that results from not unfolding a large roll of the stuff. Secure the edges with your homemade "staples," long boards, rocks, or whatever you have on hand. It's not attractive, and your neighbors will wonder if you are growing tobacco, but the only problem I have with this system is dogs padding across it with their sharp little claws.

Admittedly, it takes some time—several to many months, depending on the weather. Grass is killed fast in hot weather, slower in cold. If you start your home-style "solarization" in the fall or early winter, it should have dead grass and soft soil under it by spring. Also, the ground will be a dry island in a sea of March mud, permitting you to get out there and dig and rake when others are housebound.

HERBICIDE

I used to be such a purist that I would not even look at Roundup, a relatively benign synthetic herbicide that does not move around in the soil. I changed my mind when faced with a long and weedy gravel drive, although I still hate the stuff. It's expensive, messy, smells bad, I have to keep the dogs penned up until it dries, and it still does not knock out violets and some grasses. But this is one instance where I think the synthetic is far preferable to the old-fashioned "organic" methods. Boiling water is hard to use. Salt not only kills the weeds, but can move in the soil and mess up other plants you do like, not to mention the number it does on earthworms and the fact that salted ground is often unplantable for a long time.

POTATOES

A time-honored method of readying a bed for a hedge is to plant potatoes. It's a technique from the days of hardy, self-sufficient gardening that today's far-sighted gardeners could easily adopt if digging is their therapy.

It calls for a familiarity with the conventional method of growing potatoes rather than today's low-labor notions of spuds in soil layers in a garbage can. The old-style method calls for digging once to plant the tubers, cultivating several times to hill up around the developing stems, and a final second digging in order to harvest the full-grown potatoes. The obvious result is a long trench of well-worked soil in which it will be child's play to plant shrubs. It's a pretty good idea, as long as where you plant potatoes happens to be where you want a hedge.

JUST DIG

You can accomplish a lot with simple digging. Muscles, for one thing. A Zen sense of no-hurry, for another. Hand-digging a border is very physical and best tackled in a slow and steady rhythm with the proper equipment.

This is the place where after-dinner gardeners of the flip-flops and old spoon school grow up fast. You need thick-soled, tie-on shoes; steel shanks are not excessive. Your spade must have a pointed nose and a fairly long handle for good leverage.

Whatever method you use, begin by lifting the sod. I wasted a lot of time in the past NOT lifting sod, but simply digging up hunks of dirt with little topknots of sod attached, heaving these aside, and digging more all the way down the bed. Then I came back and had fits trying to separate sod bits from real dirt. Don't do it. Lift the sod, even if all you do with it is put it on the compost. To lift sod, it is best to have a slender, flat-nosed spade, often called a border spade or sometimes a poacher's spade. I generally use my all-purpose slender, pointed-nosed tree or transplanting spade, which is very long and narrow. What you don't want is a shovel, a squatty-nosed, broad-bellied tool that is good for general heaving about of dirt and moving other loose material, like sand or gravel. There is a special sod lifter too, which looks a lot like an edger. I've never used a sod lifter, but understand it can be just as back-breaking to use as a tree spade.

You want to chop the edges of a long rectangle about the width of your spade, then insert your spade like a blade and saw the turf loose. I find it best to do this from a kneeling position. Roll up the turf as you go and stack it in a wheelbarrow. If you just toss it aside you will not get around to picking it up before it begins to crumble, so it is worth doing right from the beginning. Now all you have to do is dig, breaking up the soil as much as possible as you go, then breaking it down into progressively finer particles, perhaps adding compost or sand to improve the texture.

Hand-digging can be satisfying, sweaty work. It can also be a waste of time if a less laborious method will do the job just as well—and it usually will if we're talking perennial or annual plants or young trees and shrubs. Exceptions would be sowing annual vegetable seed, especially root crops like carrots and beets. I personally get around this by growing them in either raised beds or big containers.

That's why I will mention double-digging only in passing. It may be some gardeners' badge of honor and even a necessity if you are confronted with horrible, horrible soil and are, for some insane reason, categorically opposed to raised beds or the use of newspaper.

RAISED BEDS

An adaptation of market-gardening techniques, raised beds are more pragmatic than elegant. If kept neatly and edged in concrete blocks or wood, with the paths between them done in shredded bark, gravel, or brick, they can be rather attractive, the basis for most cook's gardens.

You make a raised bed by simply (!) digging up all the dirt in the appropriate space, mixing in whatever amendments you want, and tossing it all into a pile that crowns a foot or so above lawn level. It stays fluffy and up there because your beds are narrow and long, so you never walk in them and compress the soil. Also, you periodically add compost and organic mulch, which helps keep the raised bed raised.

Those of us who are lazy or have bad drainage problems have been known to literally raise a bed by first forming a retaining wall and then tossing in all the ingredients for a great soil for whatever we want to grow without once digging up the ground at lawn level. However, if drainage is the problem, we may have to trench in some leach pipe or other drainage channels.

TRACTORS AND TILLERS

For many midwesterners, it's not spring until traffic starts getting tied up with the tractors out on the roads, moving from garden plot to field. In many communities you can still hire a neighbor to drop by and disc your side yard for a garden, or you can rent a heavy-duty tiller that will bust sod and grind it up. We sold our big workhorse tiller that took four men to lift, and I do not miss it. It was great when we had a large, quarter-acre vegetable garden done in conventional rows and tilled periodically for weeds, but it is of little use with my perennial borders, my nursery beds, or vegetables grown in raised beds.

Instead, what I have hung onto and love is a little tiller. It's ancient, leaks oil, and is unsightly, but it's small enough that I can pick it up and set it where I want to churn up some pre-dug dirt or incorporate compost or lime. We've used it a lot as we slowly reshape our yard into terraces and redo lawn. I don't use it for its actual purpose, to cultivate weeds from rows, as I use mulch instead to keep them from getting a hold in the first place.

Making beds for plants is just one step in making plants happy. There are lots more, as we all know.

Rethinking the Fertilizer Fix

I have only one thing to say about fertilizers: Don't fertilize if you don't have to.

The soil you have is probably not too bad. If it is bad, it is more likely a matter of compaction from walking or machinery, or depletion from lack of compost and mulch, or an issue of erosion, poor drainage, or construction backfill around the house than it is a matter of geological destiny. There are some genuinely difficult soil pockets in this country, such as the airless muds of Louisiana or the alkaline, chalky "caliche" of West Texas and other arid western regions where the lack of rain allows lime to build up in the soil. Rainy climates tend toward acid soil as rain dissolves the lime. The soil of the Lower Midwest, despite a fair amount of underlying limestone, really is not a problem unless you want to grow plants like rhododendrons and azaleas that thrive in the acid, woodsy soil of the rainy Northwest.

It is true that all soil that is actively used must be improved on an annual basis, but it doesn't need to be drenched with chemicals. You don't even have to do soil tests all the time, although you may want to do one once.

The only smart time to do a soil test is in late summer. The labs are not as busy as they are in spring. You get results back fast and in plenty of time to create the changes called for by working your garden over in the fall and having it ready to go in spring. It can take that long for some additions, such as lime, to break down and be available when your plants need them. Also, the spring soil is generally too wet to work early. Fall simply makes sense.

A soil test is best done through your local agricultural extension service office. Private labs are very expensive. The state-run programs are a bargain, usually a few dollars for each sample.

To take a sample, dig up a trowelful of dirt—no weeds or soil— from three to five spots in the planting area. Mix it together on newspaper in a dry spot and let it dry out for a week. Put this in a bag and take it to the ag office, where you will fill out forms, pay a few bucks, and get results in a week or so. Take a soil sample from each area of your garden that will have a different use; that is, a separate sample for the rose garden and one also for the vegetable patch, and another still for the rhododendron border. This will allow the lab to give you more fine-tuned and useful results.

The big secret to having good soil is to look at it, touch it, and then fix its texture. Certainly, there can be instances where the texture is right but the fertility is not. The kind of potting medium you make by combining peat moss and perlite is one example. It has no nutrients, although you can mix proportions that will be water-retentive yet drain well. Outdoors, though, most of us need to perform only a few simple annual tasks to keep soil healthy and plants happy.

Step One: Lay down a mulch every winter using good organic material like rotted or even fresh manure, alfalfa, or leaf mold, compost, or rotted wood chips. Even city dwellers with cars can get these things if they try. An apartment gardener can make compost in a bin using kitchen wastes, or buy bags of dried cow manure, compost, etc. Just check the labels to be sure you are getting the real thing and not some "hot" synthesized ammonia product laced with a little organic stuff and touted as "all-natural."

Step Two: Add compost every spring and through the growing season up to about July 4.

That's it.

Sure, you may need to augment the program occasionally if there are growth problems or if you are growing things in containers. I like to use fish emulsion or homemade manure tea in these instances, but I also have used slow-release encapsulated fertilizers with good results, as well as some of the water-soluble powders widely sold for houseplants. I just tend to underuse them or dilute the recommended strength.

You really don't have to know what the numbers mean—those 10-5-10 or 2-12-4 trios on the bags and boxes are the N-P-K ratio, of course—if you maintain a steady program of soil structure improvement or opt for the gentler, slower "natural" liquids. If you want to study agronomy, help yourself; but I usually skip the chapters on soil identification and nod off if given too many facts about nitrogen (N), phosphorus (P), and potassium (K) and which is which in the formula, which translocates and which does not in soil, which is necessary for roots and which for flowers, what yellow leaves with green veins mean versus what plain yellow leaves may mean.

What seems to work is to go out and handle your soil. It should be dampish but not wet and not bone-dry. Squeeze it. If it feels slick and gums up, it's a little bit on the clay side. If it crumbles, it's probably pretty good. If it falls apart, it's too loose and gritty, but there are things that love this kind of growing medium. I aim to err on the side of loose, airy soil whenever possible.

Take care of your soil this commonsense way and you may never buy a bag of synthetic fertilizer, like ammonium nitrate. The reason, incidentally, that such synthetic fertilizers must be stored with attention to avoiding fire is that they were developed as part of warfare chemistry and were turned to agricultural use later. They are highly concentrated and fast-acting sources of nitrogen that not only can "green up" the lawn in spring but can "burn" it and adjacent plants if applied too heavily or not watered in adequately.

Sadly, our multi-billion-dollar agricultural industry is built on what's been called a Faustian bargain with such chemicals. Man-made agrichemicals are a recent blip in our ancient agricultural tradition, and the dependence on synthesized ammonia compounds in particular seems clearly wrong-headed. The nitrogen they supply is fleeting, and as much as half of it is reckoned to wash off into groundwater, creeks, and ponds, creating a secondary problem of contamination. And a byproduct of such fertilization often is to kill the soil, to kill the fungi, earthworms, and bacteria that turn leaves and twigs and dead creatures into humus.

Also, many synthetic compounds are too simple. Offering just the big three of N-K-P is like asking a child to grow up eating mostly vitamins and water. Plants (like people) require a complex of hundreds, maybe thousands, of elements and compounds.

Compost and mulch are complex compounds. That's why they work so well. You can keep soil on the acid side for heaths and heathers, laurel, enkianthus, and rhododendron by adding coffee grounds, pine needles, and wood chips. Lime lovers (lilacs, beeches, pinks, hellebores, clematis, and peonies) can use fireplace ashes.

Be aware that organic materials take longer—about three months versus one week—to become available. What you put down in late winter is there to feed plants as they begin root activity in very early spring; what you put down in early spring keeps the larder stocked over the summer; and what you put down in early July, which is the last time to feed the garden before winter, keeps tummies full to the end of the season, but allows plants to slow down in late summer when the dormancy process begins.

Adding fertilizer or even rich compost in late summer can push some plants into unnatural top growth, which is likely to be damaged and the plant's total health compromised when the cold weather hits.

Any young tree making nine to twelve inches of twig growth is just fine, and so is an older tree or shrub making, say, six inches of twig growth. Of course, some of the dwarf varieties won't grow this fast. With bulbs, by all means buy a bag of Bulb Booster, the best product for keeping spring bloomers smiling. Scratch it in around bulbs in late winter or early spring as leaf tips emerge. Use it again in mid-fall only if growth or flowering were slow and if the bulbs are not crowded. Crowded bulbs are the main reason for lack of flowers.

If your perennials and vines, bulbs, shrubs, and trees look happy, keep them that way. Mulch them. Don't fertilize them.

Common plants can make striking combinations. Here yucca blooms, removed from normal specimen context, are mixed with ordinary orange "ditch lilies." Both are foolproof and long-lived, good friends to a beginning gardener. *Photo by Diane Heilenman.*

A root cellar partially uncovered to become a display stand for drought-resistant plants is an unconventional rock garden and a nostalgic reminder of our midwestern farm heritage. In this Kentucky garden, the dome top is covered with various small sedums, lamb's ears, and soapwort; the base is surrounded with hard-working annual salvia, annual four-o'clocks, and perennial *Sedum spectabile* 'Autumn Joy', as well as dramatic plume poppies. *Photo by Diane Heilenman.*

Smart mowing makes no-work borders. Here one at the author's house gets shaped up in spring. *Photo by Diane Heilenman.*

Old stumps and gardeners seldom get along easily. Here's one solution: a dense crop of dianthus. *Photo by Diane Heilenman.*

The moss-lined wire basket is a valuable and classic element of container gardening. Here it is planted with pink pelargoniums and pinwheel petunias and the basket is set, rather than hung, on a salvaged terra-cotta capital from a 19th-century neoclassical column. *Photo by Diane Heilenman.*

Morning glories are a standard of fencerows and porch trellises across the Midwest. *Photo by Diane Heilenman.*

Moon garden with feminist overtones at Hopscotch House, a writers' and artists' retreat near Louisville, operated by the Kentucky Foundation for Women. The full moon shape defined with river rock is cut into paths made by beds shaped like full, half, and crescent moons. The gray foliage is mostly various artemisias, while color comes from hardy hibiscus and annual petunias. *Photo by Diane Heilenman.*

Bees and errant mulberries find the fragrant spikes and big cupped leaves of *Hosta sieboldiana* irresistible. *Photo by Diane Heilenman.*

Until recently, the only way to get a hardy pink flowering begonia was to know a generous gardener. Now that the secret has reached commercial growers, you can sometimes buy these staples of the late summer shade garden. *Photo by Diane Heilenman.*

Betony, with tall purple spires of flowers, is the little-known cousin of lamb's ears and equally hard-working in a border or herb garden. *Photo by Diane Heilenman.*

A cascade of herbs and flowers grow together in a barrel at the Inn at Cedar Falls, a family farm turned bed and breakfast in Logan, Ohio. There's variegated sage, curly and flat parsley, small-leaved thyme, round-leaved dittany, and, in the foreground, purple-blue lobelia and white alyssum. *Photo by Maggie Oster.*

Vegetables can be ornamental: this garden supplies the kitchen at the Inn at Cedar Falls with food and seasonings and provides guests with a visual feast, as well. Extremely well-grown scarlet runner beans twine in the foreground; behind is a line of pink cosmos, and to the left chard and cabbage. *Photo by Maggie Oster.*

A host of hostas greet visitors to the Klehm Nursery, South Barrington, Illinois. *Photo by Michael Hayman.*

A gazebo, bench, and bee skep keep company with flowering basils in the extensive herb garden that is just one of several theme gardens at Inniswood in north suburban Columbus, Ohio. *Photo by Maggie Oster.*

Fall stains the Virginia creeper scarlet as it clambers up a tulip poplar tree and turns the leaves of young dogwoods mahogany. The arching shrub at the lip of steps to the woods and creek in the author's garden is Stephanandra, still waiting to take its fall cloak of yellow leaves against thin cinnamon-colored stems. *Photo by Diane Heilenman.*

A lush, dry meadow look that is vintage Midwest and within the reach of any gardener capable of practicing benign neglect is this combination of goldenrod and wild aster. Both are vigorous plants that can be selectively pruned and pinched for a more controlled look, and both transplant easily as large semi-shrubs in the mixed border. *Photo by Diane Heilenman.*

Compost

There is no extraneous organic matter in a yard. It's all useful. To sweep up, vacuum up, or rake up every shred of lawn debris and bag it for landfills is no longer defensible or, in many communities, permissible.

Countless books and articles have been written on this subject, and if you are intent on doing it up with a flourish, measuring potential nutrients and taking the pile's temperature, then I must confess from the onset that I am a sloppy compost maker. Sometimes it gets hot and sometimes it does not. Most of the time I am hard-pressed to patrol my five-plus acres and pick up the sticks, much less be sure all grass clippings, leaves, and soft debris make it to the compost heap and that said heap is turned by pitchfork and muscles in order to keep the invisible microbes and organisms astir so they can munch it up into rich, crumbly, sweet-smelling compost.

LEAVES

I learned my lesson when I got the notion of just raking leaves into a pile and letting nature take over. You do not get compost. You get a pile of slimy, smelly leaves. A bad odor is a good reason to suspect that the good-guy aerobic bacteria are not at work, but that the yucky, bad-guy anaerobic bacteria are. That's when you must fork the pile over a few times and let air penetrate the layers.

You can pile up leaves if you shred them first. For me, that means running the lawn tractor over them when they are dry. This raw material, by the way, is a great mulch as is. Don't worry overmuch about the relative pH of different leaves. Yes, oak leaves are a bit acid, but they don't alter the pH of your soil all that much. What's good about them is they stay so crunchy and fluffy. The leaves I don't like are maple leaves. They slime up fast and should be munched by the mower before the rain plasters them to the lawn.

GRASS CLIPPINGS

I let these stay on the lawn and decompose, a lazy country gardener's strategy that anticipated current thinking by several decades. The only time you should rake clippings is if they are as thick as hay windrows and might damage the grass. If you put them on the compost, be aware that green clippings do heat up as they decompose, so you may want to fluff up the pile a bit.

BRUSH AND WOOD

Everyone gets sloppy and puts twigs in the compost now and then, and we are all sorry later. Wood requires different microbes than soft, organic matter does for decomposition. A little bit helps lighten your compost, but you will have to dispose of large amounts of brush some other way. Piled up, it will eventually pack down and decay. In some places, you can still burn brush. I have enough space that I don't worry about the sightliness of it. In fact, I like a casual, working-place look, and I can burn brush.

Mostly, we try to leave dead trees standing and brush piles about, too, for the birds and other creatures that help make my place easy to care for because it is in balance rather than chemically controlled.

City gardeners have another problem, indeed. You have to bundle brush and get rid of it or chop it or shred it into mulch.

OTHER MATERIALS

Put on everything organic except meat and sticks larger than a straw. Whether to use animal excrement depends on the animal. I will use horse manure, but that's because I have access to it. I pile it up and let it compost separately before I add it. Cow manure too is fine to use. Pig manure is incredibly odoriferous. Chicken manure is hard to come by and, in the Ohio River Valley, I would avoid it because of the prominence of histoplasmosis.

By all means pile on kitchen scraps. Cover them with a thin layer of dirt if you are worried about insects or nocturnal visitors. To repeat, do not use meat products of any kind, and do not use cooked food, either. Coffee grounds and egg shells are great, as are fruit and vegetable parings.

Long-lived weeds such as oxalis, purslane, and Bermuda grass should not be used, unless you first wrap them in black plastic and kill them by leaving them in the sun for a month. Otherwise, simply let weeds sit in the sun for a few days before you toss them on. Avoid diseased or buggy plants. Often the disease or eggs live on and multiply.

LIME AND COMPOST STARTERS

Some people swear by lime to reduce odor and think a starter full of proper bacteria, fungi, and enzymes is necessary to kick off the decomposition process. I use neither and know lots of better composters than I who don't either. It's a suit-yourself call.

WATER

Rain does a pretty good job of keeping a pile damp enough to work. Too much rain can be a problem. Compost should be about as damp as a squeezed-out sponge. Use common sense. If it's too dry, hose it down. If it's getting soaked, throw on a tarp.

What you do with your composting materials depends on your space and inclination. I know a city gardener who simply collects bagged leaves, spreads them out to munch with the mower, rebags them, adds a little water, flips the bags and pummels them periodically, and, voila! compost.

Despite special variations like this, basically there are only two ways to go about it.

PILE AS YOU GO

This is me. Whatever is on special that week in my yard is what's on top of the heap. I do try to stab about occasionally and mix it a bit, and I hose it down if things look dry, but mostly my pile needs air rather than water. Keep soil or straw handy for a top blanket, which will keep it from getting too soaked in the rains and will add good material, too.

STOCKPILE AND MIX

It can take months to acquire enough materials, although this method will ensure a more even and quicker result once you pile it on. The notion is to start with something like leaves and woody plant stalks for an airy bottom layer, add grass clippings or other green stuff including manure and food scraps, water it, add leaves, then green stuff, water, etc. Keep going until you've got a pile no taller than you are.

A lot of gardeners like to have two or three bins with sides and to fork the layered pile over, blending it as they work, into the next bin. This allows you to effect a continuous stream of composting.

COMPOST CONTAINERS

You can simply pile up your compost in a heap, or in a hole dug in the ground for just this purpose. You can spend $100 or more on commercial systems ranging from plastic bins to crank-turned tumbler units. Or, you can make your own container by converting a plastic garbage can. Remove the bottom and drill air holes in the sides. It doesn't hurt to bury the can a few inches for stability.

Wood timbers stacked log cabin style form bins that you take down in order to easily remove the compost or turn it. Another alternative is unmortared brick or concrete block, stacked to allow ventilation. Snowdrift or other fencing bent in a circle is what I grew up with. As with the stacked wood, you have to open it to get to the compost. However, the good point is that you can grow vines around or up the side—pumpkins, squash, peas, or beans—taking full advantage of the rich nutrient leach.

In small gardens, don't even bother with a pile. Just heap the material around plants or dig it into trenches, or skim off the top of a raised bed, lay down compost, and replace soil. A final gambit for the landless gardener is to make a worm box, in which these benign and clean little creatures eat up your kitchen refuse, turning it into castings, another form of compost. The method is described in detail in a great book, Mary Appelhof's *Worms Eat My Garbage*.

Cover Crops

The idea behind planting a cover crop of clover or rye or buckwheat or whatever is to allow these plants to take atmospheric nitrogen and turn it into soil nitrogen when you mow them down and chop them into the garden. Cover crops are totally organic, a solar-powered fertilizer if you will, as opposed to a synthetic fertilizer that uses, generally, petroleum energy for production. They are to your soil what a tune-up is to your car. Although both may chug along for years without help from you, both will run better if you help out.

A cover crop, also called green manure, can be a bit of trouble if you don't pick the right one and chop it down at the right time. It's second nature for farm folks. A field of corn is followed by a field of soybeans, a legume with nitrogen-fixing abilities via root nodes that will replenish the depleted soil. Or, a field is allowed to lie out a year, planted in red clover; it is fully rested and ready to go when the clover is plowed under. At home, it goes like this:

Plant a cover crop, sometimes sowing it right over an existing crop that will shortly come out. Allow the cover crop to grow, but not to flower if you are going to chop plants down with a hoe. Power mower folks should let it grow on in order to have more green to become more humus in the soil.

Allow the cut-down crop to rot. Ethylene gas, produced as plants decay, will inhibit seed germination, so wait a week to plant. In the meantime you turn the green cuttings over into the soil.

Buckwheat and annual rye are good beginner cover crops. They die over the winter and don't set the wiry roots that winter rye and clovers do.

Rye and vetch are normally planted in late fall, allowed to get a start, and then go dormant most of the winter. They act as erosion control until spring, when they start up again, and this is when you must not let them get ahead of you. Cut and till or dig them under. Let the roots and tops rot. To speed up the process and to offset some of the temporary nitrogen depletion that occurs as all things decay, toss an inch or so of manure or compost over the area.

I do not recommend white clover. It is hard to get rid of. You can plant fast-growers like buckwheat or mustard just to cut for your compost if you are short on green material.

Mulch

There are occasional epiphanies in gardening. The summer it was me and a hoe—and a two-year-old baby—against a twenty-by-sixty-foot vegetable garden was the year I learned to love mulch. It was also the year I learned that mulch is anything that suppresses weeds, not just black plastic, pine needles, or shredded cypress. Mulch can be weeds pulled up and laid between rows. It can be old carpet, grass clippings, boards, even rocks. A satisfactory mulch is one that suppresses weeds and keeps the soil moist as surface drying is reduced. A great mulch also decomposes and adds humus to the soil.

TYPES AND USES

Permeable agriculture cloth works, but as far as I can tell it's no better, just more expensive and harder to deal with, than newspaper layers. Both have to be covered with a decorative mulch to look right.

Wood chips, bark, and nuggets are by far the most common. I don't like the nuggeted bark for aesthetic reasons—it always looks bulky and crude to me—and it tends to scatter and roll out of the beds with rain and wind. Shredded cypress stays put and mellows to a pleasant gray but it can be bunchy, too. I like the looks of wood chips obtained from the tree-trimmers, but they need to be composted for a year and turn black before you use them. Raw wood extracts a nitrogen loan from the soil as it decays.

Pine needles are great. They are airy, pretty, and stay in place. They are not cheap, but bought by the bale they do go a long way.

Straw is my vegetable garden standby, and a must if you are growing strawberries, melons, and cucumbers, crops that benefit by being lifted off the cold, wet, muddy ground. You can also use moldy hay, but lay it down in the "flakes" or little squares that pull off easily from the rectangular bales rather than pull it apart as you do with straw. Both can be seedy. I have sometimes left my bales out in the rain to sprout and die before I use them.

Leaves munched into small bits by the mower are terrific mulch if you can spare them from the compost pile. Don't use intact maple leaves. They mat, get slimy, and attract slugs.

Plastic mulches have been in the news a bit, with reports that shredded red plastic increases crops of tomatoes and so forth. Aside from the fact that I have no idea where to obtain red plastic, in sheets or shredded, I avoid plastic mulches because they neither decompose nor help the soil. At best, they get tattered and blow about; at worst, they heat up the ground and make it inhospitable to the earthworms you want out in the garden, working on your side.

Peat and grass clippings tend to mat and become impervious to water, a bad situation.

WHEN TO MULCH

It should be clear by now that mulch is not a one-time expense. You will mulch periodically through the year, sometimes removing it and other times renewing it. The old notion that three to four inches was plenty has been disputed by recent studies; feel free to heap on the great kinds of organic mulch to half a foot deep around trees and shrubs.

There are two major mulching moments.

In early spring, you gently remove winter mulch and check out the bulbs, perennials, and shrubs, giving them a little more air and light and warmth. By early summer you've got the mulch back on, probably with some new stuff added.

In late fall or early winter, you begin to mulch again, adding on as the ground begins to freeze. You don't want to put on your winter mulch until then because the idea is to keep the ground uniformly cold, even frozen, and the plants dormant. Too much mulch applied too early can keep the plants actively growing and susceptible to winter damage.

Techniques

Paths, Fences, and Treillage

It's rather an odd thing, but even a garden with almost no ornamental plants can still look grand if there are paths and fences. Trellises work, too. The way these things make people happy is obvious. They provide a sense of order, privacy, and structure and, if the paths are paved, keep your feet dry and your boots clean.

What they do for plants is more subtle. A path channels foot and cart traffic, allowing plants to grow undisturbed, which is very important. (Dogs and children do not always pay attention to this, of course, which is why there is such a thing as staking plants.) Paths, which should be laid out as part of your drainage schemes, are also an important means of getting air and light around plants so they will grow well.

Fences and walls can make a life-or-death difference in your zone. The marginal plant—a climbing rose, a rhododendron, a magnolia—can live happily on the windless side of a fence. It takes so little, sometimes, to lend protection to plants that even an open, plank fence can create a microclimate.

Treillage, which has been around since medieval times but reached a peak of sophistication in eighteenth-century France, is more than a fussy accent. In its various guises as arbors, pergolas, and freestanding plant stands, it supports climbers and vines and provides the kind of dappled shade many plants adore. In its role as a flat illusion of three-dimensional space, treillage applied to walls can lend to a small space great presence and depth.

Heeling In and the Home Nursery

Every garden needs the equivalent of a butler's pantry or backstage area. That is the home nursery, known at my house as the holding beds, and I spend as much time here, working and just looking, as I do anywhere.

This is where I temporarily place plants I can't plant because of weather or bad timing. It is where I cosset puny specimens too iffy to put in their proper place or bring along young plants recently rooted. It is where I experiment. It is where the future of my garden lies.

The home nursery is sometimes called the reserve border, because shrubs and flowers and trees are held in reserve there for future permanent sites. It's a budget thing for me. I can't often afford to buy full-size plants, so I get small, two-year-old shrubs or trees and grow them on until they are what's called "landscape size" and ready to be moved to a permanent home.

A segment of the beds is always available as propagation space. Here's where you plant out the daylily seedlings for a year to see what they do, and where you can build up a stock of perennials, like the hardy begonias, sedums, and lilies that look so silly if they are not planted in sweeps and big clumps.

Sometimes, when in doubt about the viability of a plant, you can leave it in a pot and bury the pot in the ground. Many plants like being pot-bound or snug around the roots, but it is a frequent beginner's error to plant out material that is too small to survive. If you think about it, the way seeds germinate in nature is in batches, with some of the seedlings acting as expendable nurse plants for the others that are destined to survive and grow tall and lusty.

Position your nursery beds or pots where they have the best possible conditions—which means no more than a half-day of preferably morning sun, and a wind-breaking wall or hedge—and in a place you can see daily without special effort.

My beds are strips about three feet wide separated by broader paths of cut grass, and the whole is ringed with a hedge on two sides, a fence and the garage on the other two sides. The beds get off-and-on sun all day, dappled by large trees. The only problem I have is in the summer, when the weeded and watered beds seem to attract moles, so I am constantly checking for plants upheaved.

I also have a cold frame on the other side of the yard that I wish I had put with the holding beds and will, someday.

Planting

It may come as a surprise that it takes a little education to be able to dig a proper hole for a plant. There have been a couple of small revolutions in thought on the subject, especially in regard to trees. Perennials and annuals transplanted from pots are not as tricky, or as expensive or as long-lived, but there still are some techniques to practice in order to make everybody happy.

The big thing in transplanting a potted perennial or annual is to tickle the roots. Either tease them out of the pot shape they invariably grow in or cut them in a few places with your pruners. You want to encourage new feeder-root growth and to avoid perpetuating the spiral, round-and-round-the-pot growth. If you have an annual or a small shrub, especially an azalea, that is just not expanding in a month or so, dig it up. Chances are, the roots are still spiraling around themselves and not branching out in the soil. That's why you should buy square pots instead of round pots: the plants are less likely to become root-bound.

The drill on trees goes like this:

Dig a hole that is broad and shallow. No more deep pits to China. It's been determined that, while you need to dig deep enough to accommodate the root ball, most root growth is horizontal and not vertical. There are even special tree pots in use now that are like large, flat trays. One grower pioneering this for rhododendrons is Holly Hills nursery in Evansville, Indiana. Do not augment the soil with a rich mix of peat, sand, fertilizer, and such. Trees are not dumb. If you make the planting hole too nice, the roots will happily stay in that rich prison rather than push outward, as they should, into the unknown.

Do not stake. Do not wrap. Once again, the trees must not be coddled. Stakes, if absolutely necessary, should be removed after the first year. Arborist Bob Ray of Louisville can tell tales of good-sized trees that simply fell over when their support system was removed. Wrapping will reduce surface evaporation, but it also retains moisture, gives little boring bugs a place to hide, and keeps the tree's skin too tender. Toughen up! At most you might slap on a little white latex—not oil—paint to reduce sunscald in winter.

There is a new technology to protect saplings grown in wild areas from browsing deer. They are translucent plastic tubes screwed to a stake, generally fairly expensive and useful only if deer are a big problem.

A little judicious pruning is allowed, but the old standard of cutting back the top by one-third to "balance" it with the root ball is seen as iconoclastic and disfiguring.

One thing you must do, which we did not always think we had to do, is score or remove the burlap covering the root ball. Often the fabric is plastic and it will not allow root penetration. You plant the tree first and then cut off or slip out the fabric before back-filling the hole.

If this is all beginning to seem too much like instructions for raising a successful child, I can only remind you that trees have a long history of emotional involvement with humans, from the Druids who punished tree vandals by flaying them and wrapping the person's skin about the damaged tree to today's almost metaphysical veneration for the act of tree planting as a gesture toward saving the planet.

Potting

It doesn't take long to put a plant in a pot. To do it well and to do it according to the most current thinking is another matter.

Shifts in thought in the past few years include the "low-profile" or shallow pots for trees developed in Virginia that produce anchor rather than tap roots; slotted pots to hold labels in place forever, developed in Australia, that should be a boon to the retailer, wholesaler, and gardeners, as well; and a soil core and soilless mix combination for hanging baskets and summer pots developed in Oklahoma that is a real neat trick.

In addition, you might want to know that it is no longer recommended that you use actual garden soil (too many disease problems and it's heavy and dank) or put shards or other drainage material in the bottom of your pot (they tend to keep soil too wet rather than just right). It is recommended that you buy plants grown in square rather than round pots to prevent root problems, and you may avoid conventional pots altogether, planting in "pillow-paks" and "moss walls."

Pillow-paks are made of tough black plastic sheeting folded over, filled with soilless mix, and then stapled closed. You plant seeds or plants through slits in the plastic. I have not done it, but it sounds like a terrific way to have a fast little retaining wall. It wouldn't last forever, but it would be economical and easy, perhaps a way to form a living wall for a raised bed.

A moss wall is a vertical planting contraption made of wooden slats, sometimes on wheels, covered with chicken wire and lined with plastic and sphagnum moss, then filled with a light, soilless mix. You plant at an upward slant, piercing the liner and soilless mix with plants that are relatively bushy and a bit floppy, like petunias, lettuces, and strawberries.

Yet some new features have not panned out, notably the notion of water-retentive polymers that swell with water and release moisture to plants. This has been reviewed skeptically in the scientific community, and home trials at my house do not incline me to spend money on the powders and colored "crystals" sold as water-grabbing saviors of container-grown material.

Any number of home helpers to indicate when watering is necessary, from meters to strips, simply testify to the most common cause of plant failure, too much or too little water. For my money, you can't beat sticking a finger into the soil mix to see if it's damp or dry. The appearance of automatic watering pots with wicks is merely a commercial adaptation of an old homemade idea using cloth wicks from the drainage hole to a reservoir of water in a tray. To me, it is an indication of the dangerous acceptance we have of specialization, where one buys things rather than figures out how to make things.

A case in point is the soil core or column idea developed by inno-
vative horticulturalist Carl Whitcomb of Stillwater, Oklahoma, which
reduces the amount of watering necessary for hanging baskets and
other summer containers. In essence, you make a core of garden soil
surrounded by soilless mix; your plants benefit from the moisture re-
tention of the heavier soil and the excellent aeration of the soilless
mix. The gardener benefits from a lighter-weight container that requires less watering attention. It works. I make the core by using an
old coffee tin cut open on both ends as a mold, which I fill with damp
soil, surround with soilless mix, and then remove.

Two aesthetic notions that are becoming more popular are the
globe basket and the trough.

The globe basket, which is available commercially as a cylinder
with side holes and as a sphere with side holes, allows you to plant
top, sides, and bottom, producing a baroque globe of foliage and
flowers. You can do it at home using wire baskets, which can be lined
with shade cloth or sphagnum moss and filled with potting mix, the
sides pierced where you want to plant.

Troughs, long classics for alpine and rock gardeners, are today
available as rare, old, and very expensive stone horse troughs, as
cheaper concrete facsimiles at the garden center, or as inexpensive,
light, homemade containers molded from a mix of cement, perlite,
and peat moss called "hypertufa."

The recipes vary from source to source, but the notion is the
same. You make a mold or form and fill it with hypertufa, let it dry,
and drill drainage holes. Some folks prefer to pre-set holes with small
pots set in place before they pour. You can free-form the trough upside down over a damp sand core. The carpenters among us may want
to construct a box-inside-box wooden form, but the rest of us can
make do with a pair of nesting plastic containers, leaving two to three
inches for the trough mortar.

The trough must be at least six inches deep for adequate root run
for alpines and deeper for dwarf conifers. Make your form, then prepare the mortar mix.

Recipe A:	*Recipe B:*
1 part coarse perlite	1 part coarse sand
1 part moist screened peat moss	2 parts moist screened peat
3/4 part Portland cement	1 part Portland cement

Which recipe you use is your preference, but I prefer the looks of
the sand mix, while the perlite is easier to handle. For either recipe,

mix ingredients thoroughly, then add clean water until the mixture is the consistency of toothpaste. It should not be runny. Pour and tamp the mortar in place. Big troughs usually benefit from the use of chicken wire as an internal support.

The mix will set up enough in a day to remove the form. Allow another four days before planting. Use a hammer and wood chisel to make it look like dressed stone, and round sharp edges with a damp cloth and wire brush. Paint the surface with manure tea or buttermilk to encourage moss growth. Troughs normally are displayed set up on two square stones or atop a retaining wall.

There are any number of other ideas and practices that are handy for pot gardeners.

SOILLESS MIX

You can buy it or you can make it, using stockpiles of compost, peat, sand, perlite, and bark. I keep all this around. The compost is in its heap, the sand is piled on the other side of the garage, and the rest is bought in large amounts and stored in plastic bags inside lidded garbage cans. With such a setup in your garage, basement, or back porch, you not only can create the perfect friable soil for maximum carrot germination and symmetrical size, but you can shift your proportions and pot up some acid-loving azaleas, then sidestep without missing a beat to mixing a lovely, light, and woody soil for your prize orchids.

It is hard to garden for long without needing to repot, pot up, stick cuttings, take divisions to friends, make presents, whatever. You will use this home system of supplies more than you imagine. In late winter it makes starting seeds efficient. In spring, repotting houseplants and potting up annual seedlings one pot size is easy. Again, in early summer the system is in place to start vegetables for the fall garden, and it's there in late summer for cuttings and in fall to pot up bulbs for forcing.

POTS

I use both plastic and clay pots, recycling them as I please with an occasional nod to sterilization with a bleach solution. The clay pots need a long soak, like overnight. The plastic ones, which I recycle from bought plants, seem to do well with a swish.

Sizes are a judgment call. Generally speaking, overpotting is worse than underpotting. I don't know why, but plants get insecure, or something, with too much root run. Too little pot, of course, is not good either. You repot or pot up a size when the ferns start crawling over the top of the pot, the bay trees have to be watered every day, or the orchids look sulky and undernourished. It's necessary about every two or three years, but don't fix something that ain't broke. For instance, leave clivia alone. It won't bloom—any more than agapanthus will—if it's not rootbound.

To keep a plant in the same pot, you will have to cut off some of the roots and make more room for fresh potting mix. You do this with pruning shears or a butcher knife and reduce the top growth proportionately, too. When you move a plant up, you normally go up only one size, or add an extra inch all around.

Prepare your mix before you unpot plants. Wet the mix and stir it up thoroughly with your hands or a spoon. I use an old, leaky canner, but recycled pickle and drywall-mud buckets are handy.

Gently tamp the mix in around the roots as you fill the pot. Aim for filling to within an inch of the top. Much more and you will have a watering problem as water will bounce off dry soil and come over the pot top before it can sink in.

If you need to stake a potted plant, make sure the stake is long enough to go all the way to the bottom of the pot, and if possible, find a stake with a V- or horseshoe-shaped anchor at one end to help stabilize it in the pot.

Pruning

Pruning is an irreversible process. Your shrubs and trees will tell on you for years to come if you have used your secateurs with surgical grace or indulged in indiscriminant hacking.

February and early March are the traditional times to prune most deciduous trees, shrubs, and vines; they are dormant and you don't have to deal with leaves. There are exceptions, of course. Don't cut your spring-blooming shrubs and trees in February, or you will cut off the buds for the spring bloom. If you have any doubt about when to cut a flowering plant, do it in the two weeks after the flowers fade and before the plant begins to produce buds for next season. In this way you don't have to fuss over timing and whether your subject blooms on new wood or old wood. All that means is that some plants, like forsythia, quince, dogwood, and weigela, tend to produce flower buds on wood grown the previous season, the old wood. Plants that wait until summer or fall to flower, like clethra, buddleia, and rose of Sharon, tend to produce flower buds on new wood grown that year.

The number of rules to remember in pruning can be confusing, but there is no excuse for giving any tree or shrub what amounts to a flattop haircut, which is called topping. Topping is only occasionally a necessary evil with large trees planted under utility wires—an evil smart gardeners avoid by planting short-statured trees and shrubs under utility wires. Despite clear arborist rules to the contrary, the practice of topping appears every once in a while in public and private work done by so-called arborists. If a flat-topped tree does not look awful to you, then remember that topping weakens trees and makes them susceptible to disease. The large branches seldom close over or callus, allowing rain and disease and insects to enter. The cutting encourages dense new shoots called suckers or water sprouts, which are weaker than natural branches and have larger leaves, susceptible to munching insects and blights.

There are three alternatives to topping:

1. Proper early training.
2. Selective thinning of branches.
3. Total removal of the tree.

The first two alternatives are relatively easy and inexpensive and make a nice-looking landscape.

Pruning is painless to tree and gardener if you understand some basics. Pruning confidence comes from doing. What you do depends on why you are doing it. When you stand there with a severed branch in your hand or at your feet, you should know why you cut it off. Beware cutting fever, where the hand cuts before the mind engages.

REASONS FOR PRUNING

Late-winter pruning of deciduous shrubs, trees, and vines is done for many reasons: to remove dead wood or diseased wood; to reduce size by thinning for looks or to keep a plant in bounds, as when it was planted too close to houses, walks, or utility lines; to rejuvenate by sharp cutting back to near the ground, thus giving a second chance to a senile and weary shrub or bare-bottomed hedge; to encourage production of more flowers and fruit, as in the case of brambles or apple trees; to shape for structural purposes, such as an espaliered pear on a wall or wires, or removing a weak crotch from a maple, or for aesthetic reasons, such as making lollipop-shaped standards from multi-stemmed shrubs or making multi-stemmed shrubs from small trees; to limb up, to produce more light under the pruned plant for other plants or to increase air and light generally in a garden.

BASIC TOOLS

Alert eyes and an annual routine of rubbing off buds that will turn into misplaced branches will save much labor and the purchase price of a chain saw, not to mention the services of an arborist after a bad storm has cut through the home place and felled trees.

If you don't prune, nature will do it for you.

To keep ahead of her you need to have a few cutting tools around, which may require an investment of $100 or more if you have a lot of property and pruning. Begin with hand pruners, the best you can afford, and the oil and sharpening stone to keep them sharp. Use an old sheet or a tarp or a cart to hold branches and twigs as you prune, making cleanup quick. Add a bow saw for removal of larger branches and then go for long-handled lopping shears for in-between growth.

After that, it's your call if you need a chain saw or other tools.

BASIC RULES

Be careful trimming grafted material, including roses and many special evergreens. Do not cut back below the thick graft area or you will remove the desirable plant.

Make each cut just above an outward-facing leaf node, where a bud and thus eventually a branch will appear. It is best, especially with rhododendrons, to leave three or four buds below the cut. If you cut above an inward-facing bud, you will cause a branch to grow into the middle of the tree or shrub, possibly producing crossed branches that will rub bark off each other and allow disease and insect entry.

Don't use wound paint. Current research indicates that it decreases the natural healing processes.

Prune a large branch using three cuts. Make the first a foot past where you want the final cut and only a third of the way through the underside. Then make the second cut all the way through a foot past that cut. This lightens the branch load. The final cut is made from the top down and close to the main trunk or nearest branch. This method reduces uncontrolled breaking and harmful stripping of bark.

Always cut dead wood or diseased wood to the ground or to live, good wood, which will show a green ring just under the bark. This is not just for looks. It is to prevent the spread of pathogens further into the tree and to control the spread of a disease in the neighborhood. Pruning is the control of choice for problems like fireblight on pyracantha and apples, black knot on prunes and cherries, and various cankers and blights.

Think of creating a tree with an open canopy that will allow even penetration of sunlight, which discourages mildew and other diseases to which airless, crowded leafy branches are susceptible, and also favors production of flower buds if the tree flowers.

Prune to encourage strength. You want tree branches to form angles between ten o'clock and two o'clock. Avoid sharp "V" angles, which tend to split out under wind stress as they are naturally weak joints, often filled in with extra bark.

When thinning, cut each branch individually. If a shrub is weak or you have a lot of thinning to do, prune over several years rather than all at once to give the plant a chance to produce enough leaves to keep the roots alive and well.

If you are interested in topiary, shaped plants, espalier, or just a sheared formal hedge, be aware that these require trimming twice a year. One plant is often fun; a hedge can get ahead of you faster than you can sharpen your shears.

SPECIAL TRICKS

Create a new leader or major trunk when a tree has been damaged or topped. Splint the nearest branch gently to the trunk, asking it to grow upright and take over. Remove the splint in a year or as the branch is bent and remove competitive leaders by pruning back to the trunk.

Create a standard or ball-shaped miniature tree from multi-trunk shrubs and woody perennials by rubbing off branch buds along the stem, allowing the top to grow to the desired height, at which point prune it into a nice full ball. This project will take a few seasons, and the single-stemmed plant or tree will require a stake. It is often done with herbs like rosemary, scented geraniums, and bay laurel in pots and with roses, gooseberries, and dwarf fruit trees for ornamental reasons in the herb or cook's garden.

It takes grafting high up on a mature stem to produce the now-popular mops and cascades where a juniper understock may sport a head of some other juniper cultivar or a generic cherry supports a terminal fountain of weeping cherry. Some of them look bizarre to me, especially weeping larches grafted to globular spruces or two-tone grafts of juniper varieties.

To turn a small tree or single-stem shrub into a multi-stemmed shrub, cut it back hard to encourage multiple branching and then keep it that way with selective pruning. This is a necessary step in producing a hedge of any type, particularly since they often begin with single-stemmed, rooted cuttings. It is not quite the same thing as pollarding.

Pollarding is an old-time and mostly European custom of radical topping of things like willows and poplars to encourage a gadzillion suckers. The suckers are cut back every year so you get a very gnarled and knobby post of a tree trunk, sprouting a mane of foliage. It makes an interesting winter feature, generally done in groves or as path sentinels.

To salvage a hedge that has gone bare along the bottom, you can trim off the lower two-thirds of the branches, exposing an interesting skeleton, and keep the top neatly trimmed. This is called a stilt hedge. Try it on overgrown junipers, yews, lilac, holly, or forsythia before you put a chain on the truck and try to haul them out of the ground.

For an Oriental look, you can rub off buds or cut off branches to create an evergreen or deciduous shrub that is "tufted."

Wisteria and roses, anything with long supple branches or canes, can be grown over ropes or chains, tied on with dark twine. The branches will send up shoots from the top, which you keep cut back to produce a neat, thick festoon effect.

A living arch is also possible with shrubs positioned on either side of a walk and woven together. Err on the side of a generous walk. This trick takes time and more room than you think. A wire armature or training arch is handy, too, but it is possible to do it without the guide.

Informal hedges are kept graceful by thinning dead and old wood annually and cutting back one-third of the top growth of each stem individually, following natural contours.

Shearing hedges to a formal rectangular shape is a labor of love and some skill, not to mention laying down a string guide with twine and stakes. The most important rule for formal shearing is to keep the top of the hedge slanted back slightly from the bottom, which will allow the hedge to remain full from foot to head. A totally squared hedge will eventually get ratty and leafless at the bottom because the top shades it out. Also, keep the top rounded rather than flat to minimize snow damage, an important point in northern sectors of our region.

Consider a mini-hedge, a mostly visual barrier no more than ankle to knee high à la the intricate patterns of hedges at Versailles, Blenheim Palace, and Williamsburg. If you are a hands-on gardener who loves to fuss, consider a tapestry hedge of two or more different types of plants, which also can be done tall.

Make pines bushier by shortening the new "candles" that appear in spring. Finger-pinch these when the candles are reasonably tall, but still young—between two and four inches.

Espalier is a technique that can be plain Jane or fancy-dancy. It may involve no more than keeping a dwarf apple on a stake and making it into a standard, or it can be a wall effect of pears grown along a wire fence and pruned into palmette shapes that run one into the other. If you can pay the freight—and the elaborate packaging—you can buy ready-made espaliered fruit trees. The undisputed king of the mountain is Monrovia Nursery Company in Dayton, Oregon, a vast company that seemingly supplies half the shrubs offered for sale anywhere in the U.S.

Pre-trained plants can save you ten years of work, but then again you will not have the pleasure of learning the skill.

There are probably a hundred more possible scenarios, limited only by a gardener's creativity. For all, knowing what you want to accomplish before you cut, and making cuts with sharp tools, are as important as timing. Pinching and rubbing off buds are terrific low-tech techniques that can keep the pruning shears out of your hands for years.

Editing

I have used this method of landscape design for a long time without knowing it had a name. The credit for naming it goes to Roger B. Swain, who writes a regular column as science editor of *Horticulture* magazine. I just thought of it as making do.

Whatever you call it, you simply remove what is out of place to your eye and let the survivors thrive. In this manner, you encourage a patch of ivy into a sweep, cultivate wild asters and goldenrod into a glorious fall display, let sumac run riot while pruning out wild cherries. It helps to have a bit of room to play with, but editing is what most of us do when we inherit a garden and resolve to watch it through one full year before we make changes.

A drawback of making do or editing is that you sometimes change your mind as your taste and experience evolve. I now need to remove two adolescent tulip poplars, which are constantly beset with aphids, their sticky honeydew, and the sooty mildew that excrement promotes. I will replace them with smaller, more ornamental but also native trees, perhaps halesia (silverbells).

There is a lot to be said for a tree in the yard even if it is not the one you really want. In the editing process, you can allow that tree to live while you plant another, more desirable one and then as it gets big enough, just edit out.

Mercy Killing

Mercy killing is an important concept, but it's a hard call to make.

It's easy to know what to do with a dead plant. It's not so easy to tell a dying plant from a dormant one or a diseased goner from a plant momentarily down on its luck, planted in the wrong place.

There are no hard-and-fast rules. Sometimes moving a plant to your holding beds is all it takes to perk it up. Sometimes it needs cutting back, to give roots a chance to grow without the drain of supporting top growth. Sometimes there is nothing to do for it but to toss it. Occasionally, you can reverse your thinking and learn to see a misshapen plant as an eccentric and intriguing standout in the landscape. I did that for a long time with a half-fallen mulberry until it was no longer a fun place for the kids to climb and hide, but a mere eyesore. The mulberry is gone now, but we enjoyed it supine for many years.

You will have to make your own calls. There are a few scenarios from my past where plants had to be dispatched: The lemon tree with constant scale problems that I never solved. The purple-leaf plum that the Japanese beetles defoliated like clockwork each year until I put it out of its misery. Hollyhocks disfigured each year by leaf-chewing insects. Common orange ditch daylilies, put in too prominent a place back when space was long and money was tight. A very desirable striped bark maple damaged by cicadas making slits in the bark to lay eggs. A marginally hardy shrub rose that kept dying back, and then struggled to produce one long cane each year. The pine that was stripped of all its branches by dastardly unknown visitors yet failed to die.

Variants of mercy killing include going ahead and pulling up the cucumbers when they get blight and not letting them linger on, producing an occasional misshapen fruit; replacing leggy geraniums with mums; not letting the columbine seedlings in the driveway get the wrong idea about their longevity; and thinning out a crowded thicket of redbud seedlings.

Sometimes it's hard to make a call because the plants linger on. They don't die, but they don't grow robustly. Instances in my garden include snowberry bushes planted where the water table was too high for them next to the creek, astilbe in too much shade, and hosta in too much sun.

Timely Support

Too often I've sat on my good intentions and watched an early summer storm bedraggle the peonies and lay low the raspberries. To stake or not to stake should be a moot question for everyone but tomato fanatics, who like to discuss the pros and cons as a seasonal rite.

Timely support is hard to provide, not because there is any special trick to driving a stick in the ground and tying on a rambling plant, but because even the lankiest soon-to-be rambler looks compact and sturdy during the first flush of growth. And besides, who wants to look at a flower border full of bamboo stakes?

Staking can be necessary if you are growing tall plants like foxglove, delphinium, larkspur, salvias, baby's breath, lilies, and dahlias, even cleome, especially if the border is in the path of wind gusts. The ideal time to set the stakes is as you plant or as the plants emerge in the spring. Then, all you do is tie the plant loosely to the stake, or pair of stakes or trio, with dark string.

I use bamboo and twine, both stained green, but you can buy fancy metal supports that come in various shapes, or use rebar painted green, or rig your own from those metal ring stands sold as tomato cages that are always too small. I use these for the peonies and they are great. I make tomato cages of farm fencing, rolled into a cylinder about two and a half feet in diameter and shoulder-height, or I use inch-thick, head-high wooden stakes and tie on with strips of soft cloth.

All well and good. But what do you do when you forget to stake and the winds come up and the plants flop over and any effort to make them stand up again will probably break them?

Let multi-branched plants like the salvias, dahlias, and baby's breath sprawl. They will adjust to the new orientation by sending up new vertical shoots from the now-prostrate stems. In fact, some canny gardeners trying to fill in gaps in borders take advantage of this trait and deliberately bend over a single plant to make it broader. It also is a way to rectify having planted something too tall in the front without having to snip it into submission all summer.

The prostrate stem is a strategy to get more single-stemmed roses from long arching canes, too. To be successful with roses or other plants, you may want to peg down the long, springy cane or stem. Use a discreet brick or rock, or fashion U-shaped pins from old clothes hangers and step them into the ground over the stems. Be gentle as you peg. The stem must still be connected to the main plant in order to function.

Single-stemmed plants like lilies, daylilies, and top-heavy peonies can be post-staked. I used to worry about piercing the lily bulb or the daylily tuber, but I just try to stay out six inches with my stake—or stakes, if it seems necessary to enclose the clump by encircling twine around the stakes rather than the stems.

Sometimes you want a way to lift heavy foliage up from the ground, to lighten the droopy effect. You can push branched twigs in the ground and drape the foliage over that, or rig up little undulating false floors of chicken wire. Spray-paint dark green or brown if it's too obtrusive.

There are health reasons to stake and support. Adequately supported plants get more air and light, so growth is faster, harvest increased. Supports will also decrease rotting, fungal disease, slug buildup, and insect excesses. A strategically placed two-by-four under a limb on a fruit tree overladen with fruit is a kindness to both tree and gardener.

Almost anything can be a support. I have appropriated my son's schoolyard-sized monkey bars for a ready-made arbor and old screen door guards for pea trellises. You can rig a pleasantly rural arch effect with four posts set in the ground and a canopy of farm fencing bowed over them like a ceiling. Tomatoes and cucumbers, beans and peas can clamber over bales of straw or stepladders. An existing fence or masonry wall will support most vines and climbers, as long as you tie them in with the appropriate attachments.

Much store-bought trellis is flimsy and a waste of money. The ultimate in decorative trellises are specially bought or homemade tuteurs, pyramidal and umbrella-shaped wire and wooden supports for climbing roses and vines.

Gardener's Helpers

TOOL MANIA RISES every spring with the sap. Although few gardeners will fall for claims of revolutionary, universal tools—"the only tool you'll ever need!"—even the well-seasoned are at risk faced with racks of shiny, unbattered tools at the store or photographic visions in catalogs of specialized implements. By all means, tool collectors should spend the $25 or $50 necessary to obtain a reproduction wooden seventeenth-century thistle-puller, but if it's thistles you're really after, try putting your foot on a spade. For my money, it should be a spade with a solid forged collar construction into which the wooden handle is inserted, which makes it sturdier than those with a tang or metal projection that goes up into the wooden handle.

Garden tools are one area where compromise will haunt you. I have a lot of ghosts taking up space in the toolshed, a function of buying cheap or impetuously. I used the spiked-wheel cultivator only once. I seldom use the hoe. The old wheelbarrow has become a Johnny one-note, singing only when we set postholes in concrete and need a shallow, portable basin in which to mix the glop. My rectangular garden cart is my real workhorse.

Clearly, there is no such thing as a one-tool gardener. Even in our most primitive stage we tend to have both a broken-tipped kitchen knife for weeding and a large spoon for digging. However, there is such a thing as having too many tools. Here's my list of the top ten, the ones I wish I'd started out with. The sequence is roughly in the order of most often used.

SPADE

Go for the best spade you can afford. It will be your almost constant companion. I pick up my long, slender, round-nosed transplanting or tree spade nine times out of ten. I can dig with it, move gravel with it, pop up an errant weed in the perennial border with it (without, I might mention, stooping over), and I can drag mulch around, mix compost into soil, and whack tall weeds in half, plying the spade like a grass whip. I just generally consider it my third arm. I've used it on the few occasions I have been obligated to dig postholes, finding its long, narrow nose ideal for most of the work, resorting to the muscle-building posthole digger only at the end of a two-foot-deep hole.

Shovels vary a great deal and range from those with a broad, round point or nose to those with a totally square point or nose. The first are good for lifting and moving dirt and loose sand or gravel. The second types work more like scoopers. For most gardeners, the handiest digging tool is a spade. They have shorter handles, "D" grips, and narrower points or noses. They come with deeply tapered noses or nearly flat noses.

You must have a spade. Shovels are refinements of your tool collection. I have several that get used maybe once a year. Of these, the least used in my suburban circumstances is a broad, square snow shovel. I have a gravel drive, and any paths are either grass, bark, or brick. It does come in handy sometimes as a dustpan for the broom wielded in the garage.

One reason I like my narrow-nosed spade is that I can't overload it past my ability. That is important. Don't buy a great big shovel or spade you have trouble hefting. Get one that suits you, especially in handle length, even if it breaks your muscular heart because it looks like a child's version or a ladies' spade.

GARDEN CART

My cart has a rectangular plywood body attached to two big, sturdy wheels. You pull it about by an aluminum tubular handle that is actually part of the frame. I love it. It was expensive when I got it ten years ago, one of the earliest models of its type, and it is expensive now— over $100. I expect to have it another decade, at which point it will have served me surpassingly well for a little under $5 per year. You can't beat that.

The garden cart will carry large loads of mulch. You can trot around the garden with it, stopping here and there to pick up sand, compost, soil, gravel, whatever, and make a custom mix on the spot.

I could not have built the stone retaining wall that separates the driveway from the front yard without the cart. To haul a rock too heavy to lift, you merely tilt the cart to vertical, roll the rock in, and lever the cart back to horizontal.

My cart has been commandeered as a chariot, used as casual lawn furniture, and for a long time was the only way to get the garbage cans down and up the hill on garbage day. It has hauled logs, straw bales, sticks, jugs of water, and, along with my spade and drywall bucket, is about all I need for planting in spring and fall. It has withstood abuse, having been left out in the rain and overloaded more often than it should.

PLASTIC DRYWALL BUCKETS

I favor these free buckets, which you can pick up at most construction sites. Or, look for them as recycled pickle containers at fast-food restaurants or as powdered-detergent containers bought at wholesale stores. All are sturdy, tall, and virtually indestructible, which makes them more useful than a metal bucket that will rust out on the bottom or a rubber scrub bucket that is too short to hold a cut peony straight.

I have been amused at the recent "discovery" of flat-sided barn buckets used for watering horses that are touted as easier to carry because the flat side won't bump into your legs. Having hauled a few flat-sided buckets full of water in my time, I can testify that they are harder to carry than a tall drywall bucket filled two-thirds full—or better still, two buckets for balance.

It's hard to have too many drywall buckets. They are handy at the workbench, in the kitchen, garage, and kids' playroom, too, especially for holding the gadzillion little Lego pieces or other small items. You can store potatoes in these buckets, keep goldfish in them while you change the water, use them to hold the extra three pounds of roofing nails, harvest corn, and water the St. Bernards.

Two is minimal for a gardener. Four is better. One is for carting all your gear around. The others are variously used to hold cut flowers, to transport transplants, to be a death trap for Japanese beetles as you knock them into soapy water, and to be a mixing pot for potting mix. If you can't afford a garden cart, or don't need one because your yard is small, opt for the buckets. If you don't like their practical looks, emulate the horse folks who take solid-colored white buckets and customize them with bands of plastic tape in their stable colors, sometimes going so far as to stick on initials.

KITCHEN SCISSORS

Scissors rip open plastic bags, cut string, snip off spent flowers, trim herbs, edge grass. I prefer scissors to a folding pocket knife because you can get pretty good quality for low prices—a good pocket knife is pricey—and scissors can be used one-handed, unlike knives that need to be flipped open. Also, I don't lose scissors as fast as a knife. This is one instance where moderate quality is fine, as the notion is to replace them rather than have them forever.

LEAF RAKE

There is only one sort of proper leaf rake for me. It is bamboo. I hate metal rakes. They are noisy and harsh on the ground. Bamboo does wear out, but it's cheap, another instance of buy to throw away. Yes, you can catch them on fire if you are slow while raking dry leaves onto the burn pile, but that adds to the excitement. I've found that my bamboo rakes outlast some of the rubber ones, which tend to get brittle in cold and snap.

SOIL RAKE

A soil rake is the comb-shaped implement, usually metal, used to level soil and gravel and, turned on its side, to produce furrows for planting seeds, then, turned upside down, used to rake soil back over seed and tamp in place. I don't use one a lot, but when you need it there is no substitute. The fan-shaped leaf rake is not strong enough. A soil rake of moderate quality seems to last just as long (just about forever for me) as pricey ones.

GARDEN FORK

A garden or potato fork is the sumo wrestler of pitchforks. It will turn soil, lift bulbs without slicing them to ribbons, mix your compost heap, and delve into mulch to loosen violet roots without disturbing the rest of the bed. The tines are flat and broad rather than pointed and round like a pitchfork's, and although pitchforks do a better job pitching hay, you can make the garden fork work for that rare occasion when you are tossing straw or hay around the yard.

I use mine to break up soil in new beds or in old beds where the soil is tough and to fork shredded twigs and tree parts the arborist leaves me. It's not right, but it spends a lot of its time outdoors, stuck upright in that mulch pile. Like a good spade, a good fork will be in the $50 to $100 range, but you should be able to pass both implements along to your heirs.

PRUNERS

Pruning shears come in two basic configurations, a straight anvil blade that is widely available and cheap but has limited use since it does not open very wide and tends to crush stems, and—my favorite—a sickle-shaped or bypass blade shear that is, of course, more expensive. It's hard to find these at the average garden center. You generally have to mail-order. Mine are made by Felco, a tool company that has made high-quality shears for almost half a century. They cost around $50; it was simply a matter of saying one year, "I'm worth it."

BOW SAW

I include a bow saw as one of my top ten tools, although folks with small, treeless gardens will not need it. However, those with even a few trees and shrubs to deal with will find that this handy saw will dispatch what the pruners can't and will handle up to a fair-sized branch of more than a foot diameter. Much more than that and you need a chain saw. I have many trees and shrubs and use the bow saw more often than the lopping shears, which are halfway between pruners and a saw in terms of what these two-handled pruners can cut.

A decent bow saw is moderately priced, light, easy to use, and easy to carry and store. You simply cannot use a carpenter's saw to cut green wood. The closely spaced teeth gum up quickly and make you miserable. It's worth having a bow saw even if you need it only once or twice a year after storms have littered your yard with branches.

TROWELS

A trowel is often the first garden tool purchase, but I would make it a distant tenth.

Trowels come in many shapes and degrees of sturdiness. One-piece metal construction lasts longer than those with a metal tang inserted in a wooden handle. I like the long-bodied kind in heavy-duty steel that does not immediately snap or bend if I hit a rock or some hard dirt. I try to hit a happy medium between quality and price because trowels, for me, are frequently lost—tossed on the compost by accident, left in a border all winter, or simply set down in a strange spot, like under a bush, and never seen again. You, probably, are organized enough to apply red paint to the handle periodically so your trowel is easy to spot.

Over the years I have found that the most useful occupation for my trowel is to mix potting compost and shovel compost into pots. I seldom dig with it, and when using it for transplanting I tend to use the blade to nudge loose soil out of the way, pop the plant in, and close the hole by sweeping the dirt in with my hand.

Postscript: The hoe is of course a midwestern icon. It is not on my must-have list because I tend to mulch rather than weed; and using a hoe in mulch is like swimming in mud—not worth the effort. But I concede that a hoe takes out young weeds easily in bare soil and that the repeated chop-and-drag motion can be a true gardener's mantra.

Hoses and Such

There is a lot of ado when it comes to watering. Many plants, like children and dogs, get along very well without all the baths gardeners make them take. Moreover, with potential water shortages in various areas, it makes no sense to indulge in old-fashioned watering practices. I say this, although in my heart I know that an evening's hour of hand-watering with hose in one hand and drink in the other has its place as a sanity booster. When temperatures soar, it is the poor person's equivalent of an afternoon lolling about the home swimming pool. But what is good for the gardener is not always great for the garden. Hand-watering seldom does more than rinse off the leaves and make things look nice, which is, nonetheless, a good refresher technique to employ before company comes that most gardeners seem to know innately.

Disciplined gardeners will not indulge in this, of course. They know that to be effective you are supposed to apply one inch or more at a time, measuring by letting the sprinkler drops build up in a pan. If you do this, it is tedious in the extreme with a hand-held hose and takes hours with a sprinkler. Plus, someone will admonish you for wasting water via evaporation in the air and suggest you invest in soaker hoses with or without a pricey computerized on-and-off system that gets the water to the root of things. Or they will—rightly—tell you to let the grass go naturally dormant and brown in the summer.

And then someone will invoke xeriscaping, a term so new it's not included in my personal reference bible, the 1986 edition of *Wyman's Gardening Encyclopedia*. Xeriscaping means using native and other plants suited to the conditions of your region to create a drought-resistant landscape. To me, that is all that need be said on the subject, but entire books are being written about it. Certainly there is little sense in growing much that has to be cosseted and coddled. Aside from issues of profligate use of water on this small and fragile planet, there is the common-sense issue of making gardening a pleasure rather than a burden.

Which brings us back to hoses.

Hoses were invented for humankind's pleasure. Hauling water in buckets is good for the shoulder muscles, but getting it there in a rubber tube is much easier. Sprinklers are for the birds—they love to frolic in the mist—and all the average gardener needs is a good rubber hose with a few good-quality brass attachments.

I water newly planted material fairly regularly for the first few months, I keep a keen eye out for water requirements of my container-grown stuff, and in severe droughts I will water some prized plants, such as the doublefile viburnum, which could scarcely be any farther away from the house and so requires six hoses coupled together if it is to have a drink. Other than that, most plants are on their own.

Keep nozzles down to a minimum or you will be constantly stepping on them, dulling the mower blades with them, losing them. I have two. One is all-purpose with a dial nozzle that goes from spray to stream. The other is a fogging nozzle that produces a gentle mist suitable for watering tender baby seedlings without blowing them out of the pots.

Recommended accessories include a gooseneck brass swivel connector at the spigot to avoid bending and breaking the hose there as it gets yanked about and a Y or double hose connector at the most heavily used spigot, so you can simultaneously keep two hoses connected.

Hose hangers defeat me. The majority are either adamantly in-the-way eyesores or—usually when attached to the house or garage—frustratingly out of the way behind a bush. I think I have tried all sorts, from the wind-up reel on wheels that is another way to build triceps to the open-topped basket in which you coil the hose like a domesticated snake. My favorite is a casual draping over a handy fence post or on a bought or homemade hose stand you can set in the ground just where you want it.

An alternative I have not thoroughly tried is a drip irrigation system, composed of tubes or hoses laid in or on top of the ground. I have tried it in a single S-shaped bed and concluded that it is suitable mostly for old-fashioned vegetable gardens laid out in orderly rows and for gardeners who don't constantly change their minds about what to plant where. The single hose laid under mulch to irrigate dwarf apple trees does work, but I have given up on the other one in a perennial bed because I kept slicing into it with my spade, forgetting that it was there. The sensation of slicing a hose is similar to that of slicing into a $10 Crown Imperial bulb.

Hose guides are worth having if you do a lot of watering, but, of course, none of us do. On the off chance you want them anyway, my favorites are the thick metal stakes commandeered from a set of lawn horseshoes, but you can use wooden pegs, too. I spent some cash on some fancy German-made hose guides with rollers, but find them rather obtrusive in style; and the metal shank you "step" into the ground is sometimes insufficient to hold the guide in place when you yank on the hose.

Do buy washers for the hoses. I mention this only because I grew up bereft of this bit of information and struggled too long with leaking hose connections.

Do drain and store your hoses over the winter. They last longer if they are not left out in the cold with ice inside them. The sun's rays also cause many hoses to deteriorate, and that's why rubber is better than vinyl and why you should always cover your above-ground soaker hoses with mulch.

On watering cans: You can make do with the teakettle off the stove or the lemonade pitcher, but it is nice to have a genuine, long-spouted, properly balanced watering can to water potted plants and new transplants in the yard. Beware large sizes. Water is heavy. Opt for the "long-reach" spout, and avoid metal as it inevitably rusts as you inevitably store the can with a little water left inside. (Galvanized metal cans are not supposed to rust.)

Herbicides and Pesticides

Each gardener must make her own peace with killer chemicals.

I am a convert to what I prefer to call a holistic rather than organic approach. What kills "bad" bugs and "bad" plants tends to kill good ones, too. Over the years I have settled for acceptable damage and have stopped growing a few plants, such as grapes, that are very pest-prone in my area. Japanese beetles, which may not yet have migrated to your neck of the woods, decimate grapes.

I am not weaponless. My arsenal consists of Roundup to clear actively growing weeds from the gravel drive, wettable sulfur to use as a fungicide, a soapy water spray as a deterrent for aphids and other munching bugs, and a spray with mild baking soda solution to reduce black spot on the roses. Otherwise, I weed and I hand-pick.

Regarding picking bugs: I try whenever possible to improve the local economy by offering a-penny-apiece odd jobs to the neighborhood kids, but I find that this works for only a few days, and then it's back to just me and the bugs. I was an unhappy gardener with this notion until I found that you can scrape, knock, or shake most bugs into a container partly filled with soapy water and never have to touch them. And they won't be able to fly, crawl, or inch their way back out before they drown.

A vacuum on low power also works to suck up a lot of bugs, including whitefly that may become a problem on houseplants. Just be careful around tender-leaved plants. It sucks up leaves, too.

Traps baited with sex lure or pheromones have been determined to attract more pests than they kill, so they are not a viable tool.

Gloves

Gloves are one of those gardener's helpers that make gardeners alternately happy and unhappy.

I used to be of the pooh-pooh-to-the-glove contingent, thinking of hand protectors as a barrier between me and nature. I moved over to the clean hands school a few years ago, tiring of having decades of permanent black lines scored into my index fingers and skin that absorbs lotion like blotting paper.

Clean hands and happy gardeners are hard to combine. In my search for the perfect glove I have found suede and trendy kidskin attractive but pricey and not always flexible enough. Neoprene is neat, but sweaty in summer and cold in winter. Vinyl-coated gloves tend to be hot, too, and they often split and crack. I like my rubber-impregnated canvas gloves with long, forearm-protecting cuffs only when clearing brush. They are truly a boon in briar, bramble, and thorn country. It's good to have impermeable plastic gloves for the times you use herbicides or pesticides and don't want it on your hands.

What I have settled on for general use is not elegant. It's plain cloth gloves with knit wristbands for summer work and acrylic knit gloves with little rubbery dots on the palm for winter work. Both are durable, washable, comfortable, and cheap. You can get them dirty and wet and don't have to stop. Just peel them off and toss them in the washer and put on another pair. You can have a half-dozen pairs on hand to see you through a bad day, and it's no tragedy when one gets lost in the yard or eaten by the mower, or has its fingers chewed out by the dogs. In fact, I have one pair of winter-weight gloves thus destroyed that I salvaged by cutting out all the fingertips. I find them handy to use under mittens, which are removed when I need to do fine work in the cold, like writing or tying.

Winter Protectors

I have an antidote for the postmodern dilemma of blurred lines between fiction and reality, and it's not reality-based television programming. Normal schooling for all citizens should include a three-year course in winter gardening in the Lower Midwest.

Gardeners here have to contend with cold winters and no snow, or here-today-and-gone-tomorrow snow, which is harder on plants than cold winters and constant snow, which forms a cover that keeps plants dormant and safe. In our realm, winter is the teasing season. An alluring warm spell can be followed with dizzying speed by a cold shoulder, but that can change back almost overnight, and finally the gardener gets the point. Winter is fickle, and you'd better be prepared for its freeze-and-thaw personality.

Our Zombie Zones are perfect for gardeners who like being put upon, who need to cosset and hug, who want to cling to their plants despite strong indications that the plants have to move on.

You can't call a plant hardy in your garden until it has survived three winters. As we all know, we can have one or two mild winters, where the stray dahlia tuber lives underground, or half-hardy salvias in protected sites regenerate from dead-looking woody stems. Then the third winter comes along with record cold, perhaps in late November when plants are not fully winter-dormant, and zap! Or, we get record warmth in January and the plants are fooled until February's return to reality and it's zap! once more.

Personally, I believe in erring on the side of benign neglect, not being desperate to grow many plants that don't want to grow where I live. Still, the question of how much if any winter protection you should give to make your plants reasonably happy is worth asking.

Winter protection begins with planting smart.

Plants of known marginal hardiness, like crape myrtles in our southern zones and forsythia in the northern, and those planted out late should be put in an area sheltered from wind, such as the ell of a building, near the heat-leaking foundation, or beside sheltering evergreens, walls, or fences. Watch out for soggy spots, too. Wet feet do in many a plant over the winter, when it can't respire away excess water intake since it doesn't have any leaves or, in the case of an evergreen, is in a slowed-down life-forces state. If you see water pooling, dig a diversionary ditch immediately.

Winter protection continues with knowing what plants are at risk.

Newly set material, plants in containers and window boxes, thin-skinned trees like birches, beeches, and rhododendrons, foundation plantings, and plants facing south or on hilltops all may need attention from your hose when days are warm.

There are a number of products and materials that help plants winter over. Some should be used with caution.

WATER

Lack of water over winter can be as deadly as too much. Newly set material, especially, needs to be watered consistently in the fall if there is not enough rain so it does not go into winter drought stressed. And, before you ask, No. You cannot depend on snow to water for you. It takes ten inches of snow to equal one inch of rain. It is seldom that the Lower Midwest gets that kind of snow.

PAINT AND TAPE

Plants in southern exposures can suffer sunscald, which leaves ugly and weakening scars or slits in the bark. It happens when a plant with frozen feet and no way to move water up and down its stem gets heated up above ground and the bark splits. Orchardists solve the problem by painting trunks with white latex paint. You and I might also try tree wrap, which should be removed in spring.

ANTI-TRANSPIRANTS

Anti-transpirants sprayed on needled and broad-leaved evergreens reduce moisture loss; however, some have proved to provoke a dangerous reaction to light in the sprayed plants. Three brand names shown to be OK by studies in Washington State are Wilt-Pruf, Vapor Gard, and Folicote. Under any circumstances, use an anti-transpirant very sparingly. They generally are "waxy" and work by covering up the stomata or "pores" on the leaves that allow the plant to "breathe."

All evergreens continue to transpire over winter. Things get desperate on a sunny, windy day when the ground is frozen because the plant can't replace moisture being lost up top as the water down in the ground is locked up as ice. The plant then turns to its own living tissue for replacement water, and that's what causes winter browning and death. It is not the same thing as when some junipers turn purply-brown and some arborvitae turn coppery-colored. That is natural.

MULCH

Contrary to popular myth, mulch does not keep plants warm; it keeps them evenly cold. A blanket of straw, pine needles, leaves, or wood chips helps to maintain even moisture in the ground, too, all of which helps reduce the thaw-and-freeze phenomenon of our region. This natural motion of the earth's surface can heave a plant up, exposing roots to damaging air. It's harnessed as a good force, incidentally, when you turn over soil in fall and leave it in clods for the winter to "work." Even with mulch in place, you will need to prowl your beds on warming days to see what's been heaved and tamp it back. In my garden, this is primarily in February, but winter is fickle and it can happen in December, too.

A common mistake is to put winter mulch on too early, before the ground has frozen. You must wait or you can cause too much moisture and warmth and a delayed dormancy, which can be damaging to the prematurely mulched plants.

FORTS

That's what I call anything we construct to surround a prized shrub or a planted container to help it through winter. The most prevalent is a piece of burlap wrapped around four stakes with the interior filled with dry leaves. In Louisville, such a device can winter over a tender fig planted in the city in a protected, fenced garden. In the country, these forts help newly planted rhododendrons survive winter's desiccating winds and will carry through a rose you worry may be killed to the ground.

Many rose growers buy styrofoam forts for tender tea roses, but pragmatic types can take a page from a Hoosier gardener of my acquaintance who makes her forts from folded newspaper sections and fills these with dry leaves. My approach in the Zombie Zones is to grow roses that can stand up to the winters without a lot of pampering or to put them in sites protected from the winter winds.

Forts can also be made by sticking pine branches in the ground around the plant like a tepee, then tying the boughs to the plant at the top. You can wrap the bush itself in burlap, loosely, tying in a spiral. You can make a fort of straw bales or old tires or even wet newspapers, which will freeze and are then covered with a mound of mulch. The last thing I would use is plastic, as its impermeability can cause condensation and excess heat inside the fort.

All forts must be left open at the top or otherwise ventilated well.

SNOW AND ICE BREAKDOWN

This problem for shrubs and trees, often those under eaves where snow and water can drift down, is caused by the extra weight. If you are having trouble with open-topped bushes like arborvitae and box-woods spreading and breaking, try wrapping them up with twine or soft rope for winter, so snow and ice can't get on the interior of the branches and weight them out. If you don't do this and it's just snow, go ahead and gently sweep it off. Don't try to knock off frozen snow or ice. You will probably break branches as well as the ice.

If you think the weight of the ice will break the branches anyway, you can prop them up with a forked stick or an upside-down pitch-fork. If a branch does break, go ahead and trim it off.

Watch as you shovel or blow what snow we do get that it does not go all over the plants, but only at the base where it will be a good natural winter mulch.

Sometimes, all good intentions are for naught. Winter hardiness, which is initiated by successively colder temperatures among other things, is a reversible state. You cannot stop nature running hot and cold. When she does, the best stance for gardeners is stoic—stand and watch and learn a lesson in plant realities.

Phenology

You can't be a gardener without having some facility at observation. You have to at least notice when things need water, shade, harvesting, or help getting rid of pests and disease. Gardeners who fine-tune their powers become, whether they know it or not, phenologists. Phenology is relating biological sequences such as flow-ering with seasonal sequences in order to know when to plant, har-vest, and brace for the onslaught of particular bugs. Phenology is more reliable than any book, agricultural extension agent, or gardening buddy because you do it at your place.

Phenology is an old, old notion with some contemporary updat-ing. It's the American Indian wisdom of waiting to plant corn until the oak leaves are as large as a squirrel's ear, and it's some new ideas about timing pest management to ornamental plant development that were developed in the Lower Midwest by Donald A. Orton and Thomas L. Green. Orton's observations are based on twenty years' worth of pest-checking, walking nursery fields for the Illinois Horticultural Inspection Service. Green is a research pathologist at the Morton Arboretum in Lisle, Illinois. Their collaboration has resulted in a weighty but interesting and valuable 1989 publication, *Coincide,* that can replace standard schedules or solar and lunar recommendations. By correlating insect life cycles with life cycles of well-known ornamental plants, their notion minimizes chemical pollution; you use less since the spray applications can be timed narrowly and specifically to your yard and not to the yard of the garden writer three hundred miles south of you. The book is a little difficult to get used to, but once you do, it allows you to pinpoint sprays to maximize effectiveness.

Or you can engage in phenology with less science and more structure. An April 1982 article in *Organic Gardening and Farming* suggests planting a living garden calendar. For instance, the flowering of spring crocus will suggest it is time to sow seeds of peppers and eggplants indoors. Plant the seedlings out, your garden will tell you, when the iris begin to show flowers. To create your own calendar, all you have to do is be aware of sequences of bloom and relationships of that to insects and other factors in your garden.

Stop fertilizing perennials and roses when your Peegee hydrangea blooms. Get out the horticultural oil for the fruit trees when you see the first daffodil leaves. Don't plant out your melons and tomatoes until after the lilac blooms.

Bees and Other Helpful Beasties

It should go without saying that bees and other flower-visiting insects are incredibly critical to life on earth. They are the main means of cross-pollination of the fruits and vegetables that make humans happy and healthy.

Such creatures are the main reason I seldom dust or spray with pesticides, and if I must, I do it at dark and try to use something specific to the sucking, chewing pests I want to discourage that won't affect the bees. It is a sin in my book to spray any flowering plant that the bees are working, and that includes the clover in your lawn.

The family of bats that live in my unused living room fireplace are nearly sacred residents of the neighborhood. I look forward each year to the night when I am working outside at dusk and feel as much as see the little mammals burst forth one after the other. Wings beating silently, intent on capturing literally thousands of insects, they never come close, as swallows do, but dart about busily until it has grown too dark to see them any longer. No gardener should ever do anything to harm bats, either.

Publications and Experts

I am a book person and have shelf after shelf of garden books. Others enjoy just doing or like to participate in workshops. Still others are television-trained, and these, I suspect, are the market at which the new flush of garden videos is aimed. You will figure out for yourself what in the realm of disseminated knowledge suits you; but I have a few things to say about where I think the most value lies.

Newsletters, especially those produced by plant societies, are often packed with pragmatic regional expertise with a name attached and probably a telephone number, too. I will happily spend $3 on a long-distance call to a rosarian if I'm having rose problems rather than $30 on a book of pictures of rosebushes in flower. Most local or regional chapters of national societies are great bargains, with dues of $5 to $20 per year, which includes a newsletter, plant auctions, seminars, and trips.

The USDA and its arms in the various states produce reams of literature. Check with your local agricultural extension office to see what handouts they have—often free—and if they can give you addresses to get on the mailing list for statewide newsletters that update the ag and hort industries on pests, fruit trees, woody ornamentals, annuals, and other topics.

Book clubs are a terrific way to familiarize yourself with the current literature and to build a personal library. We all need at least a modest personal library. The public library is generally closed just when you have to I.D. a bug, or the book you need has disappeared without a trace. Book clubs have a limited value as you become more sophisticated and as your personal reference library grows and you just don't need to be spoon-fed resources anymore. But do use the clubs to get big, expensive books like *Hortus Third* at a much-reduced price when they are offered as inducements to membership.

Magazines are fun. I read a half-dozen and over the years have slowly begun to lean toward more specialized journals and scientific reports. My favorite section in all is the Q&A, as this is where you find real problems and real solutions. Some I read regularly are *Fine Gardening, Horticulture, Arnoldia,* and *American Horticulturalist.* I also pick up an occasional *Organic Gardening* and *Harrowsmith's Country Journal.*

Speaking of journals, one often-touted kind I quit using is the personal journal or diary. I will jot things down on a calendar and then keep the calendar, but I don't keep up with anything I have to open and write in.

Data bases on topics like insect I.D. and tree problems, perennial selection, or available ornamentals in nursery production make a lot of sense but cost too much at $300 or so each to be in many home gardeners' software libraries. They are the kind of resource we should encourage our local libraries to obtain and update.

Herbaria are too little known. While most gardeners will never use one, we should all at least know what they are and where the closest one is. Repositories of dried plant material, they are normally connected with universities and colleges or botanic gardens. The pages of pressed plants are often a final place to search when you have a mystery plant, or think you may have discovered something wonderful and unknown.

Local experts can be an invaluable resource. Don't be afraid to phone or write experts and ask questions. Almost every community has a garden club, ag agents, botanic garden employees, newspaper columnists, television gardeners, city foresters, nursery operators, and others who can provide answers or at least put you in touch with someone who can. A lot of the joy of being a gardener is being part of a network.

Problems

ONE GARDENER'S HEADACHE is another's challenge. Some years are more challenging than others, thanks to infestations of Japanese beetles, extremes of drought, untimely cold with no snow, and other little gifts from the Zombie Zones.

The challenges are there to keep it interesting and to keep us limber. Gardening requires a commando's ability to shift directions quickly and remake plans on the go. Some gardeners seem to have a sixth sense that keeps them slightly ahead of the challenges, or perhaps they just don't blab about their failures. In reality, sometimes I rise above the problems, sometimes the problems inundate me, and sometimes I give up.

Beginners' Mistakes

The ultimate challenge is your own bad judgment. A lot of gardening is fixing mistakes. I hereby offer a list of classic errors of judgment to which I freely admit in hopes it may save someone else a little frustration and visual unhappiness. You'll be sorry if you . . .

EMPHASIZE PERENNIALS

Go ahead. Follow your instincts. Make flower bed after flower bed. It will look dandy quick depending on your eye for groupings and your budget. In three years—ten max—you'll be sorry, sorry, sorry. Your eye will begin to see what's left out—things like mass and structure, a sense of enclosure, and backgrounds to set off that riot of flowers. Gee, you'll say one dull February when there is nothing out there but horizon, if only I had planted a few inexpensive shrubs and trees at the beginning, they'd be decent-sized by now. That's where I am, playing catch-up, trying to add structure to a perennial plant collection, wishing I had started off with a firm rule to spend a third to a half of the gardening budget on shrubs and trees.

It takes three to five years for shrubs, hedges, and trees to get off the mark, find their feet, and start growing and looking as if they belong. By that time, most perennials you have planted have outgrown their homes and need dividing and replanting to look good.

BUY FOR THE BOTTOM LINE

Stinginess prompted by greed, the something-for-nothing mentality that has created a thousand suckers for real estate, medicine, diets, and food-preparation devices, is waiting to grab you in the gardening line, too. What seems like a good deal ends up costing more in the long run, like those 100 bare-root spruce and pine seedlings I bought for $30 five years ago. Only 6 have survived, and the survivors are now only knee-high. I would have been money ahead (to say nothing of the sad removal, one by one, of 94 dead seedling trees) to buy a reasonable number of landscape-size specimens in the first place.

Then I have gone to the other extreme, buying only one plant when I really needed ten, figuring I'd propagate that many in a year. While you often can—ivy, willows, barberry, and ajuga come to mind—it doesn't always work that way, and you are left looking at gaps in your border or far too many Shasta daisies.

I wanted climbing hydrangea to drape over the footbridge across the creek. Nine plants would not have been out of the question, but I bought three, despite warnings in all the literature about how slow climbing hydrangea is to get going. Now, nearly six years later, I think they are just beginning to find their roots and may be ready to put on more than six inches of top growth.

Yet, just recently I overbought on gold flame spirea, a three-foot-tall bush that loves to grow; my planting is crowded in less than a year.

Knowing when to be parsimonious and when to splurge takes a

familiarity with plants and a firm grasp of your long-range garden design plans. Getting older helps you make up your mind. I am no longer quite so willing to wait for landscape gratification. I would rather do without ten young seedlings, even rare and choice seedlings, and have my rhododendrons big enough to stumble over.

Sometimes there's nothing wrong with a we-can-wait mentality. Especially with unusual trees and shrubs, it's often the only way you can afford plants you covet, such as yellowwood, copper beech, and bottlebrush buckeye. And often with tricky trees and many perennials, a small start is as good as or better than a big start, which has so much more to keep alive while the roots get underway again. Also, the only feasible way for most of us to start a hedge is with young, inexpensive whips or single-stem youngsters. These are cut back to a few inches from the ground to encourage dense branching at planting and perhaps again the next year.

But in general, when gardening, you get what you pay for, and time is money.

SPACE PLANTS SO THEY LOOK RIGHT, RIGHT NOW

This is the pines-that-ate-the-front-yard mentality. One of the ironies of garden time is how it always seems to work against you. One day you're fussing over how small the stuff is and how bare the place looks; the next, you can't open the car door without a faceful of evergreens. Frequent crowding can occur along property lines, next to driveways and fences, at the front door, and along walks and building foundations. It happens most often when amateurs plant evergreens.

Crowding can be done on purpose. Intensive spacing is often good in the vegetable garden, as the plants' dense canopy shades out weeds and makes the most efficient use of space. New ground-cover plants can be placed a handspan apart rather than the standard one foot if you have enough plants. And lots of us try to avoid that raw, just-planted look in the perennial border by means of a little judicious crowding.

It's one thing to fudge a bit with temporary and movable plants like these. But it's foolhardy to ignore the fine print and buy a climbing rose that will ramble thirty feet if you only have a ten-foot trellis, or plant low, spreading pin oaks in a narrow driveway verge, or place a crabapple with a twenty-foot leaf canopy potential next to your front door.

And, before you plant anything large, look up and look around. If your neighbors have big trees or potentially big trees near the property line they share with you, it won't be necessary to do anything but enjoy the view. The Japanese call this the borrowed landscape, and it's a principle of design as well as common sense. Also, look for power lines, which have an inconvenient way of always running right where you want a big oak. The tree will be fine for a decade and then, zap! Fodder for the utility right-of-way trimming crew. The smart option may be to plant any of the many wonderful small shade and ornamental trees.

UNDERESTIMATE MAINTENANCE TIME

An orchard? Sounds great. I can do that. Ground-cover roses? What a wonderful change-of-pace floral notion. I can do that. A privet hedge with self-supporting arch? Go for the fast lane. Get that hedge in gear. So it has to be sheared four or five times a summer. I can do that. Three acres of lush lawn? No problem. We'll just mow it.

As with long-haired dogs and white-painted picket fences, the reality of garden maintenance is sometimes overlooked in enthusiasm for an idea. Power equipment and canny technique help, but nothing will change the fact that orchards have to be sprayed in some fashion, fruit litter removed, and the trees mowed around. Dwarf trees are just a little easier to prune, pick, and spray, but they generally need staking or tying into supports. Nothing will alter the dangers of hand-weeding a thorny ground cover or disguise the truth of incessant pruning when it comes to privet. It can be sobering to realize that it is going to take you eight hours per week to mow that big lawn.

The list goes on. The climbing roses have to be tied up and selectively pruned each year. *All* the roses are a pill in July when the Japanese beetles must be hand-picked twice a day in order to save any blooms or leaves. The herbs must be clipped, clipped, and clipped again. The strawberries force attention unless you want them all over the garden and moldy, to boot. Scented geraniums just keep growing and you keep cutting back and they keep growing and getting woody and you must renew them by starting cuttings, and the cycle continues. The ajuga does what ajuga does, getting bare in the middle where you want it to live, madly colonizing the lawn where you don't. Bearded iris reproduces faster than dahlias and cannas.

The solution to overestimating your maintenance abilities is simple. Get rid of things, or replace them with slower-growing or more mannerly plants. I no longer grow dahlias; I leave the cannas in the ground where not all survive over the winter; and I may never again buy another bearded iris (unless, of course, it's a very special color). I pull up strawberry runners. I grubbed out the raspberries a few years back. I am rethinking scented geraniums. The privet hedge has to go as soon as I can afford to replace it. I quell my mad desire to have topiary yews by means of a few topiary-esque ivy forms grown in pots. I'm not quite sure yet how I want to handle the young rock garden, which sucks up hand-weeding like a vacuum.

As for the roses, they are worth any amount of trouble to me. It's a judgment call.

However, my goal for you here is that, eventually, when you see an intoxicating color photograph of a half-acre moss garden, soft and silent, mysterious and meditative under a grove of ancient trees, you will not bounce with enthusiasm. Instead, you will ponder how many sticks you would have to pick up by hand to keep it unscarred. You will consider the amount of watering necessary in Midwest summers. You may even see clearly the amount of time involved in planting that much moss, let alone finding it. Surely you will notice that it is incompatible with children and dogs. And you will get a terrarium.

GO AU NATUREL

Just let things go. It's what nature does, isn't it?

I love my weed borders and wild bits of woods, particularly the unmowable boggy low spot by the creek, but these bits are in their own ways artificial realms in a civilized setting, and I freely confess that I don't always have my wild and civilized elements in proper balance. The wild bits do ramble on. That is the problem with this seductive notion of benign neglect.

The wild garden can be harder to pull off than the formal garden. It takes a lot of judicious "editing" and a fair amount of mercy killing. You've got to be out there, watching over things. You can't just rely on a weekly mowing and a biannual pruning schedule.

The Au Naturel attitude eventually bumps up against a basic fact of gardening. Gardens are not static. They flow like a river. Just as you can never step in the same water twice, you will never stroll the same garden twice even when you go out in your own, day after day.

ZAP BUGS THE MINUTE YOU SEE THEM

The lie you told in grade school, a padded expense account, unkind words to children and dogs, and fast-reflex bug-zapping will all come back to haunt you. Those fat striped caterpillars chomping on my lemon tree as it summered outdoors in its pot would have been a host of Eastern black swallowtail butterflies if I had let them live. Upon reflection, I see that there was enough lemon tree for us all. Nor did I have to spray the tent caterpillars; I could have just cut out the nests and burned them, thus sparing other possibly beneficial insects and me from inhaling toxic droplets. Also, all right-minded persons now know that bug-zapper lights, besides being obnoxious noisemakers and light polluters, are simply not effective at killing mosquitoes but do kill lots of good things, like moths.

Many problems tend to be self-limiting if you allow natural predators or diseases to take charge. What seems like an epidemic to the gardener often is merely nature's slow-paced checks-and-balances system getting into gear. You can help by rotating crops, keeping litter out of the garden over winter, and hand-picking the bad bugs.

WATER WEEKLY

It's like writing things on the calendar. Once having writ, you can forget them and use your brain storage space for other activities. All you have to remember to do is to check the calendar. I once thought you had to water all plants on Saturday morning, unless of course it was raining.

Waste of time. Waste of water.

Once a week can be too much water for houseplants brought indoors over winter, as they turn off under the influence of shorter days and simply can't process as much water as they did in the summer. Outdoors, once a week may not be enough in hot, windy circumstances in August for potted plants or new transplants, but it can drown plants in the ground that need to grow dry, like many bulbs and onions.

For established trees and shrubs, the most you might want to water would be one or two inches every couple of weeks. This encourages them to run roots over a deep, wide area, which will stand them in good stead in any drought. Don't bother watering the lawn. It can turn brown and go dormant and spring back. Look at your garden, not the calendar, to decide what needs water when.

One exception is what I call social watering, the wetting down of walks and walls and plants in preparation for company. There's nothing like the look of a recent rain to make your garden sparkle.

SCORN EASY-GROWERS

Here are some plants commonly scorned: marigolds, impatiens, the ordinary daylily also known as ditch lily or tiger-lily, pink rose of Sharon bushes (the white forms are acceptable), red salvia, bedding begonias, white pines, junipers of all sorts, cedar trees, mulberries, hackberry, Osage orange, and forsythia (until you reach its northern limits, when it suddenly becomes rare, lovely, and desirable). I'm a little tired of ornamental grasses, dogwoods, red geraniums, and fuchsia-colored azaleas, too.

There's nothing wrong with any of these except overuse and cliché. If you fear that using too-common plants will reflect on your lack of creativity and sophistication, try using them in uncommon ways. It's a great design challenge, and it allows you to take advantage of easy-to-find and often inexpensive and easy-to-grow plants.

How about growing forsythia as tall, mopheaded standards in a formal garden, or taming the too-too red of red salvia by combining it with purple salvia in containers festooned with ivy? Or turn up the heat and use those raucous, tall orange and yellow African marigolds with red-flowered, purple-leaved cannas. Don't falter—toss in some tasteless orange ditch lilies, too. Go for broke—add red salvia. Those despised cedar trees associated with scrub farmland can be elegant sentinels along a country allée. Hackberries and Osage oranges, if allowed to mature, become highly personable specimen trees.

WALK IN YOUR PLANTING BEDS

It doesn't take a bulldozer or a cement mixer to compact soil, although if you let them onto your lawn, they can do it very fast. Parking cars on the grass will do it. Kids and dogs taking the same path for six months around the side of the house do a dandy job, too, and so can you. Thin and fit as you are, if you constantly step into your borders and raised beds in order to work, your weight will pack down soil to the point where plants won't grow.

Soil compaction is serious, and it's laborious to correct. Prevention is the way to go. Put a strategic stepping-stone or two in your broad border so you can get in there and weed, prune, and cut flowers. Use boards in your vegetable garden. A plank giving access to an entire row will distribute your weight over a large area and allow you to change the pattern of the vegetable garden without having to always maintain paths.

Inevitable Problems

Sometimes it seems all you have to decide is which end of the boat is sinking. If it's not problems caused by you, it's problems you can't avoid. Inevitable problems include but are not limited to bugs and disease. There are many more.

JAPANESE BEETLES

If these iridescent green, shiny-backed flyers are not already in your yard each summer, they will get there eventually. Thanks to an accidental ride into New Jersey on balled nursery stock earlier this century, the beetle has spread from there to the Mississippi River and shows no signs of stopping.

The beetles, which emerge from the ground in midsummer, are merely on nature's great mission for us all, to eat and reproduce. They do it very well and very obviously. The beetles devour landscape plants voraciously and procreate with equal gusto. The female lays thousands of eggs in the lawn, preferring a well-kept, mowed lawn to a scraggly weedlot.

Solutions abound, from spraying with Sevin to hanging traps baited with sex scents to setting out enticing buckets of rotting fruit and soapy water in which the beetles drown. I have tried them all, and after talking to scientists at the University of Kentucky, who tested the sex-lure traps and determined that you attract more beetles than you kill, I am down to the final frontier of garden survival—hand-picking, which is not as unpleasant as it sounds, the way I do it. (Some people delight in squishing each beetle between thumb and forefinger, and that's OK too.)

Hand-picking the beetles becomes a surprisingly passionate commitment in late July and August. They are not quick in wit or on the wing and lie about lazily feeding and reproducing in the early morning and late evening. This is the time to go out, armed with a deep cup of soapy water and a slender stick or a knife, and simply tap the beetles into the cup, where they disappear beneath the soap suds and drown. If the neighborhood kids are industrious, offer them a penny per beetle, honor system. You'll need all the troops you can muster during the swarming.

I have tried to discourage the beetles by omitting some of their favorite plants, like grapes and purple-leaf plum trees. But I refuse to get rid of my roses or my rose of Sharon bushes or the clethra or the sassafras, so it's a matter of learning to live with them.

The best-measured judgment is that they will tend to be horrible pests for a relatively short time—five years and counting at my house—and then move along, it seems, as natural controls we have not yet identified take over.

POWDERY MILDEW

This white, flat, and dusty-looking fungus can appear on azaleas, beeches, dogwoods, elms, euonymus, holly, hydrangea, ivy, lawns, privet, roses, spireas, viburnum, you name it, and it seems inevitable on lilacs, tall garden phlox, and bee balm. A fact of life in the humid summers of our Zombie Zones, it is usually more unsightly than a danger.

A powerful infestation can cause premature leaf drop, so it's nice to know how to keep it curbed: spray with wettable sulfur once a week, but only if absolutely necessary. Often the easier and just as effective course is to pick up and burn or bury all the leaves in the fall, thus keeping the population of spores down. The time to start looking for powdery mildew is late spring, when we begin to have warmer days (above 65 degrees) and cooler nights and the rains are diminishing.

It is just one of many fungi, which come variously flaky, fuzzy, slimy, white, brown, yellow, black. Again, the best remedy is good housekeeping. With many plants, notably phlox and roses, you often can keep fungi and mildews in check by being sure the plants are pruned to an open and airy circumstance and are not jammed in an overcrowded, weedy border. Also, try to buy mildew-resistant strains of phlox, lilac, and bee balm.

If you have it badly all over your yard, the only way to stop it is by spraying with a copper fungicide just as the leaves unfurl and get large in late spring. This will save you headaches.

Some swear by a dusting of flour or baking powder under the leaves. I have not yet tried this, but plan to, as it also will create an inhospitable climate for blackspot and other molds.

APHIDS

No one gardens without aphids. They are harmless if kept in check by ladybugs and other good garden guys, but aphid populations can build up quickly, and the viral diseases they carry can cause bigger problems later.

Also, aphids in large numbers produce a highly noticeable amount of sticky honeydew—an outrageous euphemism for their excrement. However, it seems a fine descriptive term to the ants, which often appear in good numbers in order to herd the aphids and get the (to them) delectable honeydew. As if all this were not bad enough, let that honeydew stay around long enough and it will become the perfect growing medium for black, sooty mold.

Physical exertion is preferable to chemicals. The first time you see aphids, get out the hose and blow them off your plants with water pressure. They are too tiny and stupid, I presume, to find their way back. If the infestation is not stopped by this strategy, employed every other day for a week, apply insecticidal soap every other day for two weeks.

Aphids are not hard to spot. They are tiny green, brown, pink, or even black and woolly pear-shaped sap-suckers who cluster like beads on the tender new growth of just about anything. They are particularly fond of nasturtiums, which you can plant near or in your vegetable garden as a diversionary trap crop.

For a bad infestation year after year on woody plants like apples, apply horticultural oil when the plants are dormant but air temperatures are balmy, usually in late February or early March. Since aphids produce eggs on leaf and twig litter, fall cleanup is especially important.

WHITEFLY

I thought I was immune to whitefly indoors, but after twenty years they have finally found me. I think they came in last winter on the scented geraniums, which may have gotten infested by some petunias bought at the local fruit market. It was a lesson to me to look on the backs of leaves before buying plants, and then look once more before I move those plants indoors for the winter, where the whiteflies think it's heaven and build up large, flitting colonies.

Unable to spray the plants last winter because of resident cats, I vacuumed them—the plants—instead. It was much more effective than the sticky yellow strips you hang in the air or insert on a holder in the pot. This year, I am using a homemade solution recommended in Ball and Ball's *Rodale's Landscape Problem Solver:* 1 cup isopropyl alcohol and ½ teaspoon of either horticultural oil or insecticidal soap in 1 quart of water. Two applications a week apart does it. Plain old insecticidal soap works, too, but you have to spray every week to ten days for a month or so.

UNWANTED MAMMALS

Probably owing to the presence of three dogs and three cats outdoors, we are not greatly troubled by moles, raccoons, rabbits, squirrels, and other mammals. Rabbits did neatly decapitate a young, foot-tall weeping beech last winter, and they got my two baby yellowwood trees this fall. When I replace the youngsters with other seedlings or small grafts, I will be sure to protect them with a wire cage.

The moles make unsightly lumps in the lawn, but this really doesn't bother me as I am not a lawn freak and the lumps are stompable. What I dislike most is the way the dogs tear up the yard going after the moles, leaving holes that bog down wheeled mowing machines and dead moles a-moldering on the front steps. (They apparently do not taste very good, as I have never seen one eaten.) The only thing I can say about the dogs' dig, flip, and snap method is that it seems to kill the poor moles quickly. I can't stand the notion of spear traps and would rather live with the moles than watch them writhe or—shudder—try to decapitate them with a spade or toss them into a bucket of water to watch them drown. The aesthetic utility of a flawless lawn in no way mitigates causing such suffering to a creature that is simply trying to live.

On the plus side, moles aerate the ground and eat white grubs. If they are getting into your garden in their search and heaving up plants, you can dissuade them by daily stomping down the tunnels. Eventually they depart for easier burrowing. Or, if you are a real workhound, you can dig a trench around your garden and fill it with big rocks. As I understand it, most other methods, from chewing gum to milky spore to vibratory devices, are essentially ineffective time-wasters.

Deer appear in my suburban neighborhood only occasionally, but more-rural gardeners can have big problems. I have an ongoing dialogue with a colleague who has tried everything. Whatever substance you use to repel them, be sure to apply it at the deers' nose height and replenish it often. The only way to be sure of stopping deer is with a fortress-sized fence. Ten feet is not too tall. I have also heard of success if you are willing and financially able to drape fine netting over all your plants. That makes installing a ten-foot fence sound easy.

SLUGS

Slugs are in every garden. If you grow a lot of hosta and ferns, you've seen them for sure. They sleep by day under boards and leaves and love a good, rainy night to come out and make holes in plants with their little raspy tongues. Not to put too fine a point on it, I can't tolerate touching a slug, and my solution is raking up leaves and putting down twiggy mulch that they don't like to crawl over. I have no idea what kind of neurological system slugs and snails have or if they feel pain, but again I have ethical shudders at a slow death by shriveling under the salt shaker, drowning in a shallow bowl of beer, or the West Coast solution of a shot of ammonia and water in a spray bottle.

You can send slugs next door by putting down a mulch of chopped-up horsetails (*Equisitum arvense*), which contain a silicon substance from which the marsh plant derives another of its common names, scouring rush. (If you grow equisetum at home, be sure to keep it in pots, as this is a very invasive plant.) Other things to scatter about include aluminum sulfate, sand, crushed eggshells, and wood ashes. At the same time, you need to provide habitat for the garter snakes that ought to be living in every healthy garden, even in the city. They love slugs, and so do toads and turtles. If you try too hard to get rid of slugs, you may get rid of their natural enemies, too.

BROKEN TOOLS

When the problem is merely a broken handle, the temptation is to keep the pieces. You—or surely someone you know—can drill out the wood left in the metal tool and replace it with a new handle. The "Use It Up, Wear It Out, Make It Do or Do Without" mindset can give you the bright idea that that old handle can be recycled with a little clever whittling for use as a much shorter handle for another tool. Then again, it may be useful as a plant stake.

If all this fails to occur, as it generally does, the next stage is to put the broken tool in a yard sale, where someone less advanced in his gardening lessons may buy the rake head or shovel head for a pittance, thinking that he will fix it and have a wonderful tool for next to nothing.

Maybe. It can be worth your time and the cost of a new handle if you are looking at a long, solid-socket style head where the metal that attaches the head to the handle is of a piece with the head and not a separate collar. It also may be that it's not worth fiddling with and needs to go to the great metal scrap heap in the sky. Those broken handles can go to the kindling pile.

LOST TOOLS

They are either in the compost heap or lying in tall grass waiting to bite you.

Nothing works better than a firm resolve to replace all tools in the garden cart or the tool shed when you are finished with them. It can help to paint handles red, pink, or yellow, but even that does little good if you have to share tools with another whose pick-up-and-put-away habits are less developed than yours.

This is why I have two leaf rakes, two spading forks, three trowels, and two spades.

ACHES AND ITCHES

Poison ivy, blisters, splinters, bug bites, and sore muscles are badges of garden courage to be proudly displayed along with grimy hands and broken fingernails at the office show-and-tell on Monday mornings.

If you'd just as soon not, the only solution is to wear gloves, wash up right after you come in the house, and do stretching exercises before, during, and after each gardening session.

A thorough wash-up right after possible handling of poison ivy while clearing brush, grubbing around stumps, or weeding goes a long way in removing the poison ivy oils. There also is a product called Technu, which works well, costs $6 for four ounces, and has the same drawback as simple soap—you must remember to use it.

To avoid blisters, you can wear gloves, buy special rubbery slip-on grips for many hand tools, or try the old-fashioned solution and wrap the handles with friction tape.

My solution to biting bugs, which make after-work gardening pure hell, is Avon's Skin-So-Soft, a bath oil with a scent that confuses mosquitoes. Some humans find it a bit overbearing, also. I don't care. I dilute it half and half or even more with water and keep it in a spritzer bottle by the back door. It smells better and is less expensive than commercial anti-bug solutions, many of which eat holes in synthetic materials, too. I also prefer wearing a skin spray to getting dressed in an $87 head net and body suit of superfine mesh.

I do not believe in sonic insect and mosquito repellers; and, as I have mentioned, those obnoxious bug-zapper lights have been proved ineffective at killing much but good, nocturnal bugs.

THE MYSTERY OF DISAPPEARING BULBS

Blame the squirrels, not the moles. Blame the tulips, too, while you're at it. But most of all, blame yourself for planting them in a wet spot. It is possible to get bad bulbs, especially if you buy off the shelf at discount stores and groceries where the bulbs are kept hot and in bins where shoppers paw about. Most of the time the problem is drainage. Dig down and see if you have a rotted bulb. If so, don't plant there again, or fix the drainage.

If it really is squirrels who are doing the pilfering, you can soak bulbs in a product called Ro-Pel, go into home production of tiny wire cages, or buy the squirrels a special feeder and keep them otherwise occupied. I also understand that squirrels will not dig deep, past about two inches.

I have heard of rabbits eating tender tulip shoots, but normally the reason tulips don't show up is, in the first season, too much damp and, in subsequent seasons, a normal weakening of the bulb.

But moles are probably not guilty. They don't do that much plant damage unless their tunnels are running where you are planting young plants.

BURNOUT

Sometimes you feel like gardening and sometimes you wouldn't care if it all died. This is normal, especially in the heat of August, but I also have a bad, overwhelmed spell in April when spring planting and too much rain coincide with income tax time. The same feeling can occur after you have visited a fifty-year-old garden on which no expense has been spared, or spent the evening looking through marvelous garden picture books.

In August, go swimming. In April, reorganize the tool shed and make lists of what you can't afford to buy. The rest of the year, when the garden blues hit, go to the library and check out murder mysteries, which invariably take place on the estates of rich folks. See what all those bucks and great gardens got them?

BRANCHES AND TWIGS AND NO PLACE TO PUT THEM

In this great age of recycling, there is no such thing as garbage. However, it can be hard to know what to do with tree litter if you can't burn it and can't send it off to the landfill.

Stash it. Make your brush heap separate from your compost heap, which should be limited to soft, herbaceous materials like leaves, grass clippings, weeds, and kitchen waste. The pile of branches will magically disappear in a few years, becoming rich brown, springy compost/mulch. In the meantime it will be home for toads and newts and snakes, which you want to encourage in your piece of paradise.

If you are impatient for the compost or don't have much space, chop up the brush so the decay process occurs faster. There is so much hype for mechanical shredders and choppers that it seems we have forgotten those handy hand tools of our scouting youth—the hatchet and axe. It takes nothing more sophisticated than these tools and maybe a bow saw to make short work—literally—of most windfall branches. It's good exercise, too, and you won't be guilty of noise pollution or overdependence on gasoline engines. The small pieces you produce can be raked into an acceptably discreet wood compost pile.

I am not, of course, suggesting that you tackle turning a downed one-foot-diameter tree into wood chips by hand. There is a time and place for chain saws and hired help.

GRASS IN THE GRAVEL

I have this. I hate this. I have tried lots of methods, from hand-pulling to boiling water, and must say there is nothing better than Roundup, a liquid herbicide that does not move or translocate in the ground. It must be applied to uncut foliage that is actively growing. Safer's puts out a fast-acting herbicide but it is very expensive and not that much "safer," as far as I can tell, than Roundup.

I try to keep the drive neat only near the house. Further on, I have adopted a country look of a central strip of grass and weeds, which is trimmed along with the lawn.

FORGOTTEN NAMES AND LOST LABELS

This happens to everyone, usually just when a guest asks, "What's that?"

Don't fret over it. You will remember and can get a label back in place. The only way to avoid embarrassment is to memorize the names. Word associations can help: "Bet You Can't Remember Betony" or "I'll Still Be Wondering If It's Astilbe." In a dire pinch, name it yourself—yellow ruffled daylily, bee balm Cindy, Marion County iris, spiny five-leaved whatever. This is very calming and it's how common names started in the first place.

The time this is irksome is when you need to replace the plant and can't recall the variety and so, naturally, get the wrong thing. I keep meaning to create a plant list on a notepad or a computer disk, but I find the easiest way to keep track of things is to keep a file of plant orders and to insert in that file all plant labels that come with the purchase.

Wonderful Weeds and Wicked Weeds

The line between a wildflower and a weed is a matter of perspective. I count yarrow, ox-eye daisies, mullein, Queen Anne's lace, blackberry, goldenrod, ironweed, wild asters, and jewelweed as proper denizens of the often lush weed borders that mark the boundary between mown and unmown areas at my house. Wonderful as they are—as wild beauties, wildlife and insect habitat, and cut flowers—I consider them weeds if they have the cheek to show up in my proper flower and shrub borders.

As with any family, some of the members are more socially acceptable than others. There are, for instance, many varieties of desirable honeysuckle in both vine and shrub forms, but hardly anyone likes their uncontrollable Japanese relative, which thinks nothing of trespass and will strangle a young tree as soon as look at it. With the growing interest in native plants, in fact, more and more cultivated versions of such wildlings are available. Joe-Pye weed and goldenrod are now being grown as selections from the species that are shorter and easier to fit into a polite garden than their tall and gangly cousins. Indeed, it's often a matter of marketing. Call a weed a roadside beauty, a bouquet flower, an insect haven, or an edible herb—Queen Anne's lace jelly is delectable—and the scourge of farmers becomes the darling of high-society gardening.

Today's weed books and bulletins are written mostly for agricultural practitioners, not nouvelle gardeners. They often make it sound as if the weeds can not only ruin a crop—and burdock burrs mixed in with soybeans do make a dicey harvest—but take over the garden of the unwary amateur.

I am here to tell you that the average gardener can outrun the average weed. You need not be afraid of them. In fact, I maintain that the axiom "Weeds are unlikely to infest garden areas that are well tended" should be replaced with "A well-managed garden has weeds in it." We are beginning to understand that pluralism is a good thing in the garden as well as in culture and politics. Monoculture and inbreeding produce vulnerability. Horticulturally, they can be an invitation to a disease takeover or an insect epidemic.

But that does not mean you have to live with anything and everything that shows up at your garden gate. I number those that give skin rashes and those that make burrs as unsuitable company. I spade up every thistle I see and will not let them flower, much less scatter seed to the four corners of the neighborhood. Once you have tasted dandelion wine you will look upon these flowers as cheery spring companions, but I don't need much more cheer than I have and so I try to mow judiciously to get rid of the yellow mopheads before they turn into wind-tossed white seed.

Notwithstanding the charms of the common violet, it does not fool me. It is violently aggressive, a stop-at-nothing upstart that will leap into the flower beds if you turn your head. I refuse admittance to pink knotweed, which starts off looking like a passable flower of tiny balls of blooms on skinny spires, then chortles and romps all over everything. I've tried some of the so-called horticulturally valuable members of the polygonum family, such as silver lace vine and white polygonum, and found those unmannerly, too.

Don't let the French sweet-talk you into saving a spot for sorrel. Both the small wild weed and the tall kitchen garden types misbehave and form gangs. Ditto for wood sorrel, an oxalis that is a miniature lucky clover with adorable little yellow flowers and much, much seed.

There seems to be little disagreement among farmers and gardeners when it comes to multiflora roses and poison ivy, which crop up along fences, at tree bases and stumps, and—for me—in the rocks of my rock garden, where the ivy is tricky to disinvite without also waving good-bye to my fancy rockery plants. I do periodic patrols and chop the poison ivy back, applying Ortho poison ivy killer to the bleeding stub. You can lay down a dark, deep mulch of black plastic and wood chips for an entire year if you have a persistent patch.

Another persistent offender at my house is cleavers, also called bedstraw, a remnant of rural days in this neighborhood. The floppy, hairy plant leans on other plants and produces hundreds of tiny, fuzzy green balls in late spring that catch rides on your dogs and your socks. The best you can say about cleavers is that it knows rich soil when it sees it and tends to grow only there.

In fact, you can do a casual soil test on unknown land by looking at the weeds. Henbit is another that likes good soil. Ragweed and purslane are known to follow cultivation, so you can presume a gardener's presence at some time in the past by their presence and happily go scouting old roses and daylilies. Lamb's quarters and mustard tend to grow on alkaline soils. Acid is preferred by ox-eye daisy, chickweed, and sheep sorrel. The latter, a small, arrow-shaped plant that should be eliminated whenever you see it as it is a horrible self-seeder, indicates clay. Ironweed and smartweed, a relative of knotweed, mean moist to marshy soils. (Lamb's quarters is a very interesting weed, although I do not grow it on purpose. In addition to being an aphid trap, this big, meaty annual with stems streaked red, if grown on poor or nitrogen-deficient soil, will produce leaves with a distinctive red-purple sheen.)

Some weeds are helpful because they tend to bring up trace elements and minerals and so can be valuable compost additions. Plantains and dandelions tend to aerate dense soil. Plantains' liking for dense soil is evidenced by their presence on playgrounds, at the edge of driveways, and growing out of sidewalks. (The buckhorn plantain was called the white man's footstep by the American Indian.) White clover, once reviled as a too-casual, uninvited guest to the perfect lawn, deserves a special invitation. All the clovers are legumes and fix nitrogen, thus improving soil as the gardener sleeps.

And remember this if anyone gives you a rough time about the pluralistic state of affairs at your place: not only are you in tune with contemporary multicultural mandates, but your unkempt lawn and perennial borders will produce an almost perfect nouvelle cuisine salad of chickweed, very young pokeweed sprouts, lamb's quarters, tangy purslane, crunchy burdock roots, and vitamin C–rich dandelion greens.

Good Bugs, Bad Bugs

Good versus evil is no simpler in the garden than it is in the wider world of global politics and business. Even the worst scourge in your vegetable patch is food for a better, or at least bigger, bug—or a bat or bird—and so it goes. All are part of the great web of nature and its food chain that, not too incidentally, supports humans at the top. This may be the place to mention that humans are occurring in unprecedented numbers that threaten to tip the balance of nature because we are making the food chain top-heavy. Hold this thought. It will prove to be germane.

But first, there is a need for gardeners to recognize that there are indeed good bugs around, even if we cannot go so far as to say there are no bad bugs, only bugs for whom we have as yet found no redeeming value.

Insects are so often seen as the foe that some people think every one must be swatted, squashed, or sprayed upon first sight. That is a losing proposition although, to be sure, either way you lose. To borrow a particularly uncomfortable euphemism of global politics, in the battle against bugs you must resign yourself to acceptable losses.

No-kill folks will lose some plants before natural controls kick in. Usually, when populations rise to an epidemic level, some other, totally natural disaster like an increase in predatory wasps or bacterial disease arrives just in time to cut them down to size. It is a sobering thought for us humans, perched at the head of the food chain.

A more serious imbalance occurs as the kill-'em-all folks spray, spray, spray. The short-term gain of plants is earned at the expense of very important long-term losses of bugs, both "bad" and "good."

To counteract this imbalance, more of us need to implement what has come to be known as the Integrated Pest Management approach, or IPM. In this approach, gardeners and farmers try to solve problems by beginning with the least amount of firepower—benign neglect—followed by a sequence of ever-bigger guns, ending up perhaps by spraying with an organically derived pesticide that has the least possible environmental effect.

At the grassroots home gardening level, IPM means knowing what your allies look like. It would be sad to kill all the ladybugs and let the Mexican bean beetles live through mistaken identity. In my garden, I adopt the stance that everyone is a friend until proved otherwise. Over the years, yellow jackets have shown me their stripes, and so have Japanese beetles, Mexican bean beetles, and cabbageworms. I have learned that often the cavalry *does* arrive if you simply wait a week or two.

Here's an alphabetical rundown of the insect cavalry most midwestern gardeners can expect, including a few camp followers that, while not always great to have around, at least do no serious harm.

Ants are not the problem some people think they are when they show up on peony buds or rose bushes, where they are after the—to them—palatable honeydew secreted by aphids. (The presence of large numbers of ants often signals an aphid infestation.) Ants secrete formic acid, which contributes to the breakdown of lignin in wood, which helps keep the world from being piled up with brush.

Bees, it goes without saying, are quintessential good guys whose pollen-gathering mission and resultant cross-fertilization makes life possible on earth. Never spray a flowering tree or plant on which bees are working.

Braconid wasps are tiny and black with long antennae. Often no larger than the aphids they parasitize, these wasps also parasitize caterpillars, depositing egglike brown cocoons on their backs. You generally see these results rather than the wasps themselves, so be sure to leave alone any caterpillar thus fatally afflicted.

Centipedes and millipedes are those creepy, crawly things with all the legs. They do more good than harm, but if they bug you the solution is to make your garden an unpleasant place for them to crawl. Sprinkle wood ashes or cinders, if you have them, around the infested areas. This also deters slugs and snails.

Damsel bugs are small and pale-looking, with long bodies and clear wings. They are common midwestern allies in the farming counties as they like to live in unsprayed alfalfa fields and thrive on aphids, thrips, and small caterpillars.

Ground beetles are the commandos of the garden. They are voracious and swift both as larvae and as adults. Big and black, or sometimes metallic green, they come in thousands of different varieties. Please try not to kill these beneficial nocturnal hard-shelled beetles when they get in your hair at the front porch light. Some of them eat slugs. Some actually climb trees in search of a nice tent caterpillar snack.

Hoverflies, which hover over flowers like some big-headed fly-bee hybrid, are valued in the larval stage, when the sluglike green wormy things love to eat aphids.

Ichneumon wasps can be as long as your thumb or too small to see. They are elegant, red-bodied, black-winged, Dracula-style killers that, as adults, feed on the body fluids of caterpillars and, as larvae, develop inside their hapless host.

Lacewings are such good aphid controllers that they are sold commercially. The adults are fragile with oversized, transparent wings. The larvae are big-bellied brown crawlers.

Ladybugs are trickier to I.D. than you'd think. They come in many versions, from the familiar red with black spots to solid black to black with two orange dots. Also learn to recognize the bristly black and orange larvae and the orange eggs. Do not confuse these bugs with the heinous Mexican bean beetle, which is orange with black spots and has spiny, bright yellow larvae and eggs.

Parsleyworms turn into black swallowtail butterflies, which seems a fair trade for a little shared parsley, carrots, and fennel.

Praying mantises probably need no introduction. They are terrific predators. If you are lucky enough to find a brown frothy egg case glued to a twig or stem, leave it alone.

Robber flies, once seen, are never forgotten. They are very stout, make a loud buzz, and leap upon other flying insects, good and bad.

Sowbugs, also known as roly-polies at my house, are tiny armored roll-up relatives of crayfish (not bugs at all) that you often find under and in pots. They seem to like decaying compost more than plants, and are no problem unless they come indoors on potted plants in the autumn. I keep the population down in summer by elevating pots and generally trying to keep things drained.

Spiders may make some short-sighted folks think you are a bad housekeeper, but they will eat their weight in flies and insects and more than earn a spot hanging in the corner of the tool shed.

Spittle bugs, which are greenish and lozenge-shaped, protect their young in frothy masses of spittle on stems. They can cause stunting in huge numbers in strawberry fields but mostly are no trouble in the home garden.

Tachinid flies are bug-eyed and bristly-bottomed. They deposit their larvae inside grasshoppers, caterpillars, and sawflies via white eggs on their backs. Don't destroy a caterpillar with white eggs stuck to it.

Tomato hornworms are big green caterpillars that can eat a lot of tomato leaves fast. In my garden, I so often see them parasitized by wasps that I leave even the unparasitized ones alone.

Keep your allies happy. No spraying. No bug-zapper lights. Let weeds flower, and maintain permanent weedy places and sodded areas for good bugs to live. Yes, this will help the bad guys, too, but even then, when you see one, you don't have to run for a gun. Some common midwestern pests can be kept in line with benign neglect or simple physical controls.

Bagworms can be sprayed successfully only when very small. Otherwise, you need to pick them off the trees and burn them. This was my first paid job, by the way.

Fall *cankerworms,* which can defoliate various trees including apples, oaks, ash, and lindens, can be stopped if you band the trees with sticky substances like Tanglefoot in the late summer and early fall. The spring cankerworm is controlled the same way, but in spring.

Carpenter worms, which make channels inside trees and emerge as moths, can be stopped by wrapping the tree with paper to keep the moths from emerging. Simple, huh?

Elm leaf beetles can be destroyed by pouring vegetable oil or boiling water at the base of the tree to kill the larvae in the spring. The spruce needleminer, which makes brown nests parallel to the branches, can be controlled by removing the nests by hand or with a sharp stream of water. Pick up the nests and burn them.

Galls on trees are usually more unsightly than harmful, but they can be pulled off if you can't stand it and there are not too many of them.

Grasshoppers, which can be a scourge, can be lured to their deaths in sunken canning jars filled with a molasses and water bait.

Control *tent caterpillars* by picking off and destroying the webby nests.

One thing I am exceptionally afraid of is *yellow jackets.* They nest in the ground, and you invariably do not know it until you have trespassed on the home ground of these very territorial creatures. I found the last nest literally by hand, while pulling up weeds in my holding beds. Yellow jackets can and will sting repeatedly. The stings burn and the areas swell up and itch for weeks.

If you see a hole in the ground with bare earth around it, stand back and watch awhile. You will see the fleet, winged things darting in and out. I get rid of the nests in order to keep the population down to the point where we can cohabit. I have no hope of eliminating yellow jackets. The method we use—I allow my father to do the honors—is to place a clear bowl over the nest opening. The yellow jackets become confused and fly out and then back in, where they do not try to dig another opening since they think there still is one. Yes, they die. It is important to place the bowl at night, in the dark, and to be quiet and calm and leave the area quickly. You can remove the bowl in a few weeks.

Loved Ones in the Garden

Dogs, cats, spouses, and children are all loved in special ways, but they all have their own special ways to disturb your garden. Dogs dig and wear little doggy mud paths in odd corners. Children mash, decapitate, compact, dig, and wear little doggy mud paths in odd corners.

One solution is stakes. Come spring, the flower beds bristle with stakes of all description in an attempt to persuade dogs and little boys to go around the beds rather than through them. I no longer worry about the cats pawing through the shrubbery. I recently had quite a bit of fine gravel laid down to form an auto parking area, path, and terrace near the back door. I made a special trip to the quarry to find this unusual chipped stone, which packs down solid and almost flat. It is used to make concrete blocks. Looking at it now, I see it was short-sighted of me not to realize how closely my new drive, path, and terrace would resemble five tons of kitty litter. The cats knew immediately.

As far as dog trots are concerned, a few well-placed barrier plants can shape canine preferences, or you can spend a year watching where the kids and dogs cut corners and design your garden to suit their preferred paths.

Spouses are generally more trainable, but they do have privileged access to the garden, and sometimes you have to watch them like a hawk if they are not, to put it kindly, your gardening equal. My husband is a man capable of walking past wilting plants, standing on dahlias, and cutting down almost anything I value inordinately while mowing the lawn.

When visitors ask what that long row of tall wooden posts is, marching across the lawn from the shade garden and bulb bed to the sunny round patio, I am fond of saying, "That is a pergola or a divorce." The pergola, such as it is, has been left as eleven pairs of posts in the ground, untopped, for nigh on four years. It started out as my husband's project and turned into an albatross for us all.

The pergola will eventually be done and swathed in roses. I began to plant the pergola roses last summer, mentioning to the pergola builder that he'd best get a top on before the ramblers rambled. I'm sure it was unintentional, but one of the ramblers was decapitated during mowing. It is coming back strong, being of the hardy old shrub constitution.

However, he did manage to dispatch a new rose, a marvel of modern plant breeding touted as an enduring landscape shrub. I had it marked with a wooden stake, but after that and the rose were cut down several times in the course of one season, I grabbed a metal file off the work bench and stuck it in the ground next to the rose's young canes. He ran over that, too, cutting the rose in silence but making the file sink and shriek. The rose was a Meidiland type called 'Bonica'. I dub it and some Meidiland ground-cover rose relatives the roses from hell; they are that hardy and that vigorous. So it was with some detached interest that I watched 'Bonica' do silent battle with my husband and the lawn mower one summer. She gave up by August. My theory is that it was not so much the constant cutting that did 'Bonica' in as the humiliation of being completely invisible to man and machine.

That is the ultimate problem with loved ones. They simply don't see it your way.

Just the other day, my husband came in the house from a lawn-mowing stint. He looked bemused. He was holding a metal file in his hand. It had many nicks gouged out of it. "I found this stuck in the ground out back," he said. "Do you have any idea how it got there?"

The Inherited Garden

I know a woman, otherwise firmly in charge of her life, who was so intimidated by the garden presence of the former owners of her house that she could not bring herself to remove a bathtub Madonna, even though it was not to her taste or religious convictions.

You should be sensitive to the spirit of your place and to who has come before you, but it *is* your place. When gardeners inherit, what they often find is a mature garden in need of rejuvenation if not outright redesign. It is no place for the shy or softhearted. By all means take a full season to see what you have.

If it is a significant period garden, an architectural gem, or a contemporary arboretum passed on prematurely, you may have a moral obligation to see it through, or at least not ruin it, but most of us inherit something a bit less than that.

Take stock. It takes fifteen to twenty years for a garden to grow up, and in the process it can become overgrown. Weeds and volunteer trees compete with legitimate residents, and some of these—particularly small shrubs—will be passing their prime and ready to be replaced.

Identify plants, walks, and other features that are obvious keepers. Tag them. Also tag good plants in wrong places. Excluding large trees, these often can be transplanted for some big savings. Anything not on these two lists has to go. Sorry.

Don't assume trash trees are automatically out. Wild borders of volunteer hackberries and red-berried bush honeysuckles or stately groves of staghorn sumac can be cleaned up a bit and the area under them weeded and mulched. *Voilà!* A shade garden, a privacy screen, a knockout fall specimen grove, all had for almost no cost. When you look at a wildish border or grove, it may be that none of the plants in it are individually worth keeping, but you can't afford to toss out the group.

DELETE DEFECTS

Sharpen your saws and pruners or call in the tree trimmers, and get rid of the rejects and clear out overgrown areas. A good strategy is to limb up: remove lower branches on trees and large shrubs to create a light, more open look and better growing conditions. To "arborize" an overgrown shrub, you peer inside and find a good single stem or three or five good stems. (Keep the number odd. It always looks better.) Remove all extraneous growth and you should have a graceful small tree.

This may be all it takes to change dense shade in which nothing can grow to a garden of dappled shade and to find "new" space in which to install perennials, low shrubs, and ground covers. Often you will need to add an inch or two, seldom more, of soil.

SAVE THE SALVAGEABLE

Dig the material you have tagged for transplanting. If you know you will get it back in the ground the same day, you can get by with covering the roots with wet burlap. Otherwise, it's safest to pot or ball and burlap the roots and do your rearranging later. You also can set the plants in an out-of-the-way holding bed and let them live there for a year if you don't know where you want them but they are too good to toss. You also can invite your gardening buddies to come with spade in hand and have their pick of your rejects.

Remake borders and paths. Sometimes it takes just a little effort to turn a ramplike dirt path into an elegant flight of steps or to make a visual check on a hill by installing a short series of steps, which stand out like a punctuation point. Broaden and widen borders to make them balance the proportions of the house. They are seldom too large.

LOOK AT THE LAWN

The smaller the patch of grass, the more important it is that it appear flawless. A scrub bit of grass can make a $10,000 renovation look like a $1,000 Band-Aid job. With those kinds of figures, you can't afford to be meek or the only way you may get a great garden is by inheritance.

Moving

Gardening and moving are not complementary activities, which may be one reason why most of us start serious gardening only when we are past thirty, seemingly settled down on a property, and in careers that will support our true occupation: installing the perfect backdrop, the ultimate landscape, the quintessential gift to the world. Each move we make is a collision with our illusion of permanence, an illumination of the reality of our mortality and the fragile nature of our gardening gift to the world.

Having moved myself and much of a garden several times, I can attest that the activities do have two things in common. Nothing goes as planned, and you can expect to lose things. If move you must—and I swear I'll never do it again—here's how I would correct my past mistakes.

Do take plants with you, but they should be no more than part of the means for an entirely new garden. You are changing gardens more than moving one. That is the tragedy and the excitement of it all.

It is not exciting to try to dig up a sample of all your plants at the last minute and try to replant them at the new house in the period between closing the real estate deal and the arrival of movers at your old house. You usually cannot plant any earlier, as you do not own the new property until closing and anything you put on it could become someone else's property if the deal falls through.

The first step is to start taking cuttings and potting up divisions and seedlings the moment you are serious about moving. This goes for suckering shrubs, bulbs, and annuals. With these latter, if it's out of season and you just can't bear to leave it behind, try potting a hunk of undisturbed soil in the proper area where self-sowing has probably taken place. It worked for me with annual poppies.

Think small. All you need is a start, not the whole garden. And think neat. You don't need extra hassle trying to repair damage you've done in the panic of getting your plants out of what is going to be someone else's garden.

Far aside from the legal requirements that you leave the shrubbery, and leave it looking halfway decent, is the issue of your convenience. You are going to have to find a place to stash all this stuff, move it by hand, and stash it once more at the new house.

Store your inventory in your holding beds or in a cluster of pots behind the garage or some other semi-sheltered spot. Farm them out to friends.

It goes without saying that you will do this at the proper time for the plants. You may not be successful digging up plants in the dead of winter or at the height of summer.

Houseplants can be left to the last minute. If you are moving a far piece and space and weight are an issue, unpot the smaller ones and put the roots in plastic bags. They should be fine for several days to a week depending on the weather. You will have to repot them soon after you arrive at your new destination, so decide if you'll have the time before you unpot them.

The proverb "Act in haste; repent at leisure" is nowhere more true than in planting plants. In my last move, I put the bee balm in a bad place and it has jinxed me ever since. Despite starts three more times, I cannot seem to make the monarda clan happy at this house, while in the past it has been a bit of a pest. Ah, well.

As you are doing it more sensibly, your next step is to locate a spot at the new property that is out of the wind and noonday sun as much as possible but still handy to water. Temporary holding can stretch to several years.

Then, if at all feasible, you should borrow or lease a pickup truck or a van and a strong-shouldered friend when plant-moving time arrives. Set the balled and burlapped stock in first, then the potted plants, and finally, dig up the treasures in the holding beds and bag the roots in plastic if you think you can get them back in the ground pronto. Otherwise, you will have to ball and burlap or pot them, too.

If the truck is open, use a tarp, tied down, to protect your plants from wind damage. Do not expect movers to move your plants. I wouldn't let them even if they offered, which is unlikely.

All should go smoothly, but remember to let your real estate representative know what you plan to do, so that potential buyers know that the delectable array of plants in nursery beds does not stay.

It will sound selfish, but don't leave anything you love unless it is simply too big to be moved and too important to the landscape to be destroyed by the new owner. New owners have a way of butchering your viburnums on the basis that they are too dark, or they bulldoze your priceless collection of old shrub roses as too thorny, not enough flowers, and they need extra parking space, anyway.

If you are moving a long distance, consider mailing plants to a friend in the area, who will hang onto them until you get there. Or, mail them to your new address if need be. Most plants can live through UPS and post office rigors if it's not for more than a few weeks and it's not real hot.

My final advice—unless you've sold your garden to a gardening colleague you respect—is don't look back, and don't go back.

Power Lines

Nothing elicits more righteous anger than utility crews pruning trees on the utility company right-of-way. Until then, most of us have lived with the illusion that this was part of our yard. Visually, it is. Ecologically, it is. It can be a rude awakening to come home and discover that your shade trees have had their branches lowered, devastating to discover that the trees have been topped.

Unfortunately, giving trees flattop haircuts does still happen. I've seen entire decades-old hedgerows in the country reduced in a trice to a shattered mock hedge. Even when "good" selective pruning is employed, since the goal of the trimmers is to clear wires of potential branch falls for the next five years, the result can be a tree trimmed almost flat on one side to accommodate wire, but full on the other.

Not only do we need to require by cards, letters, and phone calls that utility company tree trimmers—or any tree trimmers, for that matter—engage in responsible pruning practices, but gardeners and homeowners need to shoulder their share of responsibility. The ultimate solution is buried power lines, but until that happens, avoid planting big trees under power lines. Always, always look up before you plant a shrub or tree that will get much bigger than fifteen feet tall.

Here are some that are recommended because they are short and relatively free of diseases and pests (not all will be hardy in the northern stretches of Zone 5): Japanese maples, redbuds, dogwoods of various species, halesia (silverbell), the smaller types of *Magnolia stellata*, sourwood, *Styrax japonica* and *Styrax obassia,* most viburnums, most sumacs, and the airy pagoda tree, *Sophora japonica.* There are many others with wonderful characteristics, like the hawthorns and crabapples, but be sure to get disease-resistant varieties.

If you simply must plant trees that will grow to 60 to 120 feet tall at maturity, keep them back 15 to 20 feet from the power lines.

If you ignore all this good advice, which I've been known to do, be prepared to either do or pay for your own pruning or be very cordial to the power company tree trimmers.

Hired Help

The great age of gardening help is upon us. Oh, sure, the age of having one's own gardeners, who lived in cottages far removed from the Big House, is as far removed from contemporary reality as the plot of a Gothic novel, but today we have more, maybe too much more.

We've got gardening advisors and personal trainers, not to mention the slew of garden writers arisen with the tide of new gardeners. We've got landscape architects and landscape designers. We've got venerable old plantsmen—young ones and women too—and we've got nurseries, garden centers, and mail-order firms in record numbers. We even have a small but growing cluster of garden art advisors, usually associated with sculpture galleries and architectural salvage shops that are the upscale equivalent of the Midwest's tried-and-true concrete yard ornament stores.

There is someone out there for everyone. Sometimes it adds up to a case of inferiority. What? You don't have the means for a flight of terraces with redwood Oriental-style privacy fencing? No six-foot-wide paved paths flanked by twin perennial borders? Where's your eight-foot-tall yew allée? Where's your ten-foot-tall masonry wall, on the southern face of which you of course espalier pears and grow vines, shrubs, and flowers a bit too tender for your climate zone?

Maybe that's what you'll end up with, but most gardeners I know do things in steps and often do things themselves. What they need is good advice at the right juncture, the occasional use of earth-moving equipment and stonemasons, constant access to good and uncommon plants, and, maybe, periodic help with recurring chores.

Let's say your ambitions run to an edible landscape, or you want a pond. You want to figure out what to do with the dense, dank shade of eight maples in the back or a hillside too steep to mow safely. Maybe all you want is somebody to mow the grass, keep the weeds down, and plant a few flowers each year. Whom do you call?

Landscape architects are people with specialized degrees in land use and design. They are not necessarily too big for small jobs, but many firms specialize in large-scale work. The cost is usually per hour, and they are often worth gold if you have a difficult site, with a need for drainage, grading, and engineering solutions. (If you can find one, an experienced bulldozer owner/operator willing to work with you weekends and evenings can also solve the problem.)

Most landscape architects are at heart creative problem-solvers. They love design challenges and, because they don't often also run nurseries, are in no way tied down to using only plant materials in their own nursery and greenhouse.

Landscape design is a more varied field. There is room in it for the true artist, like internationally famous garden designer Roberto Burle-Marx of Brazil, who does not have a landscape architecture degree. There also is no reason why the kid down the street with a wheelbarrow and a pickup can't advertise as a landscape designer and be one until he can't get jobs anymore. It's a real client-beware minefield, where price cannot be any kind of guide.

Nursery and garden centers often have trained or experienced folks on the payroll to do home and commercial design; but, logically enough, they also tend to have plant material on hand they would like to sell you. Sometimes what you get is what they have and not always the ideal. That's the only reason I can see for the amazing proliferation of Bradford pear trees in this world.

A fascinating frontier is the group of amateur gardener/artists who seem to exist in every community and are eager to work with and help fellow gardeners. You find out about them on the grapevine.

No matter whom you call, remember that the proof of a fit with you is in previous garden work they have done. Personalities count, but gardens speak louder than words. Always ask for references, and always follow up and go see for yourself. This is good advice with landscape architects, self-made landscape designers, and the nice nursery your Aunt Sallie always uses. The first issue is not how much it costs, but whether there is a taste fit between you and the designer.

It might be that what you really want is to tap into someone else's creativity. Inquire if they are amenable to a paid, hour-long walk through your property, talking off the tops of their heads about what immediately strikes them as good and bad, and how to improve things. It can be seriously motivating and it allows you to do the fun part, the design part. To be sure, planting and making paths and setting fence posts can be absorbing, educational, and good aerobic exercise, but most of us go crazy over the playing with possibilities.

In this process, knowledge of plants definitely pays off. That's what you have just paid someone else to tell you. In the next stage of getting it done, you have to locate the good stuff. There are a couple of other kinds of hired-help resources to consider for this and, moderately, for design ideas, too.

Local garden clubs and plant societies are terrific plant reference and maintenance resources. If you are looking to solve a special problem—a pond, rose garden, or shade garden—it may pay big to contact the appropriate society. You will join and either learn yourself or locate someone with hands-on experience who can help you.

Always talk to other gardeners. They will tell you if so-and-so is worth hiring or not. They may know about small one-person garden-maintenance firms that are a cut above the national franchise firms that are mostly lawnkeepers. They may have plants you covet and you can arrange a swap or a buy.

Check out local and regional horticulture schools, from vocational schools to university programs. There should be a few students eager to earn money and experience, *and* they should arrive at least knowing marigolds from ragweed. Some will be considerably more sophisticated than that, eager to "do" an entire garden. You may find yourself the patron of a budding genius.

Hire early. Such paragons find jobs fast by word of mouth. Don't be shy. Ask a gardener you see working in someone else's rose beds if they have any time for an extra client. Be humble.

But in the interview, be logical. Ask about background and training. Get references and call them. Get a list of drive-by places and drive by. It is important that visions merge when it comes to landscapes. Be sure your personal gardener can do the kind of work you want. It is, for instance, easier to trim hedges square and formal than it is to hand-prune them au naturel.

Take a look at equipment, if that is supplied. A shiny truck and clean, sharp tools are no guarantee, but they don't hurt.

If you want to train your own handy-dandy helper, help yourself. I have had just enough experience trying this to know that I'm safer paying someone to vacuum the house, bathe the dogs, and cook the food than to do my garden. However, if you have time to chat with an hourly worker and supervise the labor, or even work alongside, it can be a great thing. In the interview, look for an interest in plants and in obtaining a gardener's education. That is what you are going to be providing, while paying someone. If you don't think you are ready to be someone else's teacher, then you must hire someone who knows more than you do or be willing to live with mistakes.

Supervision is the key. At first you must keep tasks simple and give no more than one or two instructions at a time. Do not allow potential helpers to prune or weed until they have proved themselves hauling mulch, lifting sod, turning the compost pile, stacking wood, scrubbing pots. You must not place your garden in others' hands until you feel confident that they will follow your instructions to the letter or can be trusted with their own judgment. I must tell you that it will try the patience of most workers to be told in great detail what to do. Adolescents, in particular, find this odious. It can be best to give them hour-long or longer projects of limited scope so you aren't in the worker's face all the time with another little nagging job to do or a forgotten instruction.

Keep the jobs unchanged for a bit and then systematically add on tasks with more potential danger to your garden. Start with edging grass, move on to mowing, thence to weeding a ground cover, and if all is going well and you have not lost any shrubs or trees or flowers, progress to deadheading, a little trimming, and, maybe, actual weeding.

WAGES

The going rate around my neighborhood runs from $10 to $20 per hour for experienced help. If you are creating your own pool of skilled labor, wages need not be that high, perhaps. But make them decent—a cut above minimum for sure—and build in a trial period and raise.

Do not, I repeat, DO NOT start any worker with weeding. The chances of removal of desired plant material are too great.

A Final Note

IN THE END, the thought remains: It wouldn't be fun if gardening were easy. It wouldn't even be gardening.

The gardener is far more than a day laborer, an unpaid maintenance worker on the household payroll. The gardener is like the artist who can see something new and grand in what is alleyway trash to other, hooded eyes; like the architect who can bring forth a solid, protective, and emotionally satisfying building from a froth of ideas.

As companions of nature and cohorts of society, we gardeners have the chance in all regions and climates, indeed have the responsibility, to create as well as respond to the world, to be part of the interlocking community of like-minded souls who find their lives ennobled and enriched by days spent in the garden.

A Gardener's Calendar
for Zones 5 and 6

This is only a possible checklist of tasks to be implemented or not, as the spirit moves you. It reflects a lot of what I do, or plan to do, each year, and you may want to adapt it to suit your garden.

January

Make New Year's resolutions: to *select* plants, not settle for them; to have a plan and follow it; to keep up with maintenance; and not to start too many seedlings.

Study catalogs. Place rose orders this month to avoid sellout disappointments. Order seed for annual bedding plants now, too, as many will need to be sown between yesterday and February for spring bloom.

Get gear together for starting seeds. Don't forget labels.

Sow slow-growers like geraniums, pansies, lobelia, and dahlias.

Bring amaryllis and clivia out of dormancy if it has not been done already by upping the water, warmth, and light. Check and treat houseplants, if necessary, for spider mite, scale, and whitefly.

Check summer bulbs in storage such as dahlias, gladiolus, and canna for possible rotting. Remove any bad ones and dust the rest with sulfur.

Store wood ashes, covered, for use in spring.

Prowl your garden for microclimates—pockets of more temperate weather sheltered by shrubs or buildings—and use this knowledge in your plant ordering. Simultaneously, add to your move-it list plants that are in the wrong spot.

Check for frost-heaving and rabbit damage. Tamp heaved plants back in place and make wire cages to discourage rabbits.

Continue to remove and burn or destroy any bagworms.

Gently brush snow from trees and bushes while it is still soft. If it hardens or if the weather deposits ice, support weak branches with sticks; do not try to knock it loose.

Cold frames should be bedded down inside with straw, and covered outside with old blankets when the temperatures are brutal.

Plant those fall-ordered bulbs that got lost in the refrigerator, or pot them up for forcing indoors.

Complete plans to widen beds or start new ones. Lay down sod-killing plastic or newspaper layers if the weather cooperates.

Obtain materials like bricks, sand, bales of peat. Contact a nearby stable and arrange to get manure, which will have to be composted for nearly a year if fresh.

Notes:

February

Finalize garden orders and plans.

Check stored bulbs again. If the dahlias are sprouting, snap off and root the sprouts; or, if you have window, greenhouse, or grow-light space, go ahead and pot up the roots, along with any caladiums and begonias you want in fine fettle as soon as spring hits.

Discard forced bulbs that have finished blooming. Still hankering for summer? Dig up some perennials like primroses and astilbe, violas, and pansies, and pot them for growing inside. Mist these and all houseplants daily. Keep them all away from air vents and heat ducts.

Indoors, sow broccoli, cauliflower, and cabbage for your early vegetable garden. Also start slow-goers, like petunias and impatiens, lobelia and geranium.

Prune *Clematis jackmanii* species to just above the second or first lowest pair of strong viable buds or, if you're not sure, to within two feet of the ground. Cut back dried foliage on ornamental grasses and epimediums now or in early March in order to give borders a neater look and allow new growth to emerge cleanly.

Sow peas, lettuce, and spinach in cold frame. Begin to harden off seedlings of cold-tolerant plants, like cabbage and broccoli.

Sow Shirley poppies by tossing seed around perennials.

Prune fruit trees, brambles (if it was not done in the fall), shrubs, and trees. Do not prune spring-flowering shrubs and trees until just after they bloom, but you can cut a few branches from established spring shrubs such as forsythia, mock orange, and quince to bring indoors and force into winter bloom. Crush the stems and place in warm water to hasten the process.

Apply dormant oil spray to fruit trees when temperatures rise above 45 degrees and are supposed to stay there for a few days.

Keep an eye on the cold frame and be sure to open it on sunny, warm days.

Yard patrol: Check for frost-heaving of fall plantings, young plants, and shallow-rooted plants like iris. Tamp them back into the ground. Make a drainage inspection after a winter rain or storm and fill low spots in preparation for reseeding the lawn.

Begin to divide perennials and plant peonies.

Mulch grapes, shrubs, and trees with rotted manure or rough compost.

Turn the compost on a nice day.

Notes:

March

Sow heat-loving vegetables like tomatoes, peppers, eggplant, melons.

Begin to repot houseplants and fertilize in preparation for the summer outside.

Scratch in Bulb Booster on bulb beds and continue to apply compost mulch to perennials, shrubs, and trees. Bulb groups that are crowded and not blooming well should be marked for moving in late summer. This is the beginning of your next, season-long "move-it/improve-it" list, which identifies plants in the wrong spots or plants that need division. Use whatever system works—mental list, written list, calendar notations, color-coded stakes, even labels with messages written on them to yourself.

Fluff up mulch on all beds but do not remove it. Begin to unhill roses and rake off mulch, but keep it handy in case of a cold snap.

Put boards down in the vegetable garden to walk on, but do not till or cultivate wet soil. You should have laid down compost, crunched leaves, and rotted manure last year as a plant-through compost. If you were smart enough to plant a cover crop last fall, mow it and turn it under one day when the soil is the right consistency.

Sow peas, beets, lettuce, carrots, and spinach outdoors. Cover the rows temporarily with a board to foil hungry birds and keep moisture even. After a week check daily; remove when the first speck of green shows.

Rejuvenate overgrown deciduous hedges by cutting back hard, to perhaps a handspan above the ground, as long as there are green buds below the cut. Also, cut back buddleia, grasses, caryopteris, and overgrown red or yellow twig dogwood.

Fill low yard spots with compost, sand, and soil mix, and sow grass seed.

Yard patrol: Check trellis and fences for repairs. On dry, nice days, neaten border edges.

Continue dividing perennials, mostly summer and fall bloomers. Plant trees and roses. Late in the month sow hardy flowers and herbs where they are to grow or in cold frame to move out later. If plant orders arrive and can't be planted outside, heel them in in a sheltered spot.

Notes:

April

Groom houseplants; trim, feed, repot, and begin to move them to a sheltered porch or outdoor spot in preparation for the final move all the way outdoors in late May, when the weather is settled.

Sow tomatoes, peppers, eggplant, and other warmth-lovers if you have not done so already. Start a few new plants of broccoli and cauliflower. Sow second-crop lettuce, peas, carrots. At mid-month begin to harden off husky indoor seedlings, which you have, of course, transplanted to larger pots if necessary: On nice days, set them outside, out of the wind, and bring them back inside at night or during storms. Keep up the acclimatization for two weeks before moving them to the garden.

Last call to seed the lawn.

Apply wood ashes to your pinks, the rock garden, and unplanted beds. Fertilize acid-loving plants such as azaleas, hollies, rhododendrons, and enkianthus with special acid fertilizer. While you're at it, dig in some ashes around the peonies, too, and compost them, but do not use horse manure. Set supports around the emerging foliage before it gets too big.

Add lime to asparagus beds to deter asparagus beetles.

Outdoors, sow parsley and all other herbs except basil. Plant potatoes and rhubarb. Finish planting roses now, or wait until next year. Thin lettuce.

Take cuttings from outside of mum clumps and plant them in rows in holding beds for fall. Divide all fall-bloomers, including hardy asters, anemones, salvias, and mums. Divide Shasta daisies, too. They will be very dense. Remove all debris from iris.

Get a cutting garden lined out with extra bits of perennials and any annual seedling volunteers you are beginning to see around the yard. Sow a few annuals.

As forsythia blooms, begin to remove winter mulch and compost it or work it into the soil.

Pinch "candles" on pines to make them bushier. Trim evergreens if necessary.

Near the end of April begin applying a feeding mulch or a compost mulch to perennials and shrubs.

Notes:

May

Continue moving houseplants outdoors as night temperatures hit the 50s.

Wait for nights above 55 degrees to set out tomato seedlings. Wait for steady 70s in the daytime to set out peppers, and pick off the first ones set to encourage more production over a longer period.

Water seedlings and their garden spot right before you transplant to make the transition easier. Keep lettuce well watered for sweet flavor. Use mulch to conserve moisture. Trickle on the water. Overhead watering can encourage mildew.

If azalea leaves are yellow or other acid-lovers need a quick, safe spring tonic, mix two tablespoons of cider vinegar in a quart of water and pour it on.

Sow corn, okra, beans, squash, cucumbers by mid-month.

If you have new peonies, remove the blooms the first year to help the plant set strong roots. Cut the buds just as they begin to break, and put them in a damp plastic bag in the refrigerator. Cut the stem again and float in water. Remember, no long stems on peony cut flowers for several years. You want to leave on as much foliage as possible. Don't fret over the ants, just blow or brush or wash them off.

Resod lawns. Plant ground covers and bedding plants.

Grass mowing gets serious. Sharpen mower blades and be sure that trees and shrubs and borders are mulched far enough out to avoid mower damage.

Pot up summer bulbs or plant them out. Plant new daylilies. Pinch back mums and asters to encourage bushiness.

Keep an eye out for aphids and mildew. Knock off the aphids with a hose or use a soap-and-water spray. For mildew, start dusting with sulfur and be sure air circulation is good. Try spraying baking soda solution on the roses to fend off blackspot.

Store extra seed in airtight jars in the fridge.

Finish planting big pots, barrels, baskets, and other outside containers. Stuff them full.

Notes:

June

Make a second sowing of summer annuals in the cutting garden for fall bloom. Sow perennials and biennials, which will put on foliage growth this year and flower next year. Sow foxglove in pots or the cold frame.

Feed roses and cut back old canes. Tie in ramblers. Feed lilies for July bloom. Ditto for daylilies. I like fish emulsion or a feeding compost mulch. Clean up iris and cut off the stalks and spotted leaves. Weed but do not mulch the iris bed.

Feed the vegetable garden with fish emulsion by mid-month. Turn the compost and water it if necessary. Use it or mulch all around for summer moisture conservation.

Take cuttings from artemisias for quick-fix fillers in borders. Continue to implement your last year's move-it list. If you can't decide where something should go, plant it out in the holding beds.

Take soft wood cuttings of azaleas and other deciduous and broadleaf evergreens to start in sand in pots. Cover them with a plastic bag to hold in moisture and set them in the shade. Take stem cuttings of pinks and other flowers.

Trim back petunias and continue to pinch mums, salvias, and asters. Deadhead as necessary. Begin to divide spring-flowering bulbs as the foliage ripens or turns brown and dies back. Move in ferns to cover the bare spots in shady beds.

Check that labels and guy wires on trees and shrubs are not too tight.

Don't overwater the geraniums—that is, pelargoniums—for best flowers.

When bulb catalogs arrive, get orders out early for bulbs for fall planting. Order peonies for fall planting.

In the vegetable garden, be sure the cucumbers have a straw mulch, ditto the strawberries. Do not cut back tomatoes, but do remove the sucker at the leaf joint in indeterminate tomato types. Keep tying in the growing plants.

If you have lots of squash blooms but no baby squash, cross-pollinate by hand. Determine to plant bee-attracting plants near the garden next year, plants like clover in the lawn, dandelions, asters, bee balm, marjoram, raspberries, sage, sweet cicely, and goldenrod, also hawthorn, linden, and apple trees.

Edge out all beds.

Make hose guards from foot-tall metal stakes, old wire fence bent at a right angle, or old broomsticks painted dark green or black. Notes:

July

Garden in the early morning or, with mosquito repellent, in the evening. It's too hot to bother at midday, and it's hard on the plants, too.

Cut grass high, at three inches, to discourage weeds and to avoid stressing the grass. As summer progresses, allow the lawn to go dormant and brown. It won't hurt it, and will save on water and mowing.

Be alert to typical summer problems—mildew, drought stress, red spider mite—which often show up in the form of yellowing leaves, leaf munchers like caterpillars, and flower destroyers like Japanese beetles, which begin to emerge from the ground this month.

Watch for fire blight, a burned, blackened look at branch tips often found on fruit trees. Prune hard several inches back into good wood, disinfecting pruners in bleach solution between cuts.

Prowl the garden at dawn and dusk for Japanese beetles. Pick or knock them off into a cup of soapy water, where they will drown. Do this daily, without fail. Do not use scent or pheromone traps; they attract more than they destroy.

Keep a keen eye on containers morning and evening. They dry out quickly in summer. If watering is a problem, move the containers to a semi-shady spot, or rig up some sort of shade. Look out for shallow-rooted cucumbers. Keep these watered to avoid bitterness and keep the fruits picked to encourage a long harvest.

Muster a little energy for a second, fall garden. Sow broccoli, cabbage, carrots, cauliflower, peas, and spinach, timed to mature as the weather cools. Sow bush beans, cucumbers, and summer squash by the Fourth of July, and you should be able to squeeze in a second crop of these frost-tender plants.

Sow biennial flowers. Wait to sow ornamental cabbage until late in the month or early in August. Redo iris beds as they are dormant now.

Prune vines and begin to shear evergreen hedges. Harvest and use, freeze, or dry herbs. They need the continual trimming to grow lustily and look good. Shear box, privet, barberry, and evergreen hedges. Give vines and ground covers a trim if they need it.

No matter how ragged the peony foliage looks, let it ripen to add energy to the roots. Keep roses deadheaded unless they form attractive hips. At mid-month stop pinching mums. Take cuttings of tender plants for winter houseplants. Root in sand or perlite and peat and keep under plastic and in the shade.

Watch lilies after they flower for bulbils, which look like peas and appear at some leaf joints. When these break off easily, plant them in pots or in the ground like seeds. The seed capsules are usually not ripe until August.

Stake tall fall-bloomers such as salvias, phlox, dahlias.

Feed everything lightly with fish emulsion after the June flush, and mulch.

Add to your move-it list of plants in the wrong spot, but wait until fall to act.

Extend your strawberry beds. Root young plants formed at the tips of runners, but leave the pots in the garden and the runner intact until September, when you can sever this "umbilical cord." If you have been having any disease problems, get new plants for a new row.

Dampen a patch of sand or mud or make one in a large pot for butterflies, which like to congregate there in late morning. Watch for butterflies between 10 A.M. and 4 P.M. and do not spray pesticides. Set out orange halves, cut apples, and bananas for woodland butterflies at the woods' edge on high platforms or fence posts.

Notes:

August

Turn the compost.

Mid-month through October 15 is the time to sow grass and do lawn renovation.

Pot up strawberry runners to bring indoors after they've been touched with frost around Christmas for a small out-of-season crop in late winter or early spring.

Sow pansies for fall bloom.

Cut spent raspberry and blackberry canes to the ground.

Begin to space out and transplant perennials and biennials sown this year into holding beds or cold frames for the winter. They will go in permanent spots next spring. Take root cuttings of perennials like baby's breath, anemone, phlox, sea lavender, and Oriental poppy. Plant new poppies, iris, madonna lilies, and peonies now.

Begin to transplant mums into ornamental beds from their holding beds.

Keep azaleas well watered. They are setting spring buds.

As onion tops turn brown, knock over the entire row to encourage maturing. Remove small melons or pumpkins that won't have time to mature before frost to give others a greater share of nutrients. Put maturing melons and pumpkins on shingles, pieces of carpet, or dry straw to prevent rotten spots where they touch the damp ground.

Harvest winter squash when the vines die and the rinds are so tough they can't be pierced with a fingernail. Be sure to leave a few s:

October

Finish potting bulbs for forcing. Water well and put the s where they can form roots and experience cold-dormancy but not freeze: an old fridge, the garage, a trench, a cold frame, or ide the house under mulch.

Dig tender bulbs, and dry and store them in a cool, dark location.

Clean up the peony beds, cutting and burning foliage and feeding bone meal. Cut back mums and, if doubtful about winter toler-e, set them in a cold frame with excellent drainage. Get any other ter protection in place soon, such as a screen of burlap tacked to es around newly planted evergreens, shrubs, or rhododendrons.

Do a last lawn mowing so that the grass is not too tall over winter. e or mower-munch leaves to avoid grass kill over winter. Stockpile ves for mulching beds. Don't use maple leaves, which get slimy and t down.

Watering, if there is no rain, is crucial now for winter health.

Redo borders or sections. Prepare planting holes and new beds, ecially for roses and shrubs that you will want to plant next March fore you can work the soil.

Plant a cover crop of rye in the vegetable garden if it has not been ne already.

Dig root crops and harvest anything left to harvest, including een tomatoes to fry or ripen indoors slowly.

inches of stem when you cut them from the vin
in the sun for ten days. Allow ornamental gc
possible on the vine.

Overripe tomatoes are not safe to can. Use
summer salsa. Pull up old determinate tomat
stopped producing fruits by now.

Sow a cover crop of annual rye right aroun
to save time later.

Notes:

September

Begin to lay in manure to rot over
ered with water-repelling straw. Continue to buil
debris.

Divide and replant perennials and shrubs, usi
Get bulbs planted. Pot some for forcing.
Transplant or plant new evergreens before t
Stop fertilizing to encourage dormancy.

After you clean out the perennial beds, broadc
annuals like California poppies, larkspur, and co
next spring.

Take cuttings of tender houseplants and tende
to keep in the house over winter.

Move peonies, iris, and poppies if you have n
Set out mums.

Build a cold frame.

Late in the month or when proper, begin to
indoors before the heat is turned on. Reduce wat
clivia, fuchsia, and amaryllis to give them a rest, bu
watering Christmas cactus.

Notes:

November

Make terrariums for gifts. Use any large, watertight, clear glass container such as old aquariums, wide-mouth bowl-like vases, or even that old cliché, an oversized brandy snifter. The notion of recycling wine jugs is good, but tedious unless you really enjoy meticulously placing soil and plants with long tweezers through the narrow neck. Buy small-scale tropicals or collect such plants as mosses, violas, pussytoes, wild strawberry, and seedling evergreens from your own yard.

Begin to lay down winter mulch as the ground freezes, but not before. Old established plants may not need much mulch. Cut back roses as necessary and hill up with soil around graft on stem, or lay down mulch.

Empty hoses and store them in a heated area if possible. Turn off all but one outdoor faucet. Stockpile soil, sand, peat, etc., for winter potting and seed-starting.
Notes:

December

Start fast-growing paperwhites and hyacinths in jars of water or in pots of soil mix. Begin to bring in pots of rooted spring bulbs to warm up for budding and then blooming indoors.

Early in the month, prune your hollies, yews, etc., for holiday greens; store in water in a cool garage before the ground freezes. Take hardwood cuttings of deciduous shrubs and bundle them, labeling them according to name and which end is up. Bury them in moist sand in a trench or sunken pot. You will "stick" them or start them in spring in a cold frame outdoors.

Watch gutters and downspouts for icy water overflow on plants during the winter. Erect supports and windbreaks, do drainage as needed.

Finish planting bulbs.

Go over the houseplants carefully for whitefly and spider mite. Keep jasmine well watered, but avoid overwatering most other houseplants in winter.

Notes:

Bibliography and Recommended Reading

Allen, Oliver E. *Gardening with the New Small Plants: The Complete Guide to Growing Dwarf & Miniature Shrubs, Flowers, Trees and Vegetables*. Boston: Houghton Mifflin, 1987.

Appelhof, Mary. *Worms Eat My Garbage*. Kalamazoo, Mich.: Flower Press.

Bailey, Liberty Hyde, et al. *Hortus Third: A Concise Dictionary of Plants Cultivated in the United States and Canada*. New York: Macmillan, 1976.

Ball, Jeff, and Liz Ball. *Rodale's Landscape Problem Solver*. Emmaus, Penn.: Rodale Press, 1989.

Bartholomew, Mel. *Square Foot Gardening*. Emmaus, Penn.: Rodale Press, 1981.

Bennett, Jennifer, and Turid Forsyth. *The Harrowsmith Annual Garden*. Ontario: Camden House, 1990.

Berrall, Julia A. *The Garden: An Illustrated History*. New York: Viking Press, 1966.

Bradley, Fern Marshall, ed. *Rodale's All-New Encyclopedia of Organic Gardening*. Emmaus, Penn.: Rodale Press, 1992.

Bremness, Lesley. *The Complete Book of Herbs*. New York: Penguin Books, 1988.

Brooks, John. *The Book of Garden Design*. New York: Macmillan, 1991.

Bubel, Nancy. *The New Seed-Starters Handbook*. Emmaus, Penn.: Rodale Press, 1988.

Calkins, Carroll C. *Reader's Digest Illustrated Guide to Gardening*. Tenth edition. Pleasantville, N.Y.: Reader's Digest Association, 1989.

Clarkson, Rosetta A. *Magic Gardens: A Chronicle of Herbs and Savory Seeds*. New York: Dover Publications, 1972.

Clevely, A. M. *The Total Garden: A Complete Guide to Integrating Flowers, Herbs, Fruits and Vegetables*. New York: Crown, 1988.

Coombes, Allen J. *Dictionary of Plant Names: The Pronunciation, Derivation and Meaning of Botanical Names, and Their Common-name Equivalents*. Second edition. Portland, Ore.: Timber Press, 1987.

Cresson, Charles O. *Charles Cresson on the American Flower Garden*. Burpee Expert Gardener series. New York: Prentice Hall, 1993.

Foerster, Karl. *Rock Gardens through the Year*. Edited by Kenneth Beckett. Leipzig: Neumann Verlag, 1981. English translation, New York: Sterling Publishing, 1987.

Fox, Helen Morgenthau. *Gardening with Herbs for Flavor and Fragrance*. New York: Dover Publications, 1970.

Garden Tales: Classic Stories from Favorite Writers. New York: Penguin, 1990.

Greenlee, John. *The Encyclopedia of Ornamental Grasses*. New York: Michael Friedman Publishing Group, 1992.

Harper, Pamela J. *Designing with Perennials*. New York: Macmillan, 1991.

Heriteau, Jacqueline, et al. *The National Arboretum Book of Outstanding Garden Plants*. New York: Simon and Schuster, 1990.

Hessayon, D. G. *The Garden DIY Expert*. Waltham Cross: pbi Publications, 1992.

————. *The New House Plant Expert.* Waltham Cross: pbi Publications, 1991.

Hill, Lewis. *Secrets of Plant Propagation.* Third printing. Pownal, Vt.: Storey Communications, 1987.

Hobhouse, Penelope. *Flower Gardens.* Boston: Little, Brown, 1991.

Lacy, Allen. *The Garden in Autumn.* New York: Atlantic Monthly Press, 1990.

Lawrence, Elizabeth. *A Southern Garden: A Handbook for the Middle South.* Chapel Hill: University of North Carolina Press, 1992.

Loewer, Peter. *The Evening Garden: Flowers and Fragrance from Dusk till Dawn.* New York: Macmillan, 1993.

Lovejoy, Ann. *The American Mixed Border.* New York: Macmillan, 1993.

McGourty, Frederick. *The Perennial Gardener.* Boston: Houghton Mifflin, 1989.

Ogden, Shepherd, and Ellen Ogden. *The Cook's Garden.* Emmaus, Penn.: Rodale Press, 1987.

Orton, Donald A. *Coincide: The Orton System of Pest Management.* Introduction by Thomas Green. Flossmoor, Ill.: Plantsmen's Publications, 1989.

Piron, P. P., et al. *Tree Maintenance.* Sixth edition. New York: Oxford University Press, 1988.

Ray, Mary Helen, and Robert P. Nicholls, ed. *The Traveller's Guide to American Gardens.* Chapel Hill: University of North Carolina Press, 1988.

Rix, Martyn, and Roger Phillips. *Shrubs.* New York: Random House, 1989.

Rosenfeld, Lois G., ed. *The Garden Tourist: A Guide to Garden Tours, Garden Days, Shows and Special Events.* Portland, Ore.: Timber Press, 1993.

Sabuco, John J. *The Best of the Hardiest.* Third edition. Flossmoor, Ill.: Plantsmen's Publications, 1988.

Schenk, George. *The Complete Shade Gardener.* Second edition. Boston: Houghton Mifflin, 1984.

Schuler, Stanley. *How to Grow Almost Everything.* New York: J. P. Lippincott, 1965.

Strong, Roy. *Small Period Gardens: A Practical Guide to Design and Planting.* New York: Rizzoli, 1992.

————. *A Small Garden Designer's Handbook.* Boston: Little, Brown, 1987.

Stuart, David, and James Sutherland. *Plants from the Past: Old Flowers for New Gardens.* Middlesex, England: Penguin Books, 1987.

Verey, Rosemary. *The Art of Planting.* Boston: Little, Brown, 1990.

————. *The Flower Arranger's Garden.* Boston: Little, Brown, 1989.

————. *The Garden in Winter.* Boston: Little Brown, 1988.

Whitehead, Jeffrey. *The Hedge Book: How to Select, Plant, and Grow a Living Fence.* Pownal, Vt.: Storey Communications, 1991.

Wilder, Louise Beebe. *Adventures with Hardy Bulbs.* New York: Collier, 1990.

Wilson, Helen Van Pelt. *The New Perennials Preferred.* New York: Macmillan, 1992.

Wyman, Donald. *Trees for American Gardens.* Third edition. New York: Macmillan, 1990.

————. *Wyman's Gardening Encyclopedia.* Second edition. New York: Macmillan, 1986.

Index

DIANE HEILENMAN
is garden columnist for the
Louisville Courier Journal.